Reframings

New
American
Feminist
Photographies

Edited by
Diane Neumaier

Reframings

New
American
Feminist
Photographies

Temple University Press
Philadelphia

Temple University Press, Philadelphia 19122
Copyright © 1995 by Temple University

Published 1995

This book is printed on acid-free paper

Printed in Canada

Text designer: Tracy Baldwin

Library of Congress Cataloging-in-Publication Data

Reframings : new American feminist photographies / edited by Diane
    Neumaier.
        p.   cm.
    Includes bibliographical references.
    ISBN 1-56639-331-0
    1. Women photographers—United States.   2. Photography, Artistic.
    3. Feminism and art—United States.   4. Photography—United States.
    I. Neumaier, Diane, 1946–
TR654.R394   1995
770'.82—dc20   94–46914

This collection is dedicated
to my sisters in the Women's
Caucus of the Society for
Photographic Education

Contents

I chose to be a photohistorian because what we don't know about photography's history is greater than what we know. The medium is a frontier with a plenitude of unchartered territories, and this openness appeals to my adventurous side. Too, in the early years I perhaps knew instinctively that with so much available territory, a woman stood a better chance of staking claims.

Photography has always been open to women, at least on the level of practice. Because the medium was never appropriated by academies, women and men learned from manuals or by apprenticing. Anyone who learned technical skills could open a studio or work as a retoucher or printer. By 1890 portrait studios and magazines were offering respectable professions for single women. After a death or divorce, women often continued the photographic businesses they had shared with their husbands. Author Peter Palmquist discovered that by 1910, women made up 20 percent of the photographic work force in America.[1] Women actively participated in every significant photographic movement and school of the twentieth century. For instance, women were among the leading members of organizations such as the Photo Secession and the Photo League, and women were on the staffs of the Farm Security Administration, the Bauhaus School, and major photography magazines and newspapers.

As a young historian I discovered that a little digging in any period yielded important women who had been exhibited and published locally, nationally, and internationally. Women's representation and the acknowledgment of their contributions declined or disappeared only when later historians evaluated a movement. The more general the compendium, the less likely women were to be well represented. For instance, Beaumont Newhall's 1964 edition of the *History of Photography* included only 13 women.[2]

In arts administration, women's ranks were thin indeed. As a graduate student in the late sixties, and subsequently as an intern at the George Eastman House, in Rochester, and the Museum of Modern Art, in New York, I found few female role models. Women like Dorothy Norman, Nancy Newhall, and Alison Gernsheim had played vital roles in photography's history between the wars and through the fifties, but their accomplishments received only slighting remarks from historians and curators by the 1970s. Often, these women were dismissed as enthusiastic seconds-in-command to their male spouses and mentors: Alfred Stieglitz, Beaumont Newhall, and Helmut Gernsheim. By the time I met Nancy Newhall, her most creative period was over, but I loved hearing about her tenure as acting director of the photography department at the Museum of Modern Art and of her collaborations with Ansel Adams and Paul Strand. Still, these women have

[1] *Shadowcatchers: A Directory of Women in California Photography Before 1901* (Arcata, Calif.: Peter Palmquist, 1990), v.

[2] Evaluating Newhall's support of women is complicated. In over 400 articles written on art between 1925 and 1971, he wrote about only six women: Berenice Abbott, Margaret Bourke-White, Julia Margaret Cameron, Imogen Cunningham, Nell Dorr, and Barbara Morgan. Whatever his basis for excluding women from his publications, Newhall proudly supported his wife's career and never discriminated among his students. He generously responded to men and women equally with shared research, advice, and recommendations.

ix

received only tentative recognition for their accomplishments. In 1989, fifteen years after her death, a book of Nancy Newhall's essays was published by Aperture. Dorothy Norman's photographs recently received a retrospective at the International Center for Photography, but we still know little about Alison Gernsheim and her role in the books co-written with her husband.

As I continued to work in photography, I began to realize that the images of women usually selected for exhibition and publication were relentlessly stereotypical. They were modern representations of traditional icons, such as Eve, the Virgin Mary, or Mother Earth. Enjoying particular popularity at the time were images I dubbed "crotch in the wilderness" pictures of languid nudes in ivy beds, pools, or sand dunes. As Simone de Beauvoir had recently established, women were regarded as "other." In photographic anthologies I found few images with which I identified or wished I had made.

Those realizations led to my curating a modest show of photographs of women from the collection in the Museum of Modern Art.[3] An expanded version of this project became my master's thesis at the Visual Studies Workshop and was published as an issue of the Swiss photography magazine, Camera.[4] Those projects led to an invitation to write a book on women photographers, The Woman's Eye, which was published by Knopf in 1973.[5] Having agreed to the publisher's limit of ten photographs by each of ten women, I spanned the twentieth century with women whose works and personalities were as diverse as I could select. Featured were the lives and photographs of Gertrude Kasebier, Frances Benjamin Johnston, Berenice Abbott, Dorothea Lange, Margaret Bourke-White, Barbara Morgan, Diane Arbus, Alice Wells, Judy Dater, and Bea Nettles. Excluded were many women whose works were equally well known and deserving of inclusion, such as Imogen Cunningham, Helen Levitt, Laura Gilpin, Tina Modotti, Lisette Model, and Marion Post Wolcott. I asked whether it had mattered to the work of the women selected whether or not they were women, and concluded that it mattered most when the woman was dealing specifically with being female.

The book was widely reviewed and sold over 30,000 copies. Those knowledgeable about photography tended to dismiss it; general book reviewers and women's publications praised it highly. The most damning comments addressed the text; the greatest praise was for the photographs. Reviewers questioned why, if photographs by women were so diverse, they should have been brought together in one publication. But most critics and supporters acknowledged that the book, in the words of one reviewer, "deserve[d] credit for bringing the issue into debate and presenting the

[3] "Photographs of Women," exhibition, Museum of Modern Art, New York, Fall 1971.
[4] Camera (Feb. 1972).
[5] Anne Wilkes Tucker, The Woman's Eye (New York: Alfred A. Knopf, 1973).

lives, works, and philosophies of some great women photographers for scrutiny."[6] Similar attempts to fill the vacuums women felt keenly were occurring in every intellectual discipline. Feminist texts multiplied rapidly in the early seventies as programs in women's studies were established. The initial effort in photography was joined by more in-depth research, publications, and shows. *Women of Photography: An Historical Survey*, an exhibition and catalogue by Anne Noggle and Margery Mann in 1975, was especially important.[7]

Reframings is a substantial new anthology illustrating just how rich, diverse, and compelling the dialogue has become. It is a cliché to say that art is of its age, but the art in this book could only have been made in the 1980s and 1990s. Identifying and expressing diverse feminist priorities and issues such as those established here—according to ethnicity, sexuality, age, and class—could only have happened as the movement matured and a substantial body of literature and precedents developed. Twenty years ago the second wave of feminism was new and fragile, and that tumultuous time could not have supported the current range and complexity of feminist issues or the clarity with which they are now differentiated.

Anne Wilkes Tucker
Gus and Lyndall Wortham Curator
Museum of Fine Arts, Houston

[6] Lois Greenfield, "Books," *Changes* [1973]: 28.
[7] Anne Noggle and Margery Mann, curators, "Women of Photography: An Historical Survey," San Francisco Museum of Modern Art, 1975. The exhibition traveled to the Museum of New Mexico, Santa Fe, the University of Wisconsin–Milwaukee, and Wellesley College Museum, Massachusetts.

Acknowledgments

xii

I want to express my gratitude to Virginia Rutledge for her inexhaustible intelligent support; to Sherry Millner and Ernie Larsen for hours of discussion regarding issues that emerged in the course of preparing this volume; to Elayne Rapping for generously sharing her political wisdom and experience; to Sally Stein for many insights, including her determination that artworks and essays be presented together; to Deborah Willis for sharing her knowledge of organizing a project such as this; to Shelley Bachman for not allowing me to give up; and to Janet Francendese at Temple University Press for being such a smart and committed editor. I should have listened more carefully to each of them.

I also want to thank the contributors whose works appear here for their generosity and cooperation throughout the long process of creating and producing this book.

Finally, I thank my son, Jed Lewison, and my parents, Virginia Neumaier and John Neumaier, for their support, practical assistance, and love, which did not flag even when I allowed my workaholic ways to disrupt our holidays.

D.N.

Reframings

New
American
Feminist
Photographies

Diane Neumaier

Since the late sixties, feminists have argued, in different ways and to different degrees, that representation—visual, verbal, or any other kind— profoundly affects women's lives. As far back as can be traced, the idea of the feminine has been represented and, some would claim, controlled. Feminism questions how representation shapes women's lives, for twenty-five years consciously and vigilantly attempting to articulate what is at stake for women in visual representation. Although these attempts have not always been harmonious—one need only consider feminist debates over pornography, for example—feminists do not doubt the significance of representation, in particular visual representation.

Reframings: New American Feminist Photographies is a collection of contemporary photo artworks and critical essays grounded in feminist analyses of visual representation. The essays and the artworks explore the dynamics of visual images and ideology, how each is embedded in the other, and how together they contribute to the status of women. As a feminist artist, I have worked for more than a decade on these issues in the belief that solidarity depends on recognition of the struggles of *all* women. This principle has guided me in bringing together varied, even conflicting points of view.

The essays and photographs in *Reframings* explore a range of American feminist issues and experiences. The contributors, all women, include African Americans, Asian Americans, European Americans, Latinas, and Native Americans. Although all the contributors in some way address gender, most identify additional differences of ethnicity, sexual orientation, class, and age. At the same time the contributors bring their different feminist perspectives to bear on advertising, child care, the culture industry, everyday life, family life, food, health care, labor, public life, romance, sexuality, and myriad other concerns of women. Most often the artists in *Reframings* consider a constellation of indivisible and interrelated issues.

Most important, perhaps, the contributors to *Reframings* share the recognition that images embody, are indivisible from, politics. The artists whose works are included here make meaning through an awareness that receiving representation —working with the givens of visual culture—is a negotiable social process. Most of these works visually debate received representation. Their debates are a form of social intercourse that is also political participation. These artists share a consciousness that historically, women have been "framed" through the process of representation and can be "reframed" through the same process. They also share an understanding of photography's role in the framing and reframing processes.

1

Photography, including its immediate offspring film and the contemporary electronic variant video, is crucial to any investigation of the politics of representation. From its nineteenth-century advent, photography figured prominently in the transition to the modern world, dramatically participating in new sciences and explorations, in new forms of leisure, and in the new commercial order. Readily reproducible—a fact that facilitates the publication of this book—its vernacular visual status makes it a relevant, practical medium for an activist artist, just as it is the visual medium of choice for mass culture. Photography's efficiency as a representational tool makes it a likely medium for the artists in *Reframings*, but for these artists, photography also is an assertion of power, a way of seizing the means of production.

In Western culture, photographic images of women exist on a continuum from valued personal objects (snapshots and studio portraits) to seemingly objective documents (driver's licenses and passports) to impersonal and objectable commodities (advertising and pornographic images). At any point on the continuum of representation, however, women are objectified in a way distinct from the ways in which other groups (men, students, old people, people of color, bankers) are objectified. The determination of a woman's sexual desirability by the age and shape of her body is perhaps the most vulgar and common mechanism of the objectification of women facilitated by photography. However, the authority with which men are often represented, and the masculinized affects of the representation of authority, also profoundly affect women. For example, it is impossible to imagine pictures of the U.S. Congress or of any corporate executive officers in an annual report without imagining photographs of white men in dark suits. Absence—what we don't see—as well as presence—what we do see—in representation are formative.

In greatly varied approaches, the photographers in *Reframings* have strategically claimed photographic representation for their own ends. It is not surprising that sophisticated uses and discussions of photography lead to corrective personal applications. Self-representation—a vigilant response to oppressive patriarchal methods of representation—is at the heart of many of the essays and images collected here. The essays illuminate and interpret this activist phenomenon. Deborah Willis considers autobiographical photographic projects, whereas Julia Ballerini considers the collaborative possibilities between the photographer and photographed. Theresa Harlan and Valerie Soe respectively examine the self-assertion of Native American and Asian American women. Moira Roth explores the self-representation of women's bodies, and Lucy Lippard investigates how women identify with or are counterposed to their environments. Abigail

Solomon-Godeau theorizes the politics of self-representing social difference. Catherine Lord addresses the problem of conflicting identities and ways in which the subjugated are poised against each other, maneuvered to identify themselves against each other and ultimately against themselves. Clearly, the issue of self-representation is not restricted to literal self-portraiture. The issue is not what one looks like but how and by whom one is represented.

The possibilities of self-representation that are consciously negotiated within this book were already implicit in *The Woman's Eye*, Anne Wilkes Tucker's unprecedented collection of women's photography, published twenty years ago. The very existence of a volume that isolated women's photographs challenged received opinion about women's experience. Much has transpired since then. Today it is possible for us to call ourselves not only women, but feminists. Just as the act of naming oneself through language is empowering, so, too, is the act of visually representing oneself.

Although consciousness of sexism is at an all-time high in the popular mind, the situation of women in the arts is in many ways unimproved. Indeed, there appears to be a backlash against feminism. I suggest we consider this anxious hostility to feminism an indication of progress. The right-wing cooptation of "politically correct," initially a self-critical consciousness-raising term used by the left, illustrates just how powerful the original application of PC is. While the right has been moderately successful, it has not yet succeeded in making the attempt to "do the right thing" shameful. Misogyny in the United States may be unrelenting, but at least for now it is popularly considered to be wrong. I believe that feminist-based consciousness-raising within U.S. society must be seen as a great victory.

Reframings reveals that many women photographers are attending to a variety of problems, including racism and homophobia, to name just two issues repeatedly addressed in this book. Particularly courageous have been some African American feminist critiques of patriarchal structures. Although the aim of *Reframings* is explicitly feminist, it is also by political and ethical necessity explicitly multicultural. It is undeniably a delicate matter for struggling subjugated peoples to work together in solidarity rather than seek to subvert each other. *Reframings* is intended to contribute to an open dialogue, however difficult, in which differences between women can be fruitfully addressed. It is essential that we not blame each other for our pain: Other women are usually not the driving force behind sexism, racism, and homophobia.

In part because of standard distinctions between the practice of art and the practice of art criticism, it is the critics in this book who most directly and uncomfortably address differences among women. Without exception,

4

in every essay—each of which was written for this volume—the writer struggles with the polemics of ethnicity, culture, class and sexuality. As editor, I solicited contributors from women art critics whose perspectives covered a broad range of feminist concerns, although I did not foresee their common concern with problematizing our multicultural society. I now believe it can be said that addressing differences in ethnicity, sexual orientation, and economic opportunity (or, more precisely and negatively, addressing racism, homophobia, and class privilege) constitutes feminist art criticism today.

Over the past twenty-five years feminist cultural criticism and scholarship have dramatically transformed both the art world and academia. The effect can be traced by noting the steady increase in feminist literature published during this period, the increased feminist content of academic conferences and journals, and the increase in activity of women's caucuses. Indeed, feminist inquiries have affected general lines of inquiry throughout the humanities. Nonetheless, the moment is no longer propitious for a feminist criticism of contemporary photography. Perhaps this reflects a stalemate in photography criticism overall, perhaps a plateau in the development of feminist theories of representation, or perhaps an effect of the 1980s privatization of cultural support and a decline in support for higher education, where cultural criticism frequently originates. For example, National Endowment for the Arts (NEA) Critics Fellowships were discontinued in the early eighties, a consequence of a right-wing attack on the NEA, and through it, on progressive intellectual life. There has been little other support of feminist photography criticism. Perhaps as an indirect result, several important feminist photography critics have chosen to make their professional contributions through the discipline of art history, where their attentions must largely be devoted to critiquing a history that has denied women subjectivity, relegating them to subject matter. Ironically, addressing photography's second-rate status within art history is a real threat to that discipline, just as addressing women's second-rate position in society is a real threat to male domination.

Feminist theory has offered analytical models of mass culture upon which feminist image-makers rely, yet it has been far less thorough in its analyses of alternative feminist images. Although feminist artworks are directly informed by the intellectual work of feminists and progressives across a wide range of disciplines, the works themselves are not widely seen, even by other feminists. For the most part, feminist academics seem more interested in producing feminist critiques of dominant cultural production than in critiquing feminist alternative cultural work. This is discouraging, especially in light of the existing high level of feminist critique of dominant cultural production and the underexamined high level of existing feminist artworks. Simply put, most feminist image-makers cannot get an audience with feminist critics. Feminist cultural critics infrequently look at, much less seek out, the work of a full spectrum of feminist artists. Writers rarely view exhibitions, critics rarely visit studios. As a consequence, we are left with the frequent examination of the market-driven gallery work of a few famous feminist artists (some of whose works are reproduced here) and nearly no examination of the works of most of the artists represented in *Reframings.* Rather than hearing the system blamed for its sexism and unwillingness to reward more than a few women, we hear criticism of the rare famous feminist artist as if it were she who took something away from other women. Therefore I want to state emphatically that it is not the great success of a few women artists that causes the lack of success of other women.

Feminist academic publications are frequently ironically illustrated with sexist images "we love to hate" rather than with works by feminist artists that would make similar interventions or offer other insights. We must ask whether this eclipse of feminist artworks is a result of the powerful seductive properties of sexist imagery, is a result of ignorance regarding feminist images, is a response to marginalization on the part of feminist academics, or is an indication of failure on the part of feminist art practices to compel even a feminist audience. Toward remedying the problem, *Reframings* seeks to expose the work of feminist artists to other feminists and calls for a more developed feminist critique of feminist art documentation and distribution practices.

As another remedy to the scarcity of feminist photography criticism, some artists, such as Deborah Bright, Martha Rosler, and I, have tried to take on the task of writing ourselves, in part because feminist photography (including our own production) seldom is analyzed. While this multiple burden can strengthen both practices, it sometimes has the reverse effect, since the double burden is born at great cost. (Martha Rosler's photography and video have influenced contemporary feminist art practice as fundamentally as her critical and theoretical writing. Precisely because of its ground-breaking historical and theoretical significance, I invited her to present in a feminist context her previously published work, *Bringing the War Home: House Beautiful*, which, while it has been recently reissued, is the only project in *Reframings* that can be classified as historical.) Ultimately, however, I do not wish to argue that the practices of criticism and art-making are separate, much less contradictory. The artists in *Reframings* are clearly informed by multiple theories, although in many cases they oppose the tyranny of jargon that is sometimes associated with theory. Art and criticism are not only mutually generative but are often dependent. The cross-over practices of Bright, Rosler, Mary Kelly, Barbara Kruger, and Adrian Piper exemplify the successful joining of art and theory. The benefit of their multiple practices is especially evident in their artists' books and other phototext works that combine the visual and the verbal.

Awareness of critical work, even that which is not current, is possible for artists because of the relative accessibility of published criticism (and photocopying machines). Unfortunately, it requires much more effort to see artworks, which are usually not conveniently accessible. A primary goal of *Reframings* is to offer exposure to work that is not otherwise easily seen. *Reframings* is intended to make more visible a range of nearly invisible feminist visual art production.

In organizing *Reframings*, I became keenly aware of the differences in opportunity faced by writers and by artists. On the one hand, writers are greatly burdened by demands to publish new work; several wonderful writers wanted to but were unable to commit to this volume. Feminist writers are overworked, overcommitted, and overextended. While this is true for some feminist artists as well, the service that is demanded of writers is uniquely draining: new manuscripts are continually required to meet the needs of institutions and publications. Most artists face the opposite problem: they have little opportunity to exhibit or publish work that already exists, and even less often are they commissioned to produce projects. Thus, while a number of artworks were produced specifically for *Reframings*, many more existed well before being published here for the first time. The working conditions for artists and the systems of exhibition and distribution of their work are exceptionally uneven. I recently sat on a jury selecting work for a series of one-woman exhibitions and was stunned by the volume—thousands of slides—of works by artists with whom the entire jury was unfamiliar. Although some of the women artists included in *Reframings* are sought after like movie stars, most must solicit exhibition venues and submit slides, submit work, submit résumés, submit entry fees—submit, submit, submit—to be exhibited.

This system of distribution bears directly on the artwork itself. Those whose work circulates in pricier venues can produce pricier work. It is in the interest of the art market that successful artists work on a larger, more expensive scale—although it is often not to the works' advantage. I do not belittle the accomplishments of hardworking successful artists, nor do I chastise unknown artists for not marketing themselves better within a saturated market. For example, Cindy Sherman's earliest small-scale black-and-white work was inexpensive for her to produce, but as her success and prices increased, she could afford to hire commercial labs to make large-

scale color work, which is very expensive to produce. Interestingly, as her
production values and methods became more and more upscale and costly,
the militancy of her works' feminist position strengthened.

The material terms of art production are directly connected to the
formal material character of that production. In the arts this is nothing new:
Sistine ceilings and Hollywood blockbusters alike are not private acts of individual genius; on the contrary, they are socially produced. Like all artists
everywhere, feminist artists are hostage to the economic order. Thus, feminists whose work challenges patriarchal structures need to be especially efficient in means. And this collection is a testimony to clever efficient means!
Twenty-five years after feminism observed that most women's art is
produced not in artists' studio lofts but in kitchens, bedrooms, and living
rooms, the observation still holds true. Although we may be encouraged by
the success of several well-known women artists or discouraged by the
unofficial quotas that seem to accompany that success, a new problem has
developed: the professionalization, privatization, and commercialization of
the visual arts. Coincident with the demand for expensive methods of distribution and self-promotion is the declining economic order that further
pinches artists. The lack of public support of artists and the concomitant
market-driven standards of the art world force most artists to promote
themselves at great personal cost or to remain virtually unexhibited.

The most interesting discovery for me during the process of assembling
Reframings was a void: in my exploration of contemporary feminist photographic works, I didn't find direct, enthusiastic expressions of feminine
heterosexual desire or pleasure. I did find a few explorations by women of
the female body, most often as an isolated body outside of a social or
psychological context. Lesbian explorations of sexual pleasure made great
leaps in the past decade and have much to offer. Straight women, however,
frequently address sexuality within a context of hurt, anxiety, or rage.
Perhaps the expression of feminine heterosexual desire lags behind, since
straight women still must negotiate difficult power relations with men.
Among other problems, they (like everyone else) must contend with the
history of what passes as the expression of masculine heterosexual desire.
Perhaps the expression of their pleasure is (still) limited to display to a
masculine audience in which feminine agency is contingent on masculine
desire. Perhaps women's desire is (still) the desire to be desired. Possibly the
fear of acknowledging such dependency (acknowledging either to potentially rejecting male viewers or to potentially unsympathetic feminist politics
that has yet to work through the enormous problem of sexuality with men)
has yet to be overcome. I hope this is an area that will soon see exciting new
work.

8

The process of assembling *Reframings* yielded many other surprises as well. Not only did the collection as a whole take its own shape, but it became evident to me that many of the artists and writers went forward with their work for this volume without knowing what a particular project would become. In that sense, *Reframings* is truly vital. In selecting artwork I solicited suggestions from every imaginable source, including the most peculiar. Even my work in Russia over the past three years led to the contribution of three American women photographers represented in these pages. From the beginning, my intention was to gather a very wide, even a contradictory range of practices with which no individual, including myself, would be familiar. While the premise for *Reframings* was that gender would be central to all the works selected, it is not clear to me how many of the women included here actually identify themselves as feminists, although most certainly do.

Not all of the women included in this volume consider themselves to be photographers, either; often they are artists who use photography only in some circumstances. The formal means of expression are as diverse as the range of ideas expressed, since the choice of photographic process is always a crucial component of the formulation and articulation of the expression, whether it be black-and-white or color, documentary, photomontage, staged studio works, gallery installations, artists' books, appropriated photographic materials, or any other method, form, or process. There is no agreed-upon single principle of how to use photography well, nor are there necessarily significant differences between those who use the camera themselves and those who find and rearrange others' pictures.

One volume cannot be comprehensive, and I am extremely uncomfortable about many exclusions, intentional and otherwise. The decision to restrict myself to photographers working in the United States was based on my familiarity with the richness of what is available here. Despite the scarcity of opportunities for women in the arts, I believe that this is a historically opportune time and place for feminist art-making. I look forward to other local and international collections and to other volumes that include the work of male feminist artists who also address issues of gender. It is in the spirit of "affirmative action," especially in light of continued underexposure of women's art in America, that *Reframings* is framed.

Reframings has been organized into eight sections. However, most of the contributions could easily be moved from one section to another, and in the preparation of this book that is exactly what happened. The complexity of the projects gathered here is not restricted by their location in the book. The sections are intended to encourage the works to interact and thereby promote a kind of discussion within and among the sections.

The opening section, "Gendering Space," explores women's agency regarding social space. Contemporary theories of how social space is gendered have advanced feminist social analyses. The artists represented in this section break down earlier analyses of social space that associated feminine with domestic and masculine with public. Barbara Kruger opens with documentation of her aggressive, feminist, "woman-empowering" public billboards, bus signs, and other projects through which she reinserts into the public sphere the visual material she appropriates from it. Marilyn Nance, through classical black-and-white documentary, and Anne Noggle, through classic black-and-white studio portraiture, celebrate the strength of communities of women, in one case the women of African American spiritual congregations, in the other World War II Soviet and U.S. women pilots. The photo novella of Kaucyila Brooke transforms space by staging an erotic lesbian fantasy. Sherry Millner's photomontage redefines the space to which the media has confined women. Carol Simon Rosenblatt consciously differentiates herself from the space outside herself. In a twist on the masculinist model, Lucy R. Lippard's essay, "Undertones: Nine Cultural Landscapes," lays feminist claim to the genre of landscape.

For most women, the self-conscious identity as "female" originated in the home, a site where gendered limitations are frequently set. Thus, "Domestic Production/Reproduction/Resistance" explores some feminist relationships of women to home. Linda Brooks's black-and-white phototexts and Gail S. Rebhan's color stills from family videos consider their current family lives from their vantage points as mothers of young children. In equally complicated but graphically very different montage techniques, Nancy Barton, Clarissa Sligh, and Susan Meiselas address ways in which patriarchy orders the roles of men within the family. While Barton explores the ambivalence related to this authority, Sligh confronts its secret dangers, and Meiselas condemns its violent horror. Through her color phototexts S. A. Bachman draws out the nightmare induced by media-made fantasies of women's roles in middle-class family life. In her essay, "Women's Stories/Women's Photobiographies," Deborah Willis examines the making of alternative histories by featuring artists whose strategic placement of photography within other archival systems contextualizes personal history within a social framework.

"Identity Formations" explores ways in which identity is socially produced, even if it is individually experienced. The role of family life in producing gendered children and ultimately gendered society is examined by Sarah Hart, whose color documentary photographs investigate the everyday lives of suburban girls in consumer culture, and by Leigh Kane, whose black-and-white photomontages consider the emotional damage done by repressive sexist socializing of boys and men. Through other photomontage techniques Adrian Piper and Lorna Simpson address the centrality of racism to the complex identity formation of African Americans, and Diane Tani foregrounds the confusion and rage of an imposed immigrant identity in America several generations after the family immigrated from Japan. "As in Her Vision: Native American Women Photographers," an essay by Theresa Harlan, discusses the representation of Natives by Native women—an issue long overlooked by most critics.

"Postcolonial Legacies" assembles a range of photomontages that address specific incidents of U.S. imperialism and the inherent racism of such a policy. Martha Rosler contextualizes the Vietnam War within sexist American society. Esther Parada analyzes the sexism of media images during American actions in Nicaragua. Yong Soon Min examines ways racism alienates the Korean American community, particularly its women. Hulleah Tsinhnanjinnie explores the continuing role of the media in the eclipse of Native American culture. Pat Ward Williams's large-scale installations investigate the politics of looking and being looked at for African American men today. An essay by Julia Ballerini, "ODELLA/Carlota," complicates the dynamics of domination by investigating the politics of representation by another versus self-representation. Through her close examination of one collaboration between a photographer who makes traditional black-and-white images and an actively engaged subject who both directed and wrote about the resulting images, Ballerini problematizes issues of self-assertion, trust, and fantasy.

"Rationalizing and Realizing the Body" brings together conflicting perspectives on the experience of the body. The range of work in this section explores theories of the body by addressing bodies with which we are familiar: our own. Martha Casanave's black-and-white pinhole photographs and Linn Underhill's studio-style black-and-white photographs depict flesh-and-bone bodies, lived-in bodies. Ann Meredith's black-and-white documentary portrays women in different places and circumstances who are living with AIDS. Jin Lee and Carla Williams use graphic arts techniques to investigate how racism and sexism are rationalized through the process of representation of the body. Dorit Cypis, through complex projection installations, daringly, anxiously investigates the reality and potential of her own isolated, sexual body. Finally, an essay by Moira Roth, "A Meditation on Bearing/Baring the Body," considers how the work of feminist artists can reveal their own bodies.

"Sex and Anxiety" explores the suppression of female sexuality. Black-   **11**
and-white photographs by Connie Hatch verify the tyranny of the male
gaze over the female body. Through black-and-white phototexts, Carrie
Mae Weems confronts the compromises strong women negotiate when
engaging with men, and Tamarra Kaida cooly registers feminine heterosexual disappointment. As if excess could satisfy the problematic of desire,
Cindy Sherman's color studio photographs grotesquely exaggerate the
display of body parts in which culture trades. Hinda Schuman's photodiary
also presents sexual anxiety: the nervous passionate budding of a lesbian
love affair. As I observed earlier, not pleasure but hurt, anxiety, and rage
most often appear in photographic explorations of sexuality by heterosexual women. The riskier models offered by lesbians also take their toll. By
chronicling her own and the experiences of her friends, Nan Goldin insists
upon the urgency of sex—privileging neither hetero- nor homo-sexuality.
An essay by Catherine Lord, "This Is Not a Fairy Tale: A Middle-aged Female
Pervert (White) in the Era of Multiculturalism," investigates the censoring
and silencing of "queer" sexualities.

In "Crossing Over: Reimagining and Reimaging," Laura Aguilar gives
voice to Latina lesbians by inviting them to write directly on the black-and-
white portraits she makes of them. Through interactive installations
Margaret Stratton invites her audience to resist media images of Anita Hill
and Clarence Thomas by labeling Hill and Thomas as they wish. In the
playful, flirtatious, hand-colored stagings of Carm Little Turtle, "Earthman's" anxious passionate desire for woman is monitored, perhaps by a
distanced female audience. Catherine Opie and Coreen Simpson use
disruptive portraiture to imagine and image what seems unimaginable. In
her essay, "Turning the Tables: Three Asian American Artists," Valerie Soe
features the work of contemporary Asian American women artists who
resist racial and gender stereotypes through their complicating, analytical
photomontages that assume that identity is social, not an individual thing,
yet insist it is open to individual reconstruction.

While the entire book addresses the problem of representation, the
section "Rerepresenting Representation" focuses on interventions with
specific, existing authoritative images. Through a variety of photomontage
techniques Ann Fessler, Betty Lee, Deborah Bright and I rewrite classical art
historical canons, revealing the European patriarchal biases of those standards. Susan Jahoda's phototext exposes and subverts images of disease
that have been deployed against women for more than a century by the
medical establishment. Mary Kelly strategically withholds visual representation of women's bodies in order to explore how feminine socialization,

including the distancing of women from their own bodies, takes place through the process of representation. An essay by Abigail Solomon-Godeau, "Representing Women: The Politics of Self-Representation," considers how identity is constructed through representation and how that process can be complicated and interrupted through self-representation.

Reframings: New American Feminist Photographies is not only a collection of individual artworks and critical essays. It is a collection of pro-active works that seek social redress through representation. In aggregate the diverse feminist work presented in this book constitutes a self-consciously engaged and, I hope, engaging political practice.

Gendering Space

14

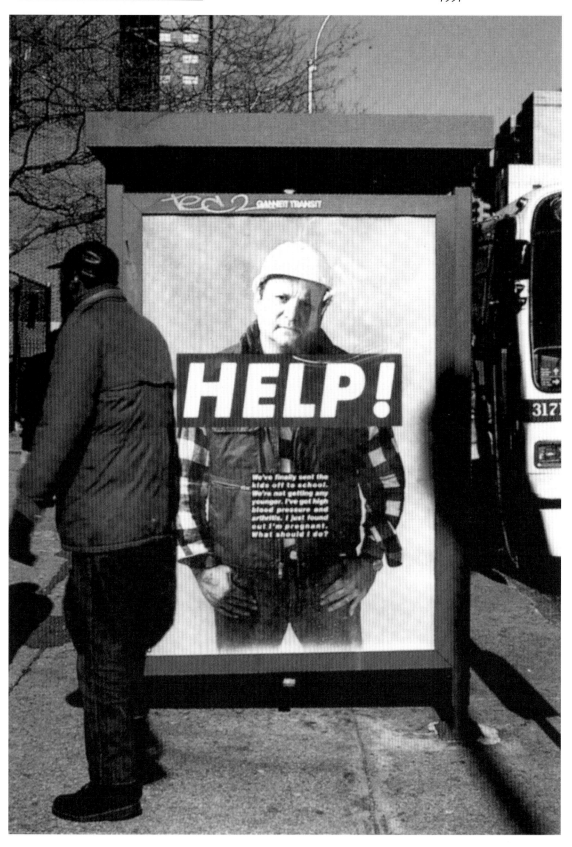

Campaign for Legal Abortion and Women's Reproductive Rights, New York City, poster, 1990

Public Art Fund, New York City, billboard, 1989

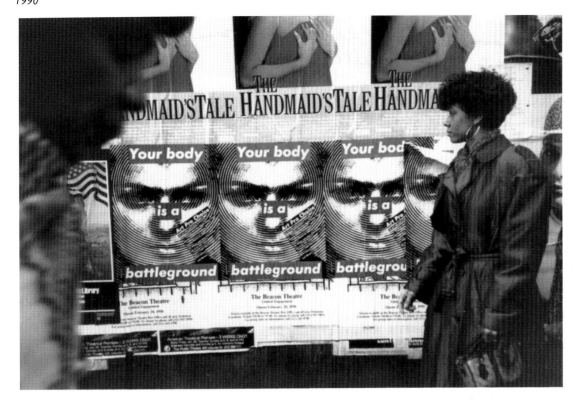

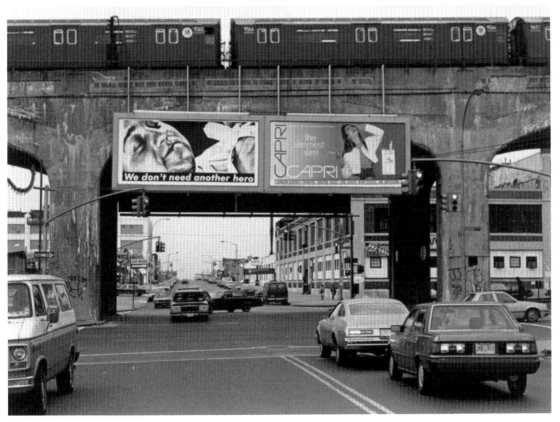

London, billboard, 1986

Against the AntiGay Referendum, Portland, Oregon, bus placard, 1992

16

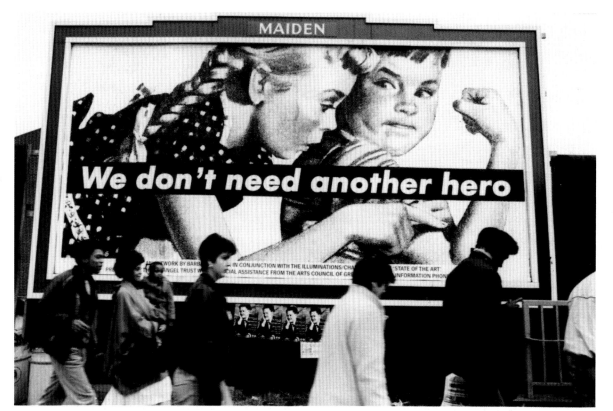

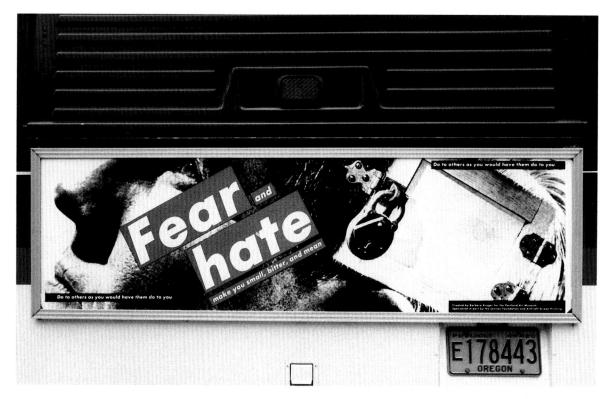

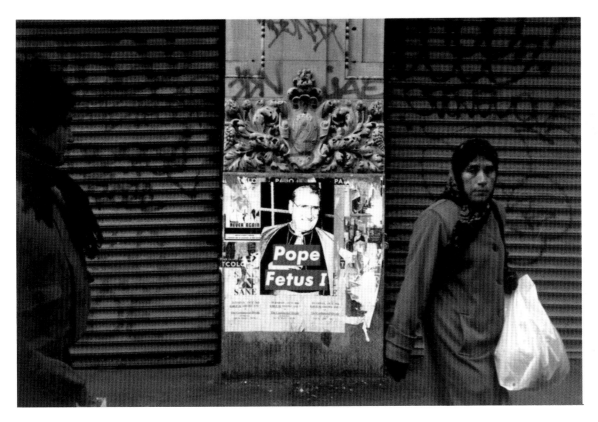

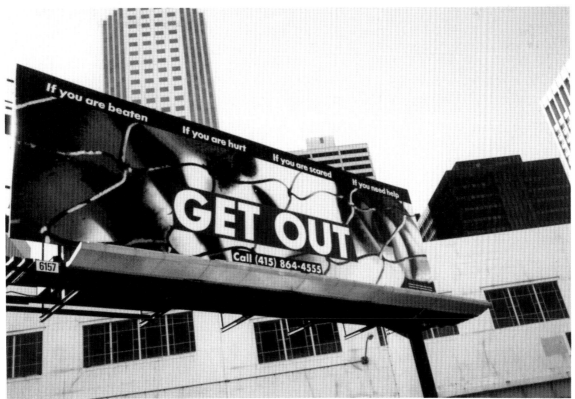

from *African American Spirit*

Deaconess Rosa Williams, Women's Day, Progressive Baptist Church, Brooklyn, NY

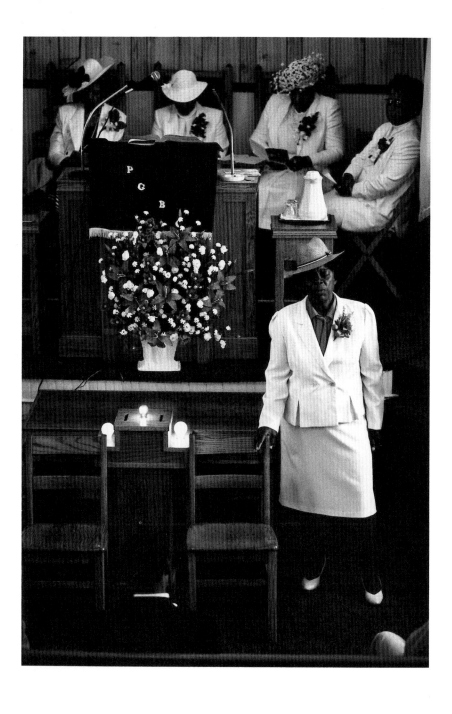

First Annual Community Baptism for the Afrikan Family, Midnight Healing Session, Brooklyn, NY

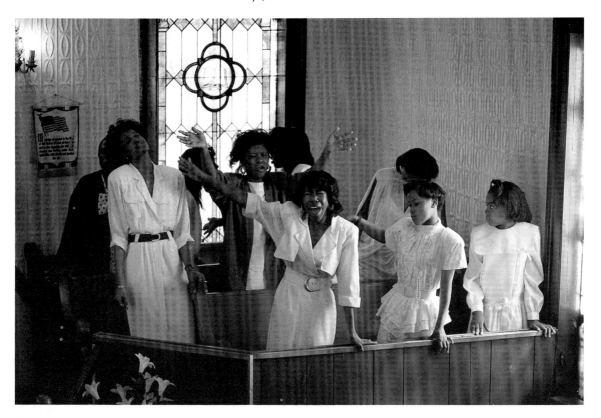

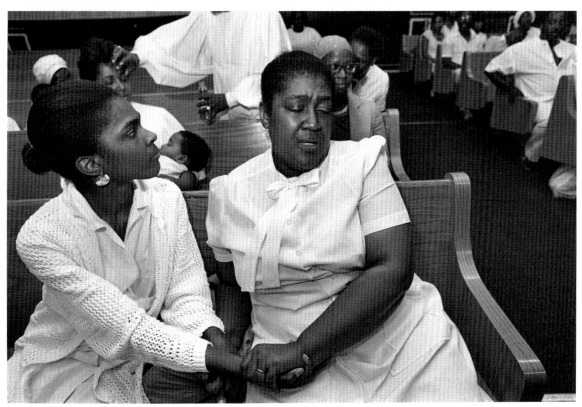

20

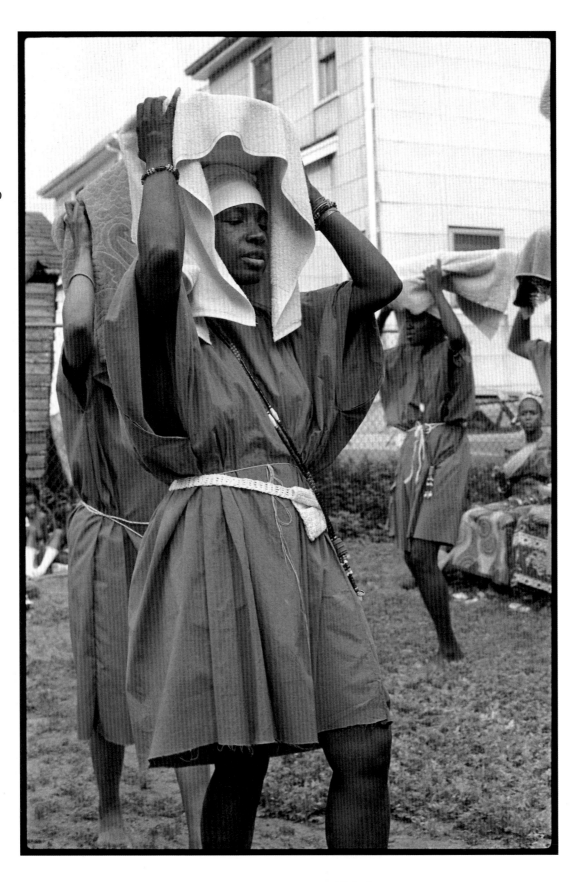

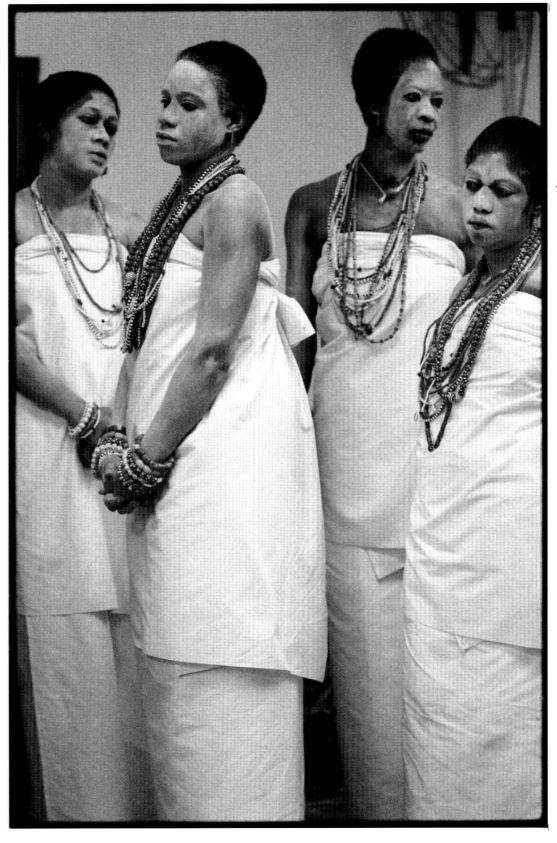

from *WWII American and Soviet Women Pilots*

Geraldine Bowen Olinger, Woman Air Force Service Pilot, USA, WWII, 1986

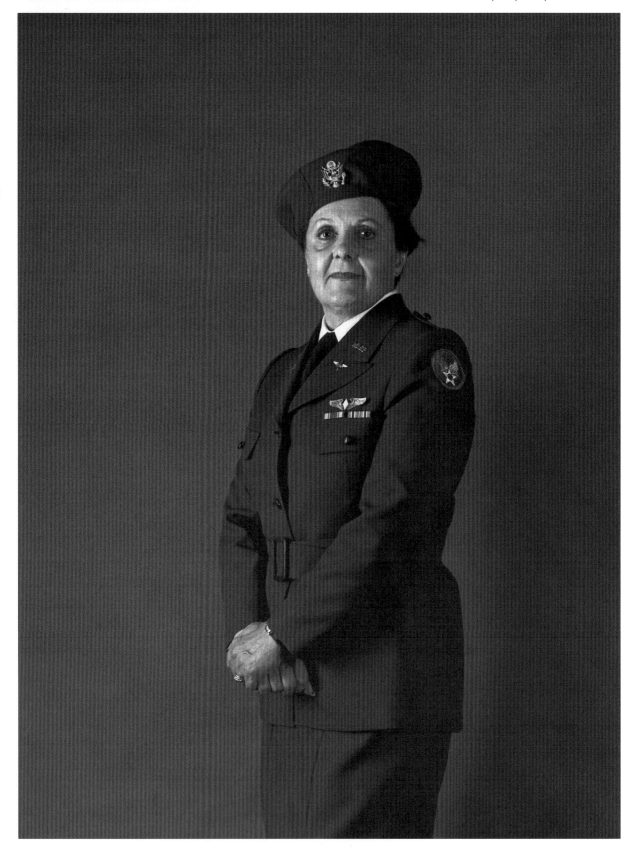

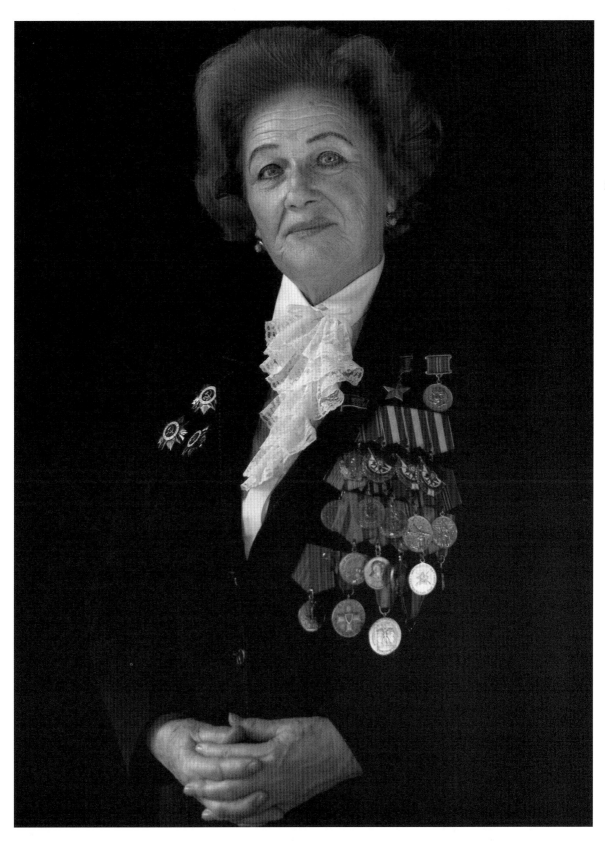

Nadezhda Popova, pilot, Hero of the Soviet Union, Soviet Air Force Army, WWII, 1991

*Mariya Akilina, bomber pilot, Soviet Air Force
Army, WWII, 1991*

24

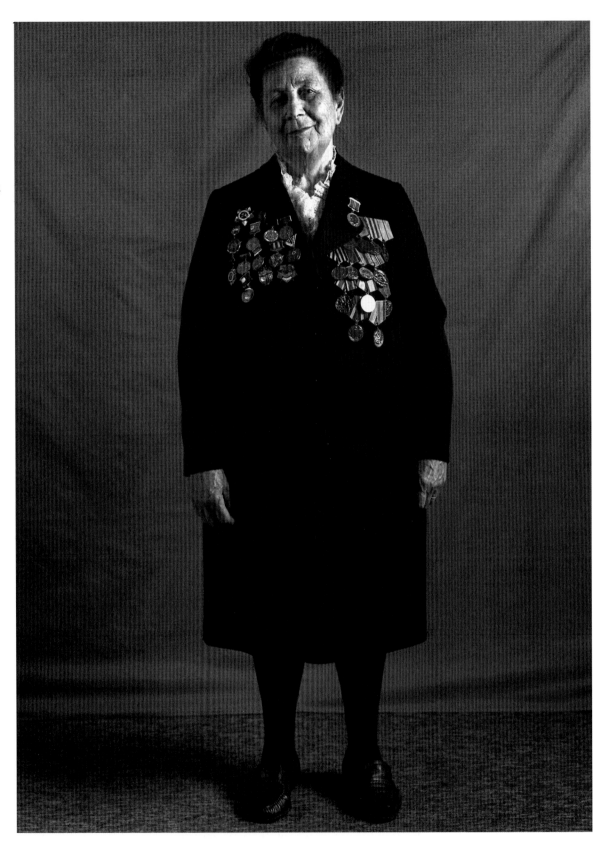

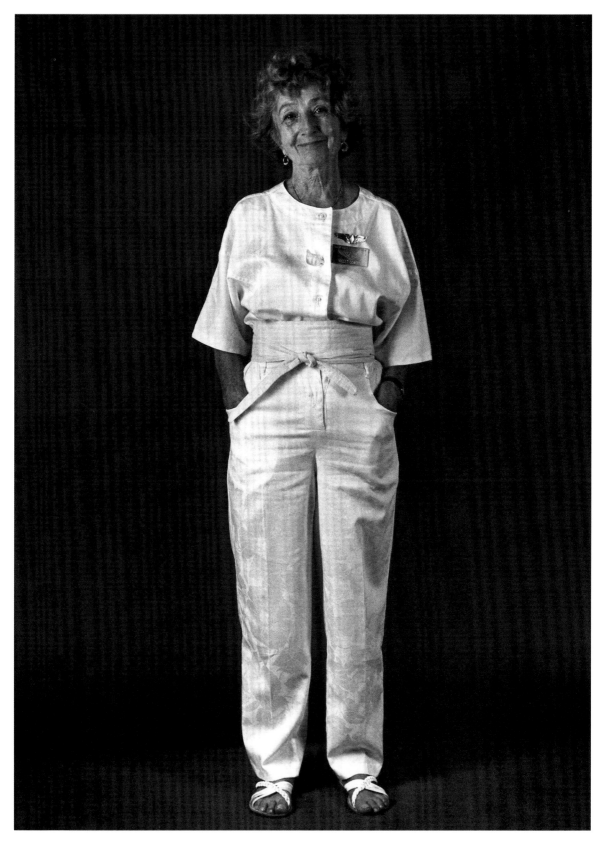

from *Making the Most of Your Backyard:
The Story Behind an Ideal Beauty*

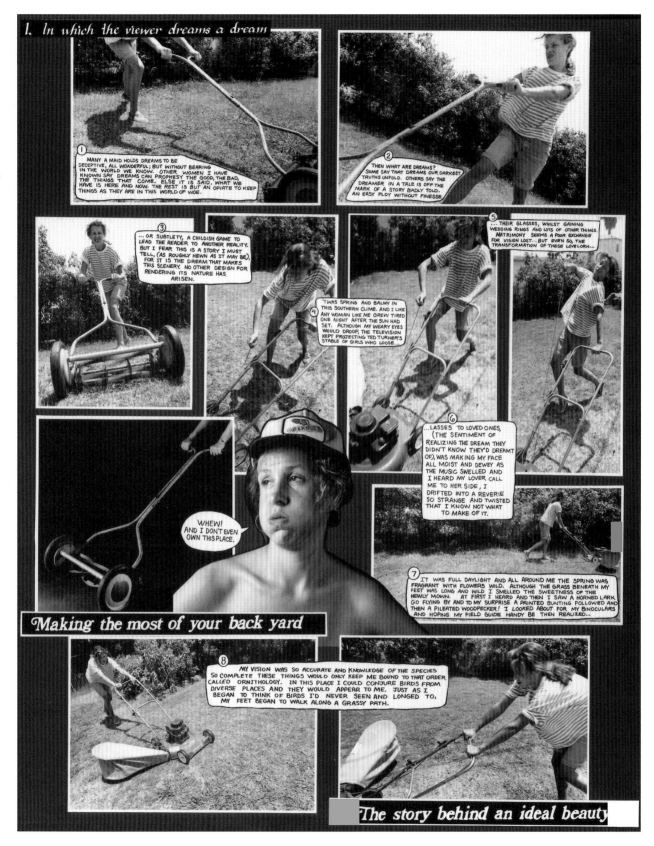

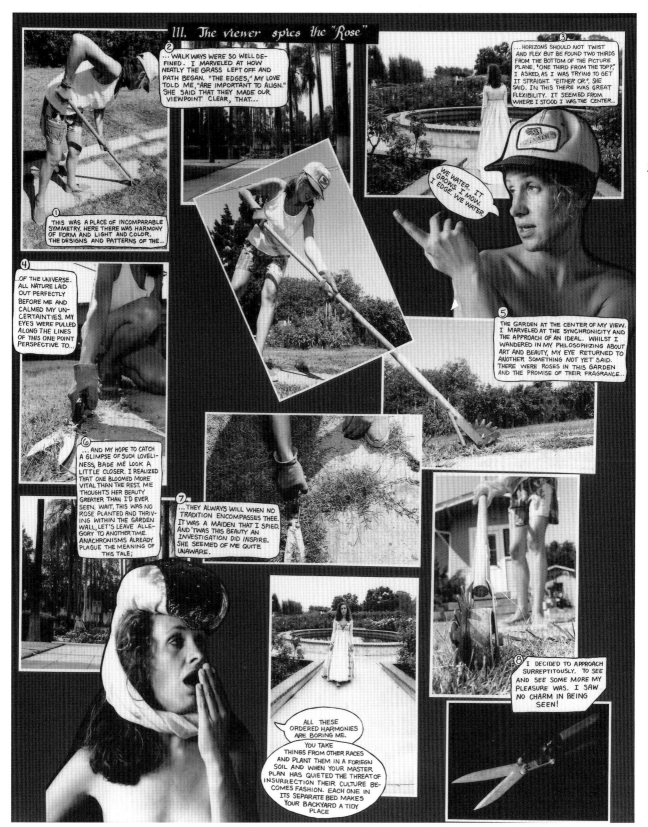

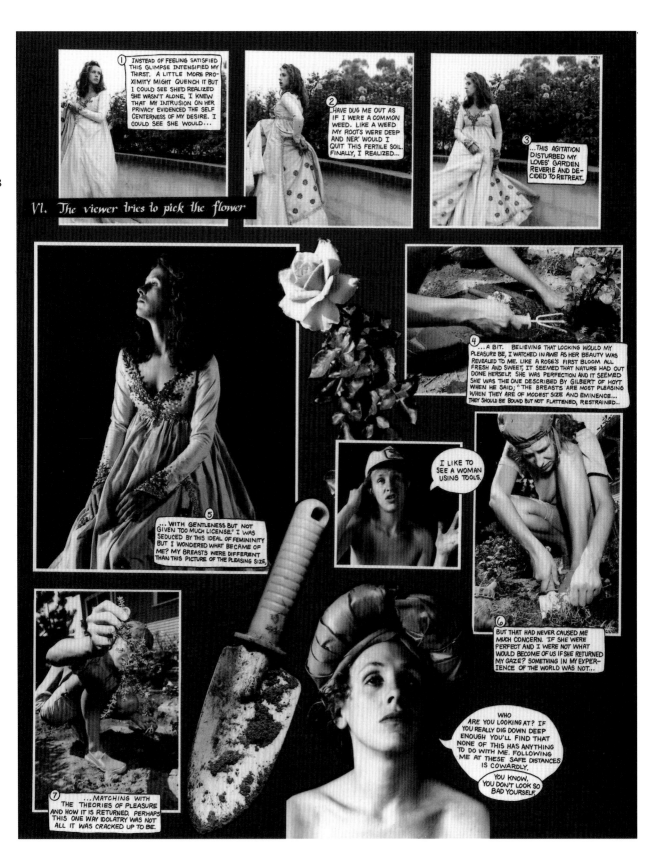

1. INSTEAD OF FEELING SATISFIED THIS GLIMPSE INTENSIFIED MY THIRST. A LITTLE MORE PROXIMITY MIGHT QUENCH IT BUT I COULD SEE SHE'D REALIZED SHE WASN'T ALONE. I KNEW THAT MY INTRUSION ON HER PRIVACY EVIDENCED THE SELF CENTERNESS OF MY DESIRE. I COULD SEE SHE WOULD...

2. ...HAVE DUG ME OUT AS IF I WERE A COMMON WEED. LIKE A WEED MY ROOTS WERE DEEP AND NER' WOULD I QUIT THIS FERTILE SOIL. FINALLY, I REALIZED...

3. ...THIS AGITATION DISTURBED MY LOVES' GARDEN REVERIE AND DECIDED TO RETREAT...

VI. The viewer tries to pick the flower

4. ...A BIT. BELIEVING THAT LOOKING WOULD MY PLEASURE BE, I WATCHED IN AWE AS HER BEAUTY WAS REVEALED TO ME. LIKE A ROSE'S FIRST BLOOM ALL FRESH AND SWEET, IT SEEMED THAT NATURE HAD OUT DONE HERSELF. SHE WAS PERFECTION AND IT SEEMED SHE WAS THE ONE DESCRIBED BY GILBERT OF HOYT WHEN HE SAID; " THE BREASTS ARE MOST PLEASING WHEN THEY ARE OF MODEST SIZE AND EMINENCE... THEY SHOULD BE BOUND BUT NOT FLATTENED, RESTRAINED...

5. ...WITH GENTLENESS BUT NOT GIVEN TOO MUCH LICENSE." I WAS SEDUCED BY THIS IDEAL OF FEMININITY BUT I WONDERED WHAT BECAME OF ME? MY BREASTS WERE DIFFERENT THAN THIS PICTURE OF THE PLEASING SIZE,

I LIKE TO SEE A WOMAN USING TOOLS.

6. BUT THAT HAD NEVER CAUSED ME MUCH CONCERN. IF SHE WERE PERFECT AND I WERE NOT WHAT WOULD BECOME OF US IF SHE RETURNED MY GAZE? SOMETHING IN MY EXPERIENCE OF THE WORLD WAS NOT...

WHO ARE YOU LOOKING AT? IF YOU REALLY DIG DOWN DEEP ENOUGH YOU'LL FIND THAT NONE OF THIS HAS ANYTHING TO DO WITH ME. FOLLOWING ME AT THESE SAFE DISTANCES IS COWARDLY.

YOU KNOW, YOU DON'T LOOK SO BAD YOURSELF.

7. ...MATCHING WITH THE THEORIES OF PLEASURE AND HOW IT IS RETURNED, PERHAPS THIS ONE WAY IDOLATRY WAS NOT ALL IT WAS CRACKED UP TO BE.

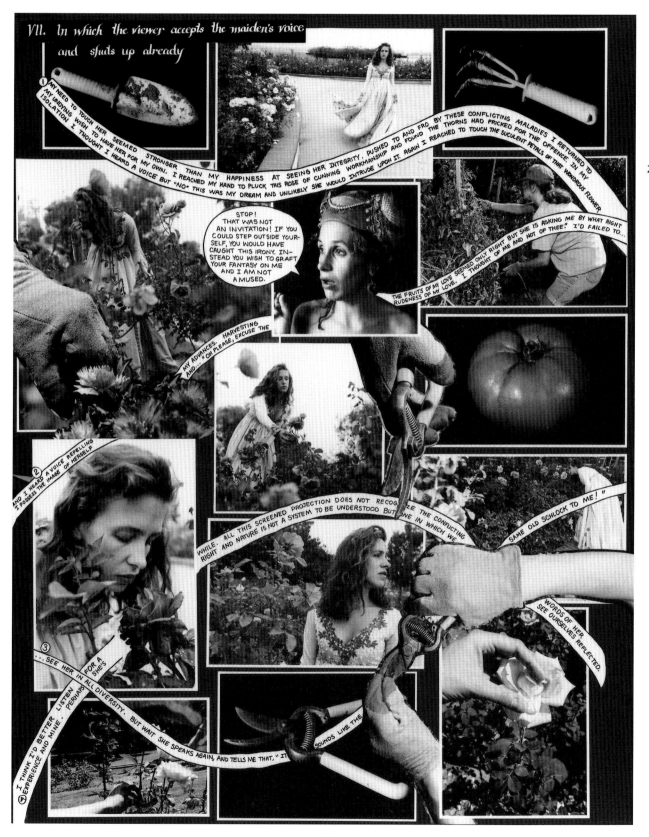

30

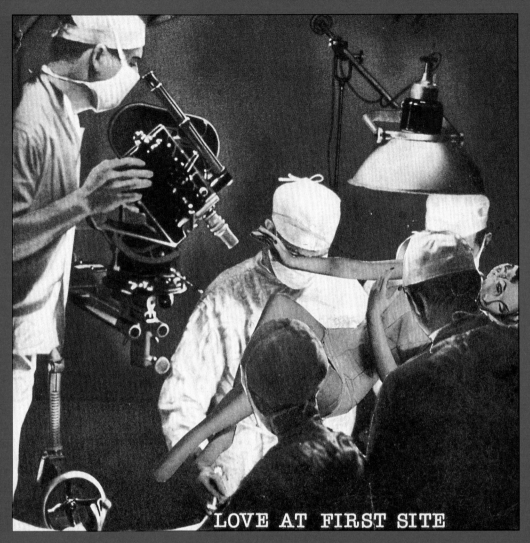

LOVE AT FIRST SITE

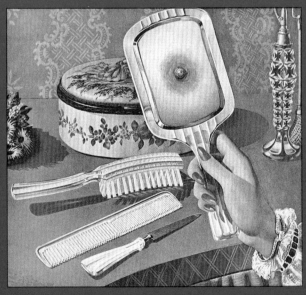

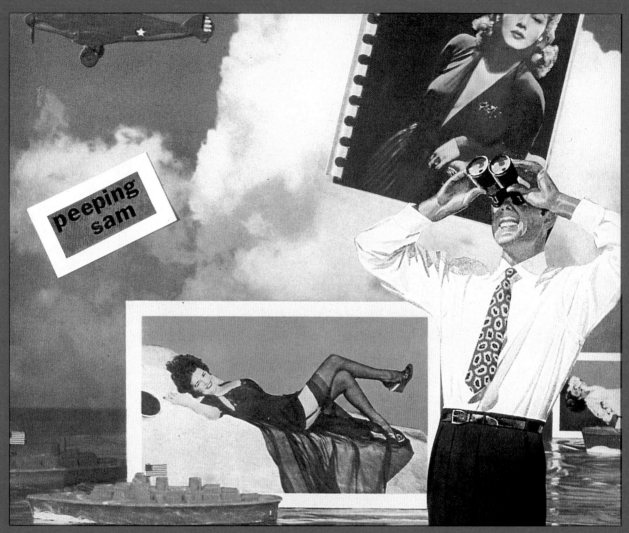

peeping sam

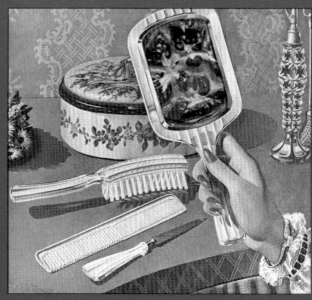

32

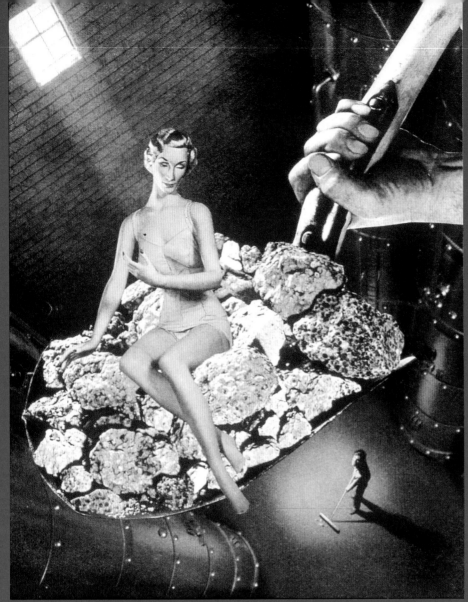

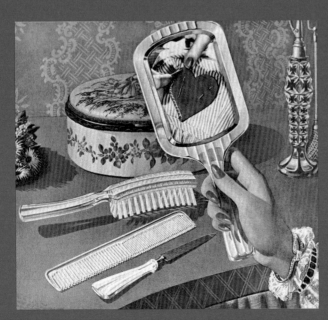

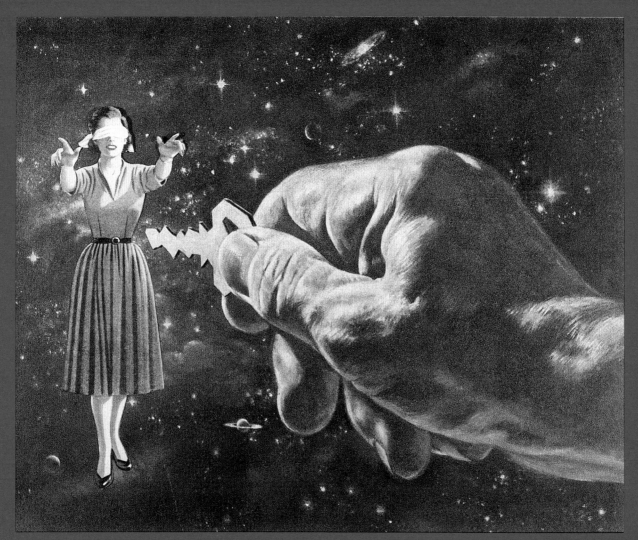

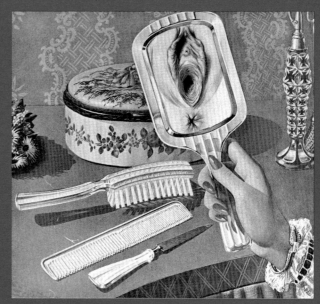

34

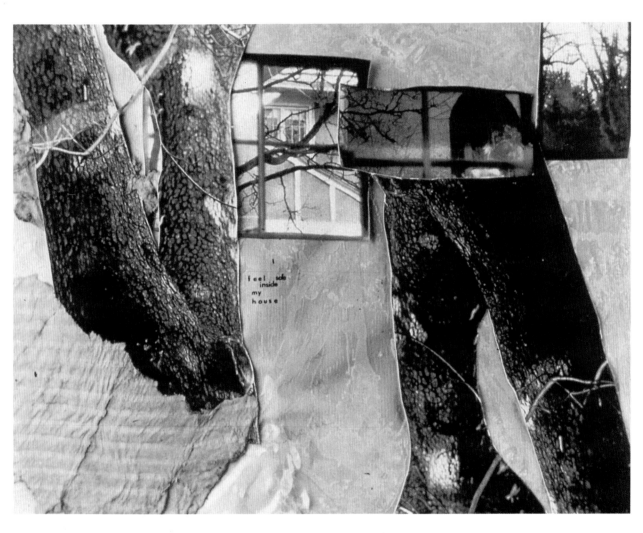

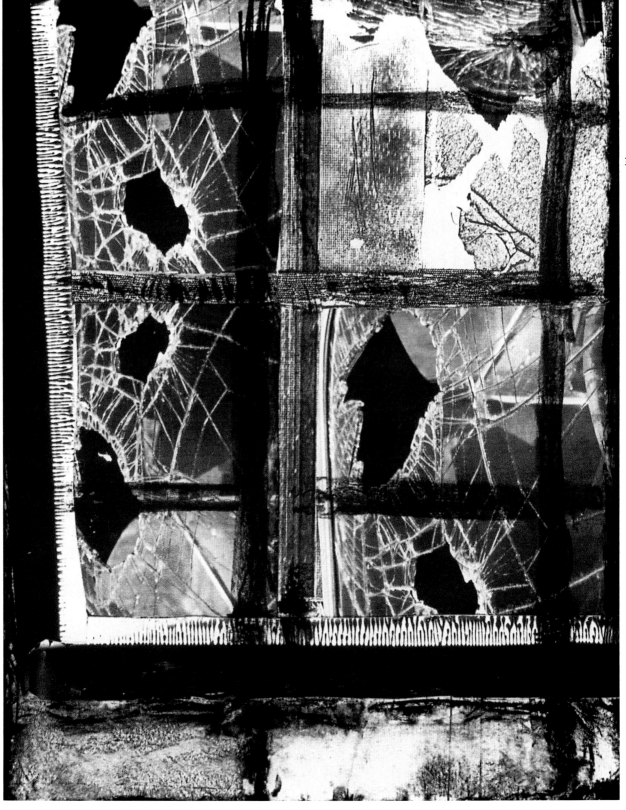

36

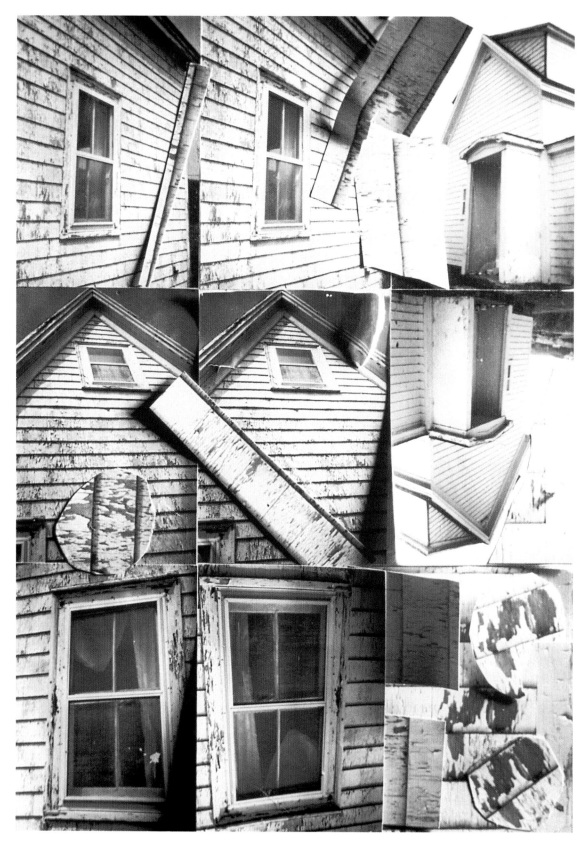

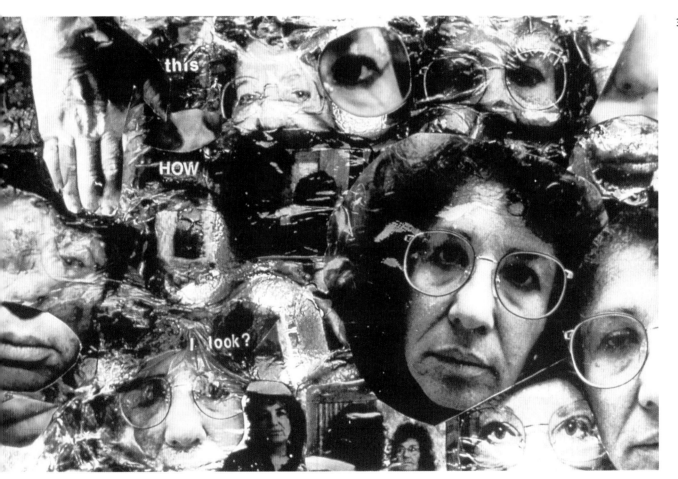

Lucy R. Lippard

38

Although there is a long history of women artists who have, for better and worse, identified with or been identified with nature and land forms, very few female photographers are included in the rolls of old or "new topographers." Men have dominated the field of landscape photography just as men have dominated the land itself. Thus "shooting" a "virgin" landscape has been man's work—hunting, not gardening. It is as though the outdoors, especially in the western United States, were the only remaining male sanctuary among the domesticated interiors of home and workplace. While a large number of women photographers has gathered outdoor images, their failure to impress the art and journalism markets suggests that landscapes are still perceived as trophies from the battle of culture with nature.

Perhaps the calmer, more intimate approach to "nature" offered by many women artists is not exciting enough to appeal to a public taste formed by the dramatic spectacles of the BLM (Boys' Landscape Movement), by the banal beauties of *National Geographic,* and the glamorous oranges and blues featured in *Arizona Highways,* all of which constitute an aftertaste of frontier heroics in which the bigger the land looked, the bigger the men who conquered it were reflected. If Laura Gilpin's loving portraits of the West,[1] Marilyn Bridges's aerial views of ancient civilizations and sacred places, Joan Myers's images of southwestern landmarks, Lyn Davis's monumental interpretations of landscape and ruin, and Linda Connor's formal evocations of time and place have received a certain acclaim, they have not been permitted even to play Eve to the two generations of Adams (Ansel and Robert).

Only recently have women photographers in North America been cutting their own paths into the land-mined "wilderness" of landscape photography, and they have done so not as an influential group but as isolated individuals—unnamed, perhaps in their diversity unnameable—responding to and critiquing their own cultural circumstances as echoed in the environment. Although most of these artists are feminists, their work is not necessarily "feminist landscape."

And what would that be, anyway—a feminist landscape? Something intimate and comfortable, either the opposite of the Marlboro man's domain or a subtle intervention therein? A landscape seen as the body of a woman? A critique of the landscape photography made by men? A critique of landscape art or of "landscape" altogether? The creation of or the dismissal of the notion of gendered landscapes? Postcolonial vignettes? Analyses of the politics of space? Or just the stuff that men aren't doing?

Or perhaps the feminist landscape is an acculturated landscape. Landscape is where culture and nature meet, though both terms are problematic. Photographers dealing with the whole rather than the parts turn to the

[1] Martha Sandweiss writes about Gilpin's interest in "the cultural significance of the landscape" and "in the land as an environment that shaped human activity," and J. B. Jackson said her book on the Rio Grand "established Gilpin as a cultural geographer" ("Laura Gilpin and American Landscape Photography," in Vera Norwood and Janice Monk, eds., *The Desert Is No Lady* [New Haven: Yale University Press, 1987], 62–73).

landscape of culture, which defines place and its meaning to people rather than *viewing* everything from the outside. People (and their ideologies) are often left out of art and criticism about land, the landscape, and place.[2] The idea of landscape must include the ways that land is formed by social relations and the ways social relations are formed by the land.[3] (The scape, or scope, is broad indeed, ranging from archaism to futurology.)

Few of the women whose work I discuss here are even landscape photographers in the conventional sense. They are doing something else. First and foremost, the not quite extant feminist landscape tends to include people, although people may or may not be included in the pictures. The focus is what is seen from the inside, from the viewpoint of people familiar with it, rather than a record of its otherness. At the risk of being accused (yet again) of dread "essentialism," I contend that many women photographers, like many women public artists, are more interested in the local/personal/political aspects of landscape than in the godlike big picture, and tend to be more attuned to the reciprocity inherent in the process of looking into places.[4] Their approach might be called vernacular.

Most of these artists have been led into the political from personal concerns. They are more likely to picture the ways in which landscape is a collective and interactive production—the land affecting those who land on it, and vice versa, offering clues to the cultures that have formed it. This does not exclude acute social criticism, and it certainly includes an awareness of power relations as the agent of spatial production. In almost all of their work there is a dialectic between compassion, memory, continuity, and connectedness on one hand, and, on the other, the looming shadow of an ominous future imposed by forces uncontrollable or uncontrolled (acts of god being secondary to acts of greed). But even when the message comes through loud and clear, the undertones are often as important as the overview.

The intercultural contributions that have opened up a certain cross-ventilation in the arts over the last decade have also shed new light on the incredibly complex politics of nature and place. A major part of the cultural ecology is our relationships to each other, as well as our mutual relationships to place, all of which are defined by social privilege and spatial distribution. To be ignorant of one is to misunderstand the other. If only Euro-American history is studied, the place remains hidden. A culturally inclusive (or culturally specific) landscape aesthetic is only beginning to be revealed. Until there is increased access to education, equipment, and distribution for a broader economic spectrum of women, the picture will be partial.

Because the ground for this subject is still in a rough state, and generalizations are dangerous in such an early stage of discussion, I am going to

[2] Jeff Kelley has distinguished the notion of place from that of site, made popular in the late 1960s by the term site-specific sculpture. A site, says Kelley, "represents the constituent physical properties of a place, while places are the reservoirs of human content." (*Headlands Journal, 1980–84* [San Francisco: Headlands Art Center, 1991], 34–38.)

[3] Daphne Spain offers a variation on this common idea: "Although space is constructed by social behavior at a particular point in time, its legacy may persist (seemingly as an absolute) to shape the behavior of future generations" (*Gendered Spaces* [Chapel Hill: University of North Carolina Press, 1992], 6).

[4] This is borne out by the massive amount of material I have been compiling for a book on land, history, culture, and place. There are more women working in site and photography in this area, as in "real" public art—art that takes into account, involves and responds to the place where it is put and to the people who are there.

pursue these ideas through specific images by specific artists. One of my own first inklings of these issues occurred in the early 1980s, when Jolene Rickard spoke at a PADD Second Sunday about some photographs she had taken on the Tuscarora Nation, where she was raised. They depicted old cars and trucks rusting away amid weeds and shrubs, and what she said about them completely reversed the Euro-American view of such remnants as a "blight on the landscape." On the reservation, she said (I'm paraphrasing from memory), these old trucks were honored reminders of their function, returning slowly to "nature" (with less self-consciousness, I'd add, than the old boats and bathtubs used as planters in white people's yards). Their parts having migrated to other vehicles, they were there for the same reasons an old horse, no longer useful, might be pastured until its death.[5]

Another Native American image that has influenced my thinking is a photograph by Hulleah Tsinhnahjinnie (Navajo/Creek/Seminole) from her "Metropolitan Indian" series of the late 1980s. A handsome Native woman dressed in traditional Plains buckskins is mounted on a horse on a rounded California hill overlooking a freeway. Although she is of course there—a point made by the image—the effect is that of a collage: the "vanished" Indian superimposed on the modern landscape that has replaced the decidedly vanished Native landscape. The emphasis is less on beauty and nobility (although they too play a part) than on survival and, in other pictures in the series, on the near invisibility of the urban Indian population within the spaces created from their own lands.

While conventional "landscape" is rare in modernist Indian art,[6] the land on which Native people live or once lived remains primary—its presence, spirit, and beauty often presented with humor or irony. (Tsinhnahjinnie herself shoots only "pure landscape" of Navajoland in slides, for home consumption rather than as art.) The role of the landscape in this image might be assumed to be peripheral, a mere background. Yet place is a consistent subtext, as important as the handsome figure; a displaced person proudly re-placing herself is a central theme of the series.

Patricia Deadman's "Beyond Saddleback" is a series of portraits of nature blurred in movement. They contain some of the mystery of a bush moving in a sudden breeze, subtly conveying the fact that the movement is internal, taking place within the landscape, within the glowing trees and shadowy mountain or thicket, rather than being externally imposed by a modern time sense, a hurried photographer, an uninterested passerby.

In fact, Deadman does not move her lense, but manipulates the photograph while printing, shifting it four times to achieve a curious combination of focus and lack of focus. She prints her black and white negatives on color

5 Jolene Rickard speaking at a PADD Second Sunday, Franklin Furnace, New York City, Winter 1982–83. Rickard has since made a series on land use/landscape from the Native viewpoint.
6 See the exhibition catalogue *Our Land, Ourselves* (Albany: University Art Gallery, State University of New York at Albany, 1991).

Patricia Deadman
Beyond Saddleback, III
from the series **Beyond Saddleback**, 1991
color photograph, 24″ × 20″.

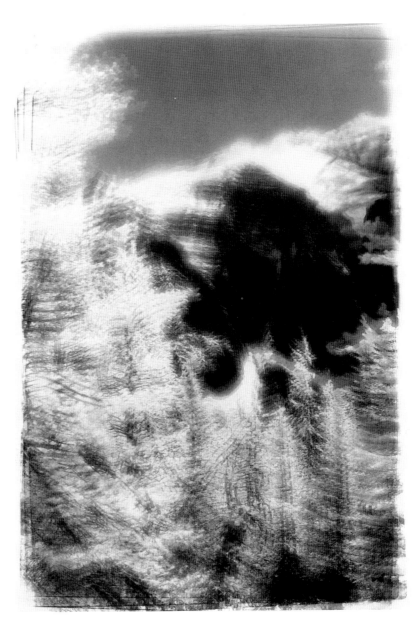

paper, causing an additional imbalance or loss of equilibrium, as Theresa Harlan has pointed out, and challenging 'the notion of the familiar a step further by reminding us that if we stray from the path or underestimate our environment, we can easily become lost and confused, and thus vulnerable."[7] The process permits relatively ordinary images to take on an extraordinary emotional intensity, drawing the viewer into the pulsating scene. Deadman says she intends "to monumentalize these ambiguous qualities, in order to recognize the sublime and the elusive in the experience of landscape."[8]

Deadman (who is Tuscarora, raised on the Six Nations Reserve in Canada) made her earlier work at pow wows, where motion and energy were also her subjects. Painting over small photographs of dancers, she stirred up hidden rhythms with flurries of paint, sucking the figures into colorful abstract whirlwinds that transcended physical movement to reach for the spirit and meaning of Indian people dancing. Although landscape per se is absent from these images, and photography itself is only the point of departure, they presage the "Saddleback" series by suggesting connections between the human heartbeats and those of the terrain being activated by the dance. Dancers and landscape are made indistinguishable, which is also the philosophical point, as time and place are blurred into a timeless and placeless energy zone.[9] In some of these works, says Janet Clark, Deadman is also "commenting on the women participants and their role in dance and in traditional Native society, [representing] a positive link with the past . . . the stability that holds cultures together."[10]

Family history and culture are at the heart of Marlene Creates's recent work about place as repository of memory. Her early work involved peopleless places, slightly altered prehistoric sites. In 1982 she made *Sleeping Places, Newfoundland*—25 black and white photographs depicting the matted grass where Creates bedded down in her sleeping bag while traveling alone. She saw them as "one more layer, a mark, laid upon the thousands of other layers of human and geographic history on the surface of the land."[11]

During a sojourn on Baffin Island in 1985, Creates solicited directions from local people and was taken by two strikingly different maps of the open tundra, one by a white man, the other by an Inuit man. The former depended on labels, the latter on contours and topographic features. This was the beginning of a series called "The Distance Between Two Points is Measured in Memories," which Creates worked with elderly country people displaced into town or cities,[12] setting up a counterpoint between lived space, recalled space, and "natural" space. One of her intentions was to resurrect human history, to dispel prevailing images of Labrador as "a pris-

[7] Theresa Harlan, "Message Carriers: Native Photographic Messages," *Views* (Winter 1993): 7.

[8] Patricia Deadman, in *Fringe Momentum: The Photocollages of Patricia Deadman* (Thunder Bay: Thunder Bay Art Gallery, 1990), 14.

[9] Vincent Scully's *Pueblo: Mountain, Village, Dance* (New York: Viking, 1975), which relates southwestern topography to pueblo architecture to dance, comes to mind.

[10] Janet Clark, in *Fringe Momentum*, 9.

[11] Marlene Creates, *The Distance Between Two Points Is Measured in Memories* (St. John: Sir Wilfred Grenfell College Art Gallery Memorial University of Newfoundland, 1989). This piece recalls Susan Hiller's 1974 *Dream Mapping*, in which parallel dreams were recorded after several people slept overnight in "fairy circles" in England.

[12] In a 1988 installation and artist's book, Creates interviewed the former inhabitants (Naskapi Innu, Inuit, and Euro-Canadian settlers) of an isolated area in Labrador; they told stories and penciled tentative maps from memory. These maps were then installed with a portrait of the storyteller in her or his living room, a brief reminiscence, a photograph of the mapped place today, and a natural object such as a bundle of grass, a rock, dried flowers.

Marlene Creates
from *where my grandmother was born*
from the series ***Places of Presence:***
Newfoundland kin and ancestral land,
Newfoundland 1989–91, 1989–91
assemblage of photographs, memory map
drawings, story panels, natural objects
63.5" × 7.25" × 20' overall.

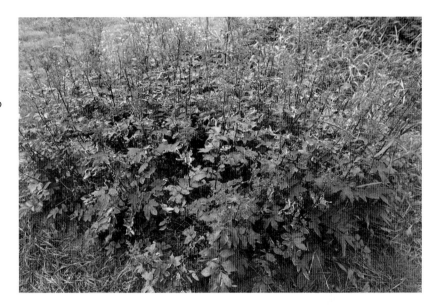

tine untouched wilderness where there is no one and where no one has lived."[13] There is another layer to the piece as well. The nostalgic coziness of place gives way not only to the melancholy of lost pasts, but also to the threat of more drastic change. In the 1940s, an airforce base was established in Labrador, and since a NATO agreement around 1981, militarization has increased with vast bombing ranges and low level flying, about which few Canadians are aware. This is the ominous, untold background theme of the apparently intimate stories recounted.

People, and the ways their narratives are told and remembered become the mediums through which place is perceived, are also the subject of Creates' next series "Places of Presence: Newfoundland kin and ancestral land" (1989–91). It focuses on "three precise bits of 'landscape'" where her grandmother, grandfather, and great grandmother were born. Aside from the personal aspects of this "poetic inheritance," Creates's photographs also reveal "a pattern of land use in rural Newfoundland where land has been passed down from generation to generation, divided into smaller and smaller pieces among sons and nephews and, with some interesting exceptions, inherited by daughters."[14]

She compares these stories and photographs to "a net that was set up at one point in the flow of people, events, and natural changes that make up the history of these three places." They are palimpsests, impressed with

13 Marlene Creates, "Statement" (unpublished), December 1990.
14 Marlene Creates, artist's statement (unpublished), 1991.

lost or barely recalled histories. The images themselves are most evocative when a trace remains, such as the flowers her grandmother planted in a garden long since "gone back to nature."

Carrie Mae Weems "went looking for Africa" in the Gullah (from Gola, Angola) community off the South Carolina Coast. In her 1992 installation *Sea Islands*, the landscapes might be seen as incidental to her postmodern folklore, but that would be missing the point where the two come together. As the daughter of Mississippi sharecroppers who migrated to Portland, Oregon in the 1950s, as a trained ethnicist long involved with African American folklore, and inspired by Zora Neale Hurston, Weems pictures places that are entirely acculturated. It is not the history of their colonization that concerns her, but the maintenance of culture, and of a powerfully different sense of place and nature beneath colonization. Weems has frequently used family history as a lever into general Black American experience, which has often been land-based even when land-deprived. Like Rickard's and Tsinhnahjinnie's art, hers is also about survival, integrated with the land on which the process "takes place." In a way, the culture *is* the landscape in these photographs, even when the landscape itself is a very real presence, an integral part of the enterprise. Recognizably southern (live oaks and spanish moss), the land and the buildings are the containers of imported knowledge; they hold ancient, elusive meanings, including the terrible oppression of displacement. One of the most evocative images is that of huge old palm trees at Ebo Landing, where a cargo of Ibo men declined to be slaves and walked back into the sea to their deaths, saying, "The water brought us, the water will take us away." Some of the trees stand solid and straight, others sway and are about to fall.

People occasionally appear like the phantom child in Julie Dash's film *Daughters of the Dust.* Even without them, the landscape is clearly a lived one, a place filled with rather than emptied of meaning. The cool, matter-of-fact documentary format of the images co-exists with this layer of undertones and simultaneously offsets it, as do the cryptic texts, which are less captions than parallel poetry, sharing the lucid understatement of the images. Weems went "looking for Africa," and found

> A bowl of butter beans / on a grave / newspapered walls / for the spirits to read / rice in the corners / a pan / of vinegar water / up under the / bed.

Elevating "superstition" to spirituality—"the opening up of yourself"—Weems asks, "How do you get closer? . . . How do you spin in and unravel?"[15] By going to local sources, her "Sea Islands" show provides

15 Carrie Mae Weems, *Artweek*, 1992.

Carrie Mae Weems
from *Sea Island Series*, 1992
black-and-white photograph,
20″ × 20″.

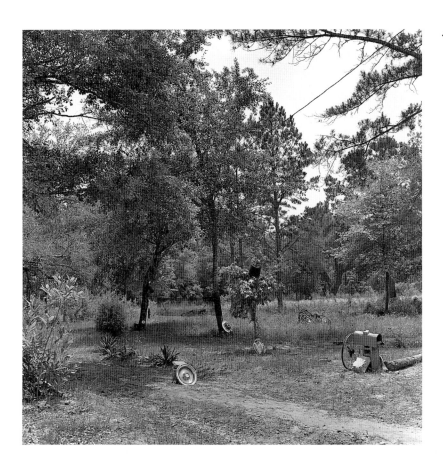

new ground for contemporary black artists' scrutiny of their historical and spiritual roots—from "picturesque" brick slave houses to hubcaps on the lawn (providing a "flash of the spirit" to repel evil spirits), to a bedspring in a tree, literally embedding culture in the landscape. At the same time, there is a political task yet to be done. Weems feels she needs to add something that might help fend off the impending threat posed by suburban golf courses in this ancient acculturated landscape.

In the late 1980s, Masumi Hayashi made panoramic photocollages of Superfund toxic waste sites in the postindustrial midwestern landscape. Her recent work concerns similarly infamous locations, but now they are particularly pertinent to Asian Americans, and to her family—Angel Island,

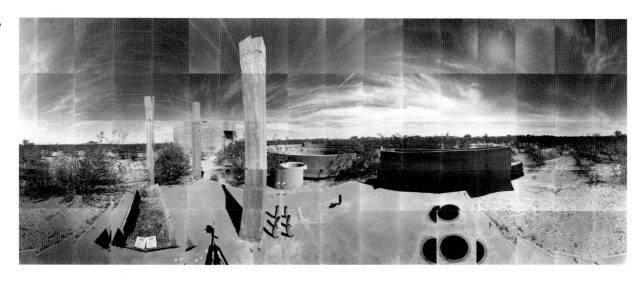

Masumi Hayashi

Gila River Relocation Camp, 1990
photocollage, 22″ × 56″.

where her grandmother came as a "picture bride," and her own birthplace, the Gila River Relocation Camp. This series reflects "the struggles my family members have passed through."[16] She has heard the testimony of those who experienced the concentration camps, including in her installations audio interviews with survivors, friends and relatives.

Beginning with the personal—Gila River—Hayashi moved into a series of works on nine other internment camps, in order to mark a historical moment when, as she says, "racism and nationalism outweighed moral judgment, civil liberties and logic." In an amnesiac late 20th-century society, there is, as J. B. Jackson suggests, a "necessity for ruins."[17] Works like Hayashi's constitute a social archaeology, conveying a relationship between the metal, concrete, wooden ruins and the desert landscape that differs from an external perception of the scene as simply picturesque, melancholy, historical. Perhaps because of her personal involvement, she has downplayed the eerie beauty of the Gila River camp, while creating desolate sculptural parallels. The dramatic skies also evoke the site's ominous history. She is not picturing the power of "nature" to transcend that history so much as insisting on the remains to tell or cue in the stories that Asian Americans know but not enough other people have heard or remember. Her gridded photocollage technique, which sometimes includes double images of one form through slight overlapping, may allude to scientific mapping techniques that filter ourviews. It also suggests the multiple viewpoint of traditional Asian landscape aesthetics, or the double-

[16] Masumi Hayashi, in *Centered Margins: Contemporary Art of the Americas* (Bowling Green: Dorothy Uber Byron Gallery, 1992).

[17] J. B. Jackson, *The Necessity for Ruins* (Amherst: University of Massachusetts Press, 1979), 89–102.

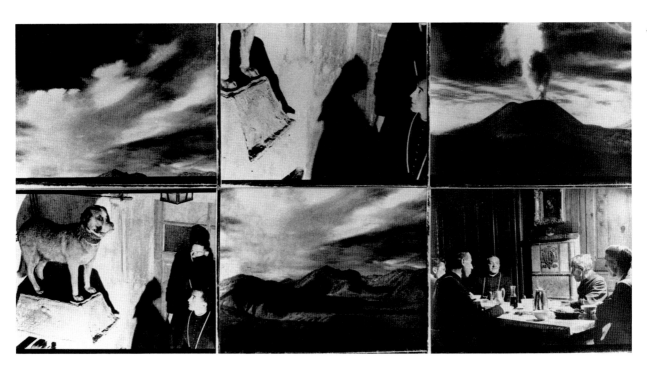

Caroline Hinkley

Death of the Master Narrative, 1991
installation of black-and-white photographs, 32″ × 60″.

exposure quality of memory itself. The viewer is not quite "there"; the
vantage point is disturbed, in transition, potentially catastrophic. Beauty is
used to draw the viewer into a politically contested space.

Landscapes often appear in Caroline Hinkley's gridded works about authority conflicts as terrains of psychic terror, but only as equal elements within a
hermetic whole. A longtime scholar of landscape and photography who has
taught environmental design, Hinkley is interested in exposing the dominance of the masculine gaze and its corollary: the exclusion of women from
representation as subject. She quotes Michele Montrelay's notion that
women are "the ruin of representation" because they have nothing to lose
and their exteriority to western representation exposes its limits.[18]
 Hinkley lists her devices for the dismantling of cultural and ethnographic authority (what she calls "visual swipes" at men in suits, uniforms,
robes): repetition of symbolic gestures and objects, appropriation, seriality,
truncation, amplification, reduction. Her usual format is six or nine horizontal photographs, most of them appropriated; the apparently unrelated
images are connected by details or close-ups that revise their meanings.

[18] Michele Montrelay, quoted in Caroline
Hinkley, "Work in Progress"
(unpublished), 1990.

48

The landscapes, although reduced in scale, tend to determine the (usually dark) mood. As a lesbian, Hinkley also slyly confuses gender and gender references in subtle (almost invisible) digs at the dominant culture and its scenic overlook.

There are three landscapes in *Death of the Master Narrative* (1991): clouds almost hiding a bare slope, mountains with dramatic sky, and a volcano. Each image is striking in itself, but each part is subordinated to the political allusions of the whole. All the pictures in this piece are appropriated from the *National Geographic,* epitome of imperialist pictorialism, the master narrative. (Having played god to the extent of moving pyramids and re-arranging sunsets on a cover, *National Geographic* is fair game for feminist appropriation.) The three decontextualized landscapes (one a different view of another) are juxtaposed against three views of Catholic priests. In the lower right several priests (one with a particularly sinister face; one with a gap toothed smile, a minor reference to the stereotypical lasciviousness usually applied to women, as in Les Blank's film) sit around an altar featuring the Madonna, whose force lines direct our gaze up to the steaming volcano above. In the lower left image, two young monks stare up at a stuffed dog (mascot of the St. Bernard hospice monastery) who might be awaiting his master's voice or might represent the moribund rigidity of the master narrative. A close-up of the dog's feet from this picture is repeated above and locates the gaze and emphasizes the two ominous shadows. Aside from their formal power, these juxtapositions and repetitions communicate a forceful message: man's thwarted desire for control over nature and spirituality. The distant clouds, rugged mountain landscape, and angry volcano imply the defeat of patriarchal domination.

The feminist photographer who has most extensively thought through, written about, and practiced a postmodern landscape photography in relation to local political histories is Deborah Bright. In an attempt to move the ailing documentary photography tradition into a more precarious and layered place, she has worked primarily with installation and "textual landscapes," beginning with the "Battlefield Panorama" series (1981–1984) in which history was recalled through texts that made the vicious events of the past rise from bland images of the now domesticated grounds on which they were fought.

Bright's turf is the apparently innocuous landscape charged by its history. In *How the West Was Won* (*Caution—Do Not Dig*) (1985), ordinary color photographs were made subversive by texts explaining their political contexts and revealing the underlying ideologies of what had happened there. The story begins with General Groves of atomic bomb fame reminiscing about having been brought up in the west early in this century and worrying that there was nothing left for *him* to conquer. The cowboy gods were to offer up a reward for such faith in manifest destiny and he became top administrator of the U.S. nuclear program, managing the world's first nuclear reactor, which was installed in 1943 some 20 miles from Chicago; around 1950 it was bulldozed under what is now "park" land. **49**

Bright's piece is bracketed by two artificially rustic stone monuments, one commemorating the landmark and the other admonishing "CAUTION— DO NOT DIG," while insisting in smaller print that "there is no danger to visitors." In between are the Groves texts and the landscapes. Nancy Gonchar writes that "what is most compelling about this piece is the sparseness of the information displayed, in contrast to the enormity of the project and its implications for the future." She points out, however, that "the visual image becomes the backdrop for the unfolding text."[19] There is a certain deliberate bloodlessness about the overall installation which stems, perhaps, from the fact that form, text, and substance are in reaction to the dominant culture and therefore mirror its emphasis on objectivity at all costs.

In Bright's brilliant writings on the history of the arranged marriage between photography and nature, she interrogates her own and other photographers' work with questions about the ideologies perpetuated by all photographs "in whose interests they were conceived; why we still desire to make and consume them; and why the art of landscape photography remains so singularly identified with a masculine eye."[20]

In "Elements of a New Landscape,"[21] Rebecca Solnit, the other major feminist writer on landscape photography, writes that "as an analysis of entrenched structures of belief, feminism reached far deeper to disrupt the binary relationships around which the culture organized itself," and "the explosion of the bomb is the moment when two traditions of thought collided: the world of dead fragments of Descartes and Bacon and the world of interconnected systems of quantum physics, of ecology, and later of postmodern theory" (to which I would add feminism).

Feminist landscape and the bomb do seem deeply connected, not just theoretically, but also emotionally. From an eco-feminist viewpoint, the brutality with which the new weaponry treated Mother Earth has been viscerally felt by women (already culturally charged with "horticulture," maintenance, nurture), whose bodies had so long been identified with the hills and valleys under siege. (Neil Smith has coined the composite "M/Other Nature.")[22] Power, but not necessarily the balance of power, is the key to looking at almost every "natural" landscape, and power is always a feminist issue.

19 Nancy Gonchar, *Deborah Bright: Textual Landscapes* (Binghamton, N.Y.: University Art Gallery, 1988).
20 Deborah Bright, "Of Mother Nature and Marlboro Men: An Inquiry into the Cultural Meanings of Landscape Photography," *Exposure* (Winter, 1985).
21 Rebecca Solnit, "Elements of a New Landscape" (manuscript): 5,4.
22 Neil Smith, "Making M/Other Nature," *Artforum* (Dec. 1989): 17–19.

Deborah Bright
How the West Was Won, 1985
phototext installation.

50

In a remote spot in the middle of a forest preserve about 20 miles west of Chicago lies the abandoned site of the world's first nuclear reactor.

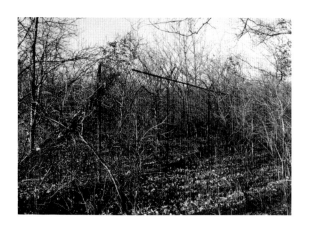

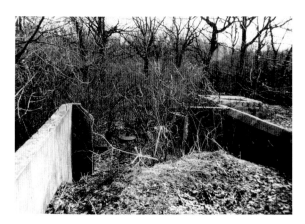

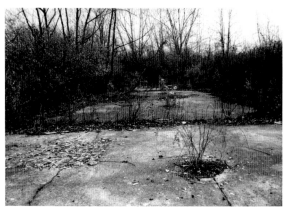

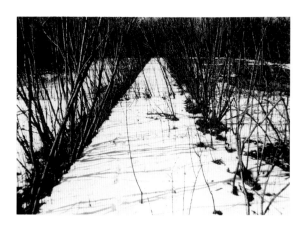

Gen. Groves: Compton raised the question: "Why wait for Argonne?" There was no reason to wait, except for our uncertainty about whether the planned experiment might not prove hazardous to the surrounding community.

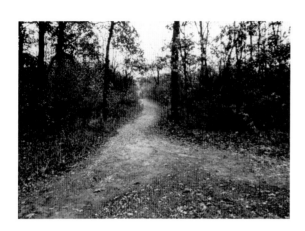

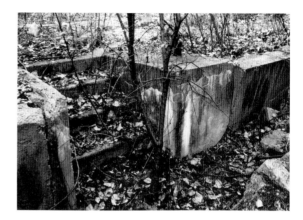

If the pile should explode, no one knew just how far the danger would extend.

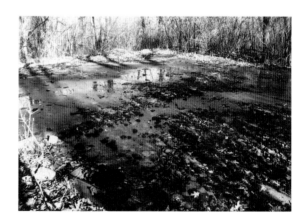

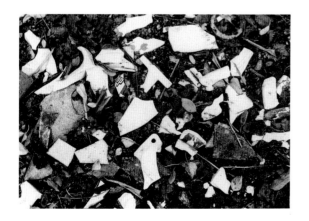

With the establishment of the Argonne National Laboratory in 1954, this site was returned to forest—the reactor buildings and laboratories were bulldozed into the ground.

For several years, Meridel Rubinstein (in collaboration with performance artist Ellen Zweig and videographers Steina and Woody Vasulka) worked on *Critical Mass*, a multimedia installation about the intersection around Los Alamos of the terrains and territories of Native American and nuclear scientific cultures. Rubinstein came to this project after years of photographing Northern New Mexico and its inhabitants. Her narrative is centered on the story of Edith Warner, the "Woman at Otowi Crossing," a refugee from the East who in the 1920s moved to a cottage near the Rio Grande and became close to both the Pueblos at San Ildefonso and the top-secret-ridden inmates of Los Alamos. A number of crossings are the subject of this work, and the Rio Grande runs through it. A vortex is established between two ways of experiencing the land—nothing so simple as past/future.

Rubinstein's landscapes reflect two conflicting belief systems entangled in power, doubt, fear, beauty on a cosmic scale. Her work is usually multipartite and layered, offering multiple viewpoints on a subject or place, interweaving disparate realities. The images in "Critical Mass" combine portraits, still lifes, and landscapes. As Rebecca Solnit has observed, Rubinstein's photography

> postulates a kind of subjective nonfiction that dissolves the distinctions between the personal and the documentary, the made and the found. . . . Photographs—and by extension, witnessing and vision—are revealed as far more complex phenomena, shaped by the artist and viewer as invested participants. . . . All of Rubinstein's work of the past decade can be said to describe a world that shapes its inhabitants as they construct it, and to explore the resonance between place, action and belief.[23]

Broken Landscape (1990) includes not people, but cultural artifacts. It is a panoramic view of bare hills in the Pajarito plateau interrupted by a picture of an old jail cell, the horizon line moving from exterior to interior and back out again; below these three rectangles is a long, low, horizontal but still suggestively phallic missile, serpentlike with its needle-pointed nose, lurking in the underworld, a literal subtext. This is a landscape "broken" in several senses. Its lunar appearance (not a tree in sight) suggests that the land might have been subjected to actual testing. The prison suggests the fate of the land—cordoned off from its own past and from ordinary life—as well as the fate of those protesting the nuclear enterprise and those who would suffer if a disaster occurred.

[23] Rebecca Solnit, "Meridel Rubinstein: Critical Mass," *Artspace* (July-Aug. 1992): 47.

Meridel Rubenstein
Broken Landscape, 1990
pd prints on steel, 36″ × 60″.

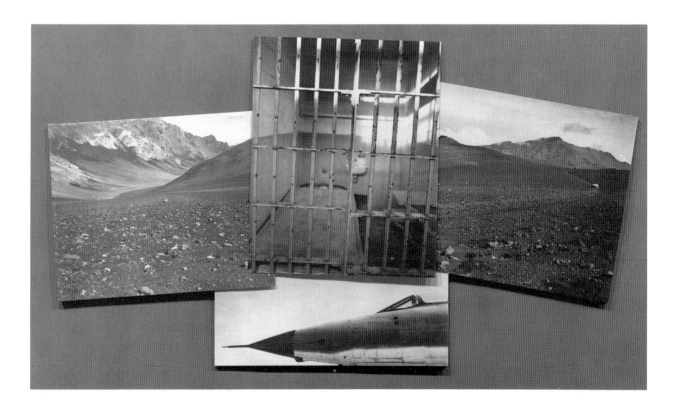

The paradox buried in the late twentieth-century landscape is that earlier ruminations on the sublime and cosmic natural beauty have given way to a discourse about poisons. The beauty is still there in many cases, but it has been (literally) undermined. Carole Gallagher's book *American Ground Zero: The Secret Nuclear War*,[24] and Sharon Stewart's "Toxic Tour of Texas"[25] take on the future. These two projects bear witness to the parallel destruction of people's lives and the land they live on. They are devastating indictments of the wilful disregard for lives and land by the powers that be—public and private, governmental and corporate. Neither work can be done justice in this brief space, since the detailed information behind the pictures is as significant as the images. The voices of victims, witnesses, and activists (sometimes the same people), as heard in interviews, echo through the vast spaces surrounding them: downwind (mostly in Utah) from the Nevada test site in Gallagher's work, which also includes atomic veterans and test site workers; waste disposal sites all over Texas in Stewart's.

Texas, Stewart points out, is indeed biggest and best in some distressing categories: Its industries discharge "the highest level of toxic air emissions in the country"; it has "the largest concentration of oil refineries and chemical plants in the nation . . . [and it] ranks first in the amount of known or suspected carcinogens in the number of hazardous waste disposal sites, seventy percent of which leak and threaten groundwater." The guides on her "tour" are "farmers, priests, mothers, ranchers, engineers, nurses and teachers intent on protecting their land, their children, their homes and their communities." Each photograph (some are of apparently bucolic vistas, others of people) is accompanied by grisly testimony. For example, in the haunting image unpoetically titled *Chevron's 160 Acre Uranium Mill Tailings Pond; Contents: Six Million Tons of Radioactive Waste and Chemical Solvents*, a branch fence, partly submerged, leads symbolically from a foreground littered with empty drums into the lethal waters, toward the other shore of this contemporary Styx.

Gallagher's book (also an exhibition) was begun in 1981, when she dropped out of her life as a SoHo artist and rented a basement room in St. George, Utah. She remained in the area for most of eight years. This monumental decision to embark on a private anti-nuclear humanitarian crusade was inspired by her discovery of some declassified Atomic Energy Commission documents from the 1950s and a quote from Francis Bacon cherished by Dorothea Lange, a documentary photographer's credo:

> the contemplation of things as they are, without error or confusion, without substitution or imposture, is in itself a nobler thing than a whole harvest of invention.

[24] Carole Gallagher, *American Ground Zero: The Secret Nuclear War* (Cambridge: MIT Press, 1993).

[25] Sharon Stewart, *Toxic Tour of Texas* (Houston: published by the author, 1992).

Sharon Stewart

Chevron's 160 Acre Uranium Mill Tailings
Pond; Contents: Six Million Tons of
Radioactive Waste and Chemical Solvents
from *Toxic Tour of Texas* (Houston, 1992).

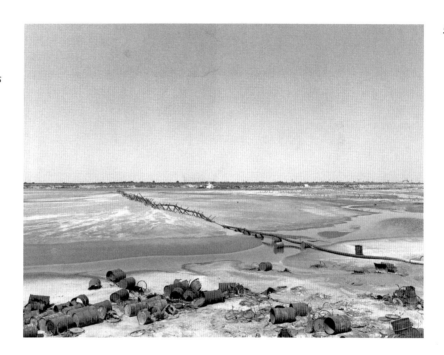

In the documents Gallagher found the people living downwind of the Nevada nuclear testing site described as "a low-use segment of the population." Mormon Utah was apparently chosen as a sacrifice area because its religious/patriotic (and extraordinarily naive) population would not question the government that planned to kill them, their livestock, and their land. (According to Gallagher, Eisenhower is alleged to have said: "we can afford to sacrifice a few thousand people out there in the interest of national security.") Until recently, the perpetrators were right.

It is the rural Mormon culture that emerges from the faces, surrounding landscapes, and texts. Gallagher's photos primarily document and take testimony from people dying and dead from unheard-of types and rates of cancer, some of whom still cannot or will not believe that their government would do such things to them. As a feminist, she makes sure that women get equal time, citing, for instance, the ways women with all the symptoms of severe radiation sickness were diagnosed as neurotic or as having "housewife syndrome."

The last section of the book includes the images of some heartrendingly beautiful landscapes, all profoundly contaminated. These include pictures of the animal cages near ground zero at Frenchman Flat (atomic

56 Carole Gallagher

*Animal Cages, Frenchman's Flat, Site of 27
   Detonations, Nevada Test Site*
from *American Ground Zero: The Secret
   Nuclear War* (Cambridge: MIT Press,
   1993)
black-and-white photograph.

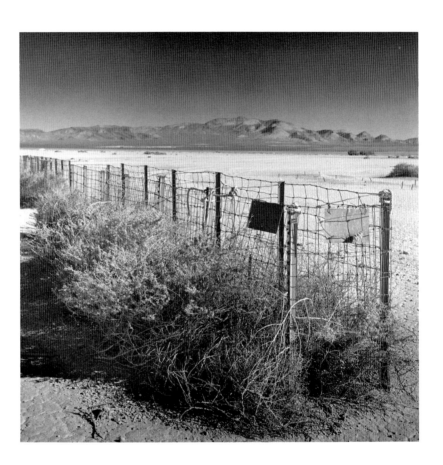

veterans have testified that they saw both animals *and humans* chained in
cages on this site of 27 detonations), an abandoned schoolyard,
condemned sheep ranches, downwind grain elevators and fruit orchards,
still functioning, still in our lives, still "out there" in the silent West,
described in a 1950s issue of *Armed Forces Talk* as "a damned good place to
dump used razorblades." This scorned land has become a vortex of crucial
issues, since much of it is still legally owned[26] by the Western Shoshone,
who feel differently about it.

   "Death by geography," comments Gallagher. Her book, like Stewart's
tour, is a call to action. She details the despicable history of court cases
against the government ("the fox guarding the chicken coop"), but *American Ground Zero* should help blow the door off the closet in which these
scandals have been kept. Although the landscapes she pictures are in the

26 The U.S. government contends that it
   has legally bought the lands deeded to
   the Shoshone by the 1863 Treaty of
   Ruby Valley. The Shoshone contend that
   the land was never for sale and they
   wanted not money, but the return of
   their land.

West, she also quotes an Air Force colonel who told her "there isn't anyone in the United States who isn't a downwinder."

The loss of paradise has been a constant theme in American art at least since the end of the nineteenth century. And the farther we get from "paradise," the less we are connected to the land we live on and the less we understand how it came to be as it is. Geographers have argued that to "explain why something occurs is to explain why it occurs where it does."[27] Landscape itself might be defined as place at a distance, framed with some objectivity, whereas the concept of place leans to the subjective, the intimate, the marked, the recalled, and by implication, the female. Annette Kolodny has written that American women have inhabited a metaphorical landscape they had no part in creating and "to escape the psychology of captivity, women set about making their own mark on the landscape, reserving to themselves the language of gardening."[28] Judith Fryer writes poignantly about the "felicitous spaces" created by Willa Cather and Edith Wharton, where intimacy centered in vastness, defined by a sensuous expansion from visual perception to information learned from touch, smell, sound, the better to perceive "a world in flux, of connectedness."[29]

Outside of literary criticism, analyses of contemporary gendered space have usually focused on home and workplace, urban and suburban experience.[30] While intimacy has been women's (socially constructed but not entirely evil) terrain, less attention has been paid to women's perception of "open" space and place outdoors—in the public domain or in less circumscribed locations defined by an artist's eye. Temporal and spatial distance within photographic images is a crucial element in this new arena. The psychological ambiguities of spatial interpretation have further confused research into landed desire.

Do women photographers still reserve "the language of gardening"? If interior divisions have to do with labor and childbearing/caring, does landscape invoke freedom, and is freedom still by definition a masculine reward? Are women psychologically excluded from the Great Outdoors by constructed (sexual) fears? How do acculturated spaces perceived from the inside differ from the views from the outside?

The forms society makes and takes when overlaid on what's left of nature are pre-eminently artistic turf. The challenge now is to translate segregation and exclusion from interior to exterior through the eyes/lenses of women. Through the work of the women discussed here, among others, a different set of lived experiences of land and place is edging its way into contemporary aesthetics, exposing the deeper layers of life that form a cultural landscape.

Robert David Sack, *Conceptions of Space in Social Thought* (Minneapolis: University of Minnesota Press, 1980), 70.

[28] Annette Kolodny, *The Land Before Her* (Chapel Hill: University of North Carolina Press, 1984), 6–7.

[29] Judith Fryer, *Felicitous Space: The Imaginative Structures of Edith Wharton and Willa Cather* (Chapel Hill: University of North Carolina Press, 1986), 290.

[30] See, for instance, Daphne Spain, *Gendered Spaces*; Peter Jackson, *Maps of Meaning* (London: Unwin Hyman, 1989), chap. 5; Alexander Wilson, *The Culture of Nature* (Cambridge: Blackwell, 1992) on the women/gardens and men/lawns syndrome, p. 99; and Dolores Hayden's *The Power of Place* (Cambridge: MIT Press, 1995). The exception is the Sandweiss article referred to in note 1.

57

Gendering Space

Domestic Production/Reproduction/Resistance

ARTWORKS
Linda Brooks   from *between the birthdays*
Gail S. Rebhan   from *The Family Tapes*
Nancy Barton   from *Live and Let Die*
Clarissa Sligh   from *Reframing the Past*
Susan Meiselas   from *Archiving Abuse*
S. A. Bachman   from *It's All There in Black and White*

ESSAY
Deborah Willis   Women's Stories/Women's Photobiographies

60

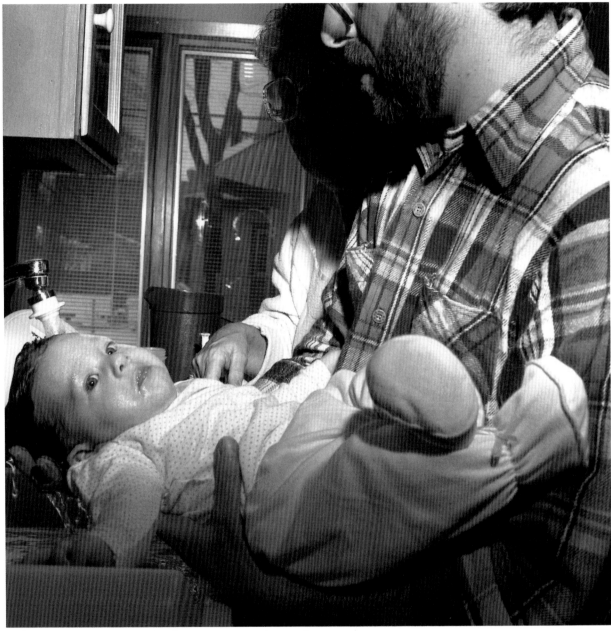

Joe washed Ana's hair, Grandma Renee watched
They came in late December. Traveling north in winter is something
Floridians never do unless they have to. Grandma fed Ana her first
bowls of rice cereal and taught her how to sputter her lips with a
mouthful. She also took great pleasure in 'training' Ana's wet hair with
a comb after her bath.

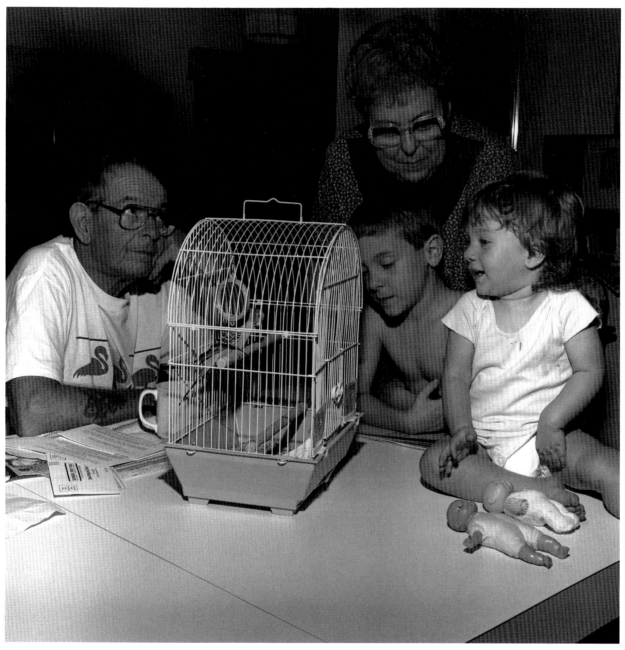

Grandpa Billy bought a parakeet for the kids

His plan to fly 'Pepe' home with us to Minneapolis was doomed from the start. Grandma knew, as soon as she saw that bird, she would be cleaning the cage. She finally agreed to let the bird stay after he convinced her that he would take care of it. A few weeks later he brought home a mate for Pepe. Several months later, he tried to give the birds to his other grandchildren. He wanted them to take the birds back to NY in the car. When that failed, he gave the birds to someone who would give them a good home.

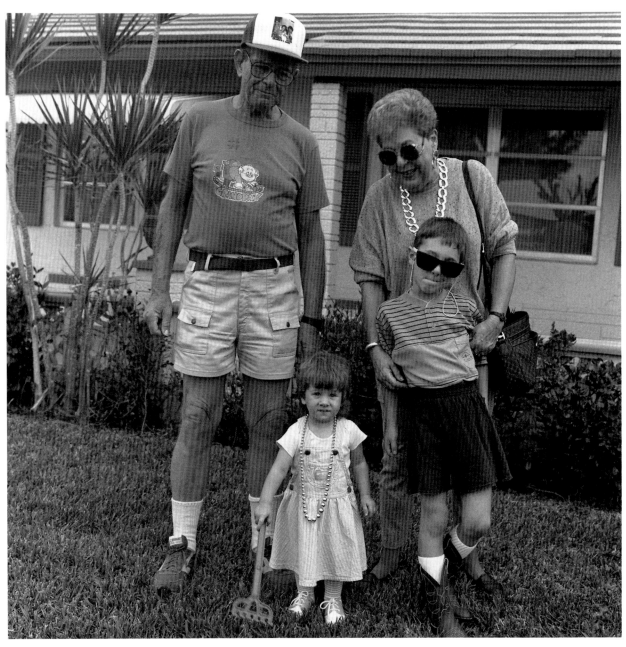

Grandpa Billy, Grandma Renee, Ana and Aaron, front lawn
Grandpa took Aaron to the mall and returned with a pair of cowboy boots for
him. The selection was too macho for my tastes, but Aaron thought they were
pretty cool. Ana was attracted to Grandma's shiny jewelry. Grandma took
advantage of the attention and let her wear some of her 'pretties.' Aaron
was also attracted to the jewelry, but Grandma rejected the idea of
engaging him with 'feminine' objects.

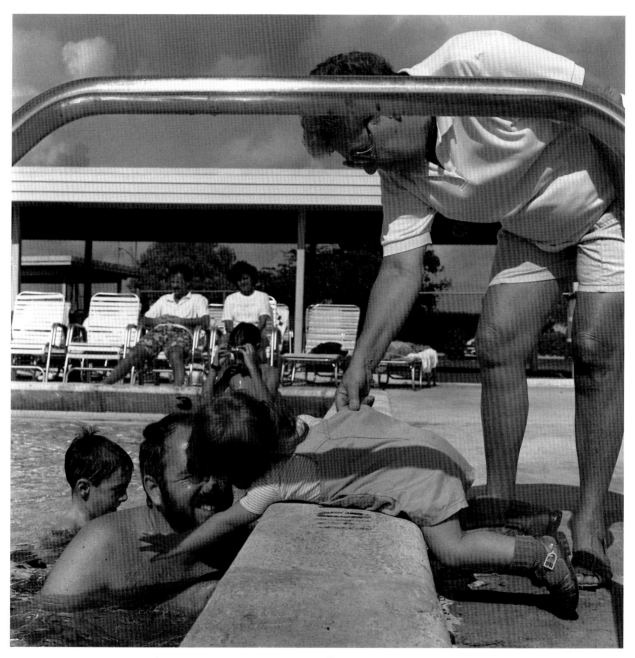

Grandma Renee holding Ana (17 months) at the edge of the pool
One of the strict rules of the adult community where my parents live is
that only children who are toilet trained may enter the pool. She
constantly asks if Ana is trained yet, while reminding me that I was
trained at 18 months.

from *The Family Tapes*

64

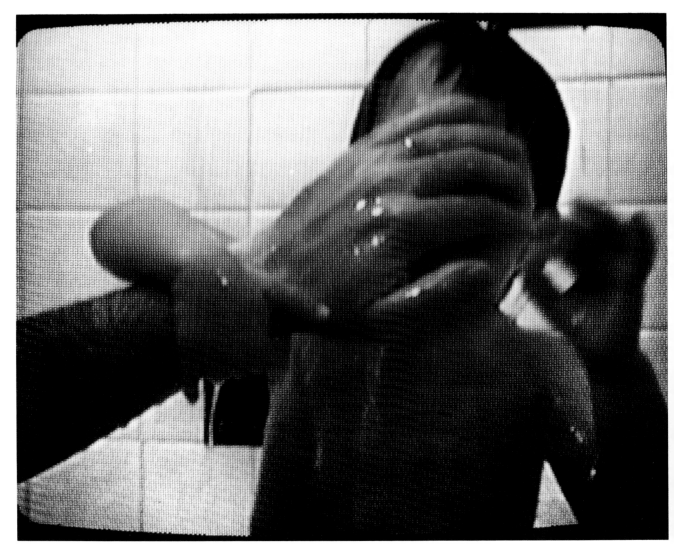

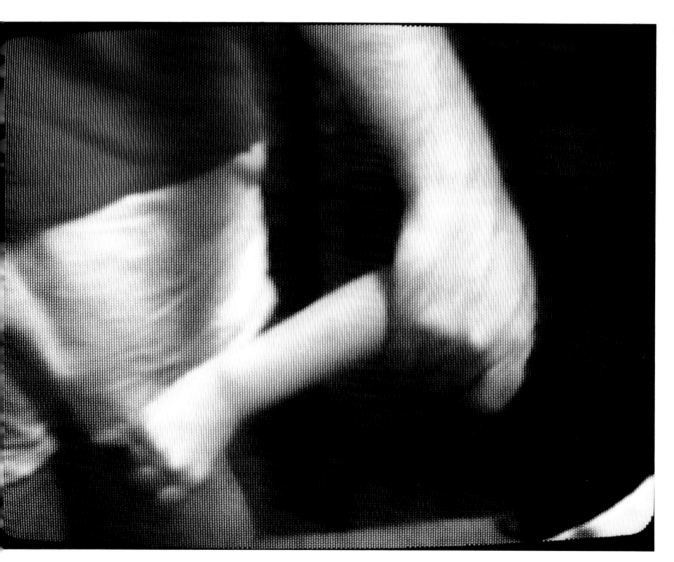

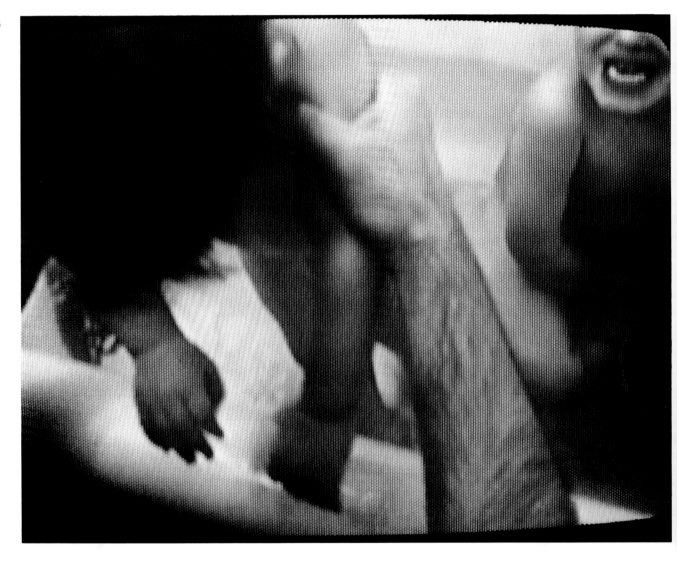

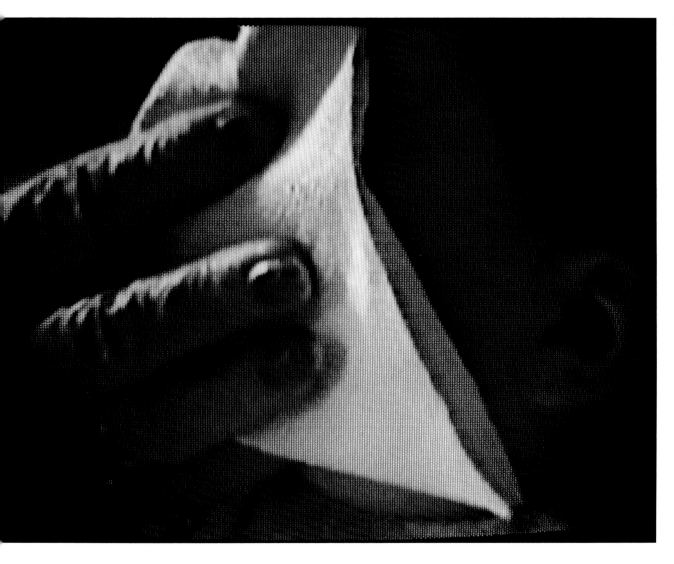

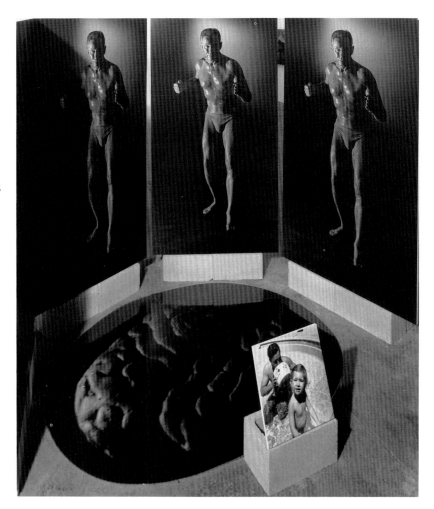

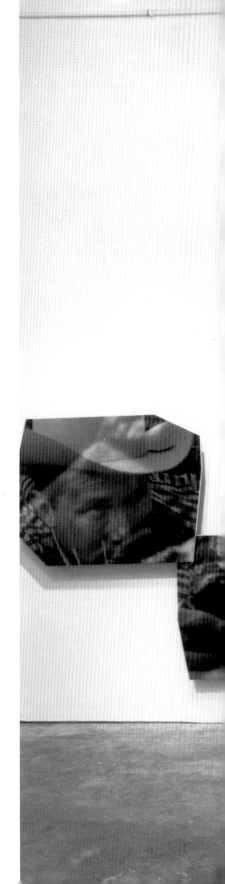

My favorite thing though was to pee in the swimming pool. It was my secret pleasure, perhaps the most real contact I and my father had. A pale yellow stream invisibly gluing us together. Veins were forming on his legs. In his own terms, his aging was beginning to reveal his real lack of authority, and I was responding, forming my own language.

A private language. I developed at the age of seventeen, a strict regime of self-discipline. I bought a handgun, two rifles and filled a room with bottled water. I could eat only two pieces of fruit a day. Not bulimia, not whatever teen girl phenomena you might be thinking of, it was my decision and I was proud of it. This plan progressed over many months. Until most of my hair had fallen out.

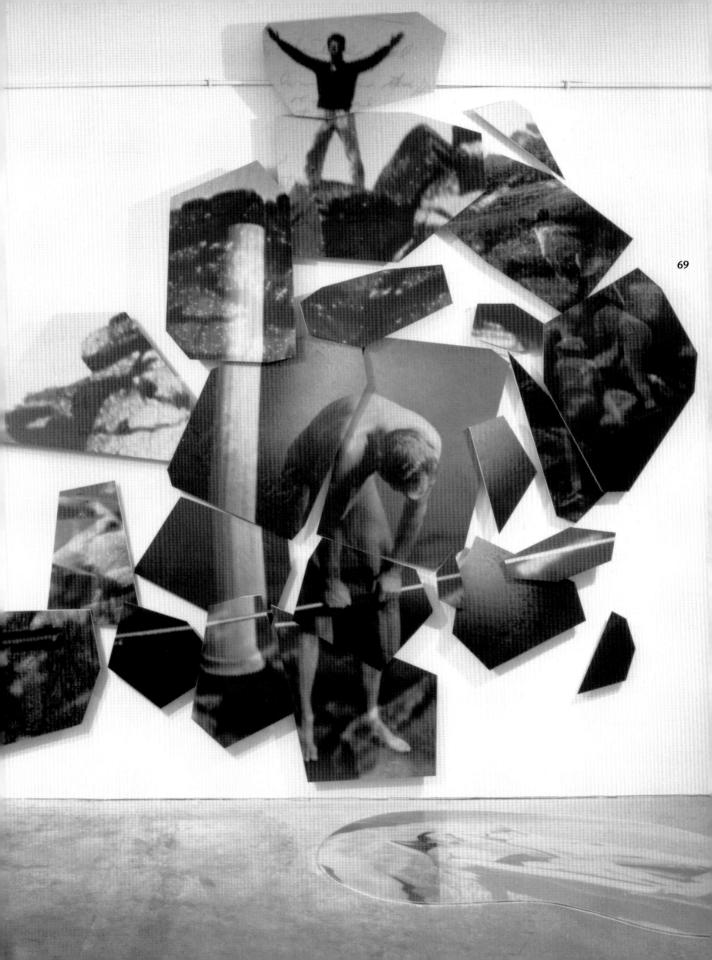

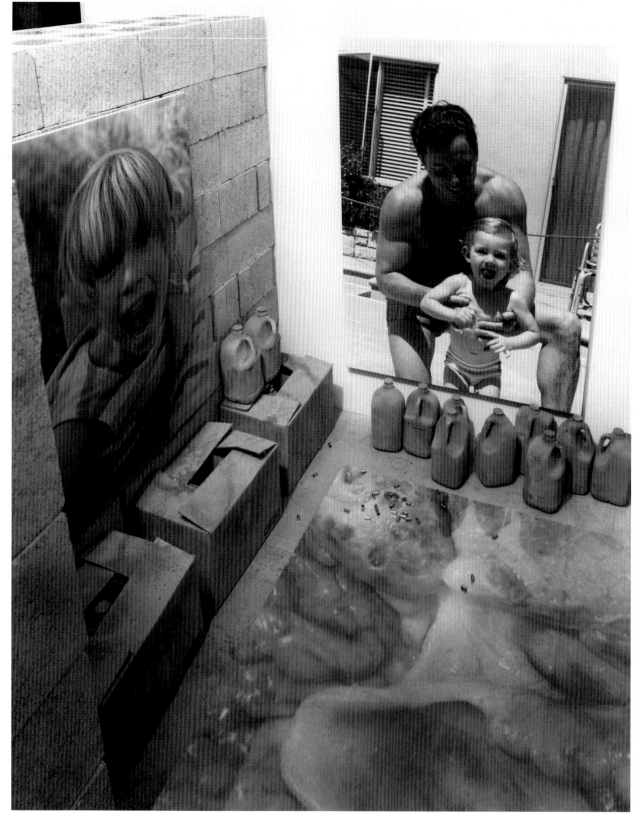

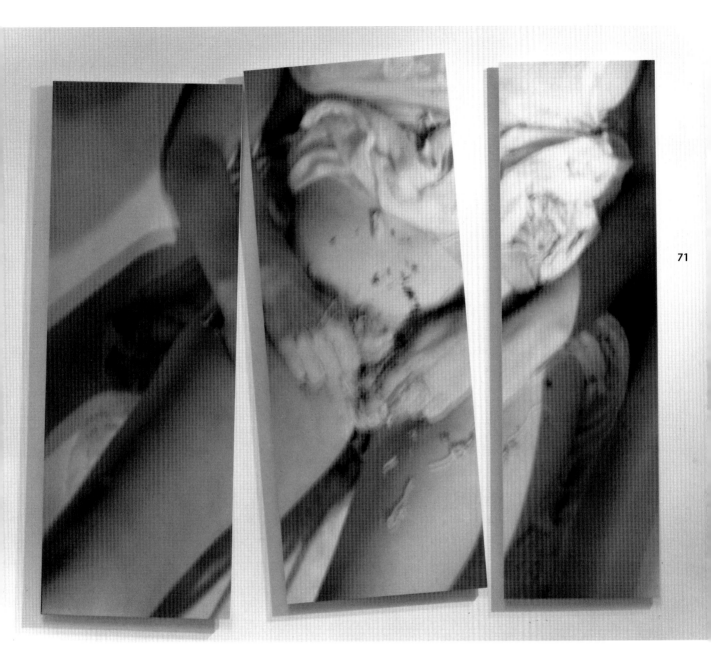

I look at the lines etching themselves on his face. He's receding from the world, I'm watching him decay inward. I don't want to believe what I'm seeing because I am him. I see myself decaying in his shrinking frame and clouding eyes. Somehow I know from these cracks in my mirror that there is no mastery. He who I have struggled to impress is lost in chaos. In my intellect, I can reiterate clearly the ways in which men merely use their logocentric systems as a defense and an escape. I can demonstrate why the need for control is a sickness. But when I feel the truth of this insight, I panic, because now no one is responsible. He is a corpse killed by the pressure of being "the father" which he is too weak to withstand, withering in his shell, rotting, filling me, decaying me, and identity composed of a seething slimy mass of fragments, that's my inheritance, this wormy corpse is my father of individual prehistory. But I love him.

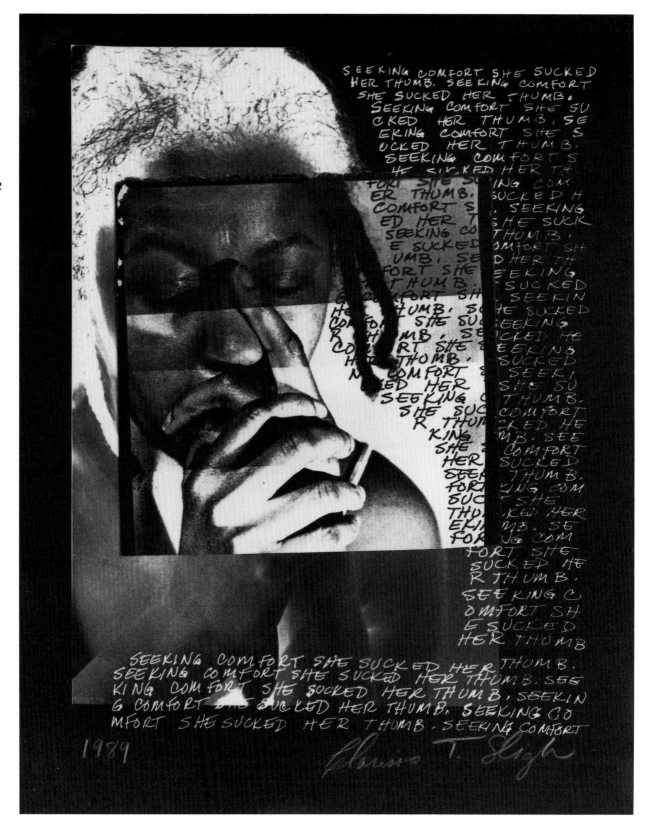

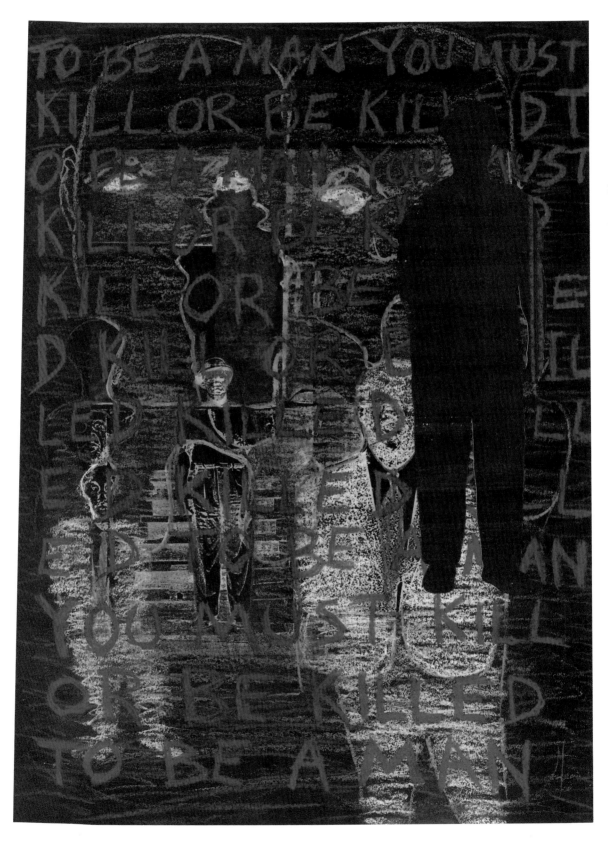

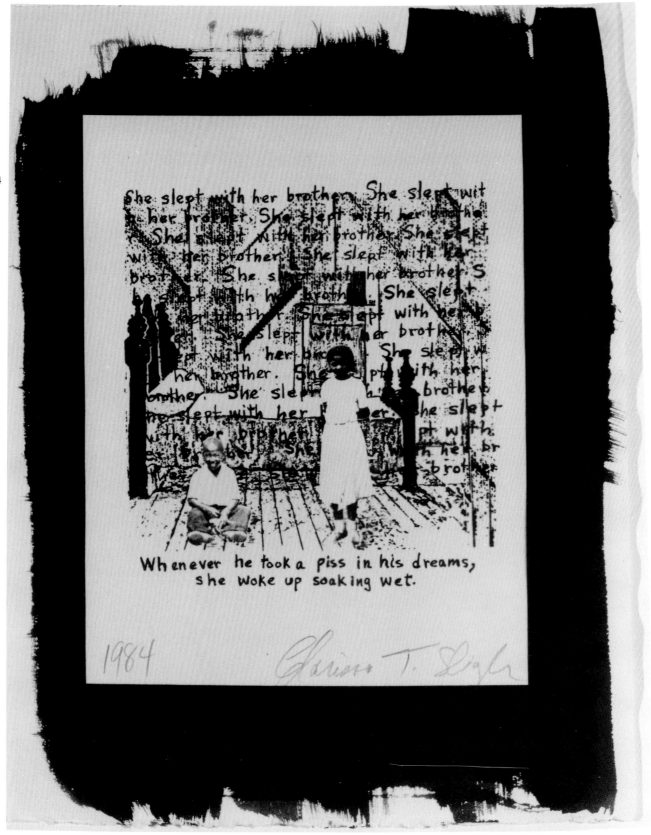

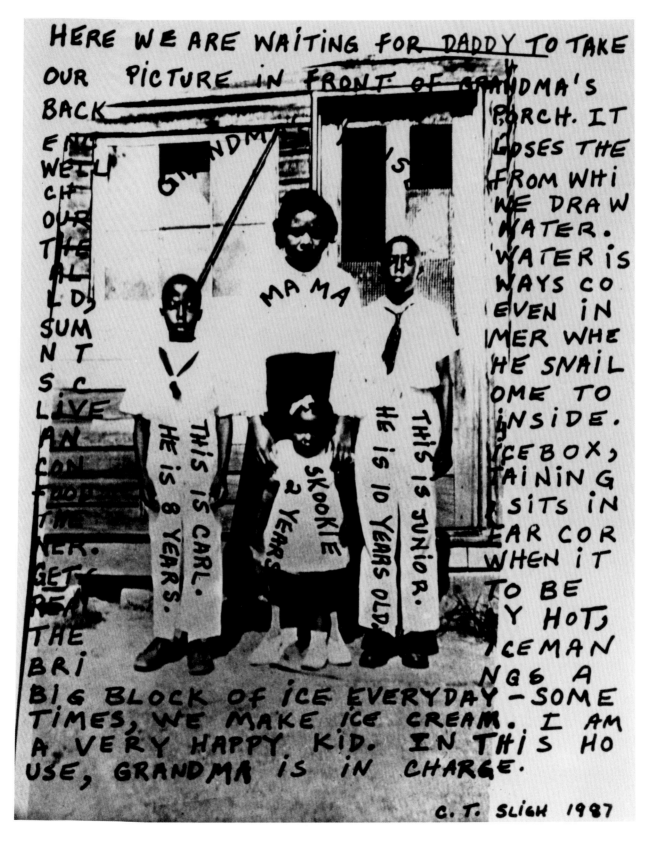

HERE WE ARE WAITING FOR DADDY TO TAKE
OUR PICTURE IN FRONT OF GRANDMA'S
BACK PORCH. IT
END CLOSES THE
WELL FROM WHI
CH WE DRAW
OUR WATER.
THE WATER IS
ALD, ALWAYS CO
SUM EVEN IN
NT MER WHE
S. C HE SNAIL
LIVE OME TO
AN INSIDE.
CON CEBOX,
FROM TAINING
THE SITS IN
NER. EAR COR
GET WHEN IT
REA TO BE
THE Y HOT,
BRI CEMAN
NG6 A
BIG BLOCK OF ICE EVERYDAY — SOME
TIMES, WE MAKE ICE CREAM. I AM
A VERY HAPPY KID. IN THIS HO
USE, GRANDMA IS IN CHARGE.

GRANDMA'S
MAMA
HE IS 8 YEARS.
THIS IS CARL.
SKOOKIE 2 YEARS
HE IS 10 YEARS OLD.
THIS IS JUNIOR.

C. T. SLIGH 1987

DISTRICT ATTORNEY

ARLO SMITH
DISTRICT ATTORNEY

ROBERT M. PODESTA
CHIEF ASSISTANT
DISTRICT ATTORNEY

76

SAN FRANCISCO

880 BRYANT STREET, SAN FRANCISCO 94103 TEL. (415) 553-1752

April 20, 1992

Ms. Susan Meiselas
Magnum Photos
72 Spring Street
NY, NY 10012

Dear Susan,

Here are the statistics you wanted:

1. Every year it is estimated that 2.1 million married,
separated, or divorced women in the US are beaten by their
partners. (Patrick Langar, Christopher Innes: Bureau of Justice
Statistics Special Report, "Preventing Violence Against Women",
Washington, D.C., U.S. D.O.J. August, 1986, p.3.).

2. F.B.I. Reports that almost 1/3 of all homicide victims in
the US are killed by a husband or boyfriend (FBI, Uniform Crime
Reports, 1984).

3. 22-35% of women going to hospital emergency rooms are there
because of domestic violence (JAMA, August 22/29, 1990, Vol. 264,
No. 8, P. 943).

4. Battering is the single most major cause of violence/injury
to women, even more major than the numbers injured in muggings,
rapes, or auto accidents combined (J.O'Reilly, "Wife Beating:
Silent Crime" Time Magazine, September 5, 1983).

5. 95% of spouse abuse victims are women. (P. Klaus, M. Rand
"Family Violence" Bureau of Justice Statistics Special Reports,
U.S. D.O.J., Wash. D.C., 1984, p.4).

THE FOLLOWING PHOTOGRAPHS & TEXT HAVE BEEN RECOVERED FROM THE FILES OF THE SAN FRANCISCO POLICE DEPARTMENT

INCIDENT NO.	REPORTING OFFICER	STAR	DATE(S) & TIME(S) OF OCCURRENCE
███ ███ ███	██████████	███	12/27/91 1806HRS

NARRATIVE:

████████████████ STEPPED BETWEEN ██████████ AND

████████████, ███████████ STABBED HER ONCE IN THE

ABDOMINAL AREA. ██████████ AND ████████████ BOTH ATTEMPTED

TO STOP ███████████ FROM FURTHER ATTACKING. ████████████

BEGAN TO CUT ███████████ IN HIS ATTEMPT TO HARM

████████████, ███████████ STATED THAT ███████████ STATED

THAT HE WAS GOING TO CUT HER THROAT. ████████████

CONTINUED TO STRUGGLE WITH ███████ AND ████████████

████████ STATED THAT SHE TOLD THE CHILDREN TO CALL FOR

THE POLICE. THE STRUGGLE BETWEEN ██████ AND ██████████

CONTINUED UNTIL BOTH WERE FOUND BEHIND THE COUNTER

BY

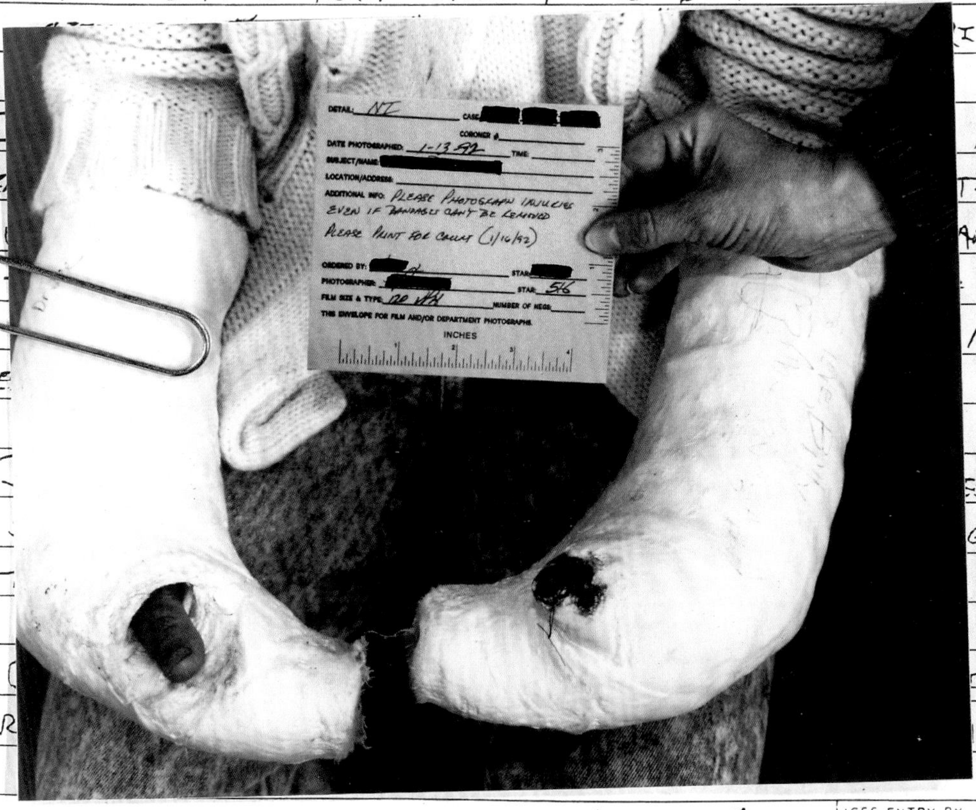

PAGE __4__ OF __5__

INCIDENT NO	REPORTING OFFICER	STAR	DATE(S) & TIME(S) OF OCCURRENCE
████████████	██████████	████	10-30-99, 2245

████ WAS IN THE DINING AREA OF APARTMENT. ████

WAS THERE ALSO. BOTH ████████ GOT INTO A

VERBAL ARGUMENT. ██ GRABBED A POT OF

BOILING WATER THAT WAS ATOP THE STOVE AND

THREW THE WATER UPON ███ CHEST. ██ THEN

LEFT THE BUILDING. ████████ HAVE BEEN

HAVING A RELATIONSHIP, BUT DO NOT LIVE TOGETHER.

██ WAS TAKEN TO ST. FRANCIS HOSPITAL BY

H 87 FOR BURNS ON THE CHEST.

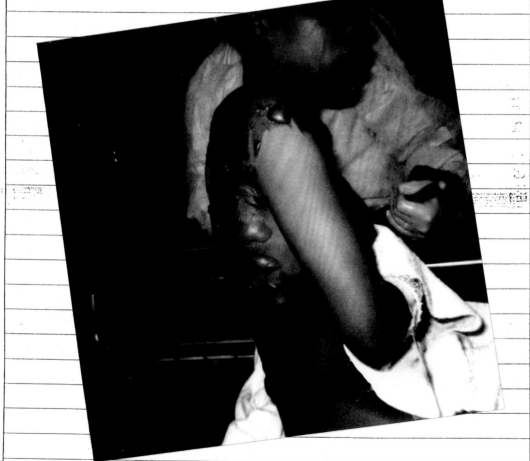

NOTES

INCIDENT NO	REPORTING OFFICER	STAR	DATE(S) & TIME(S) OF OCCURRENCE
██████████████	████████	███	10-21-91, 1730 - 10-22-91, 0130

NARRATIVE: SUBSEQUENT TO CLEANING UP HER RESIDENCE AFTER HER EX-HUSBAND VANDALIZED IT, ████ ████ FOUND THE FOLLOWING WRITTEN ON HER KITCHEN FLOOR, "DON'T FUCK W/A CRAZY MAN I'LL TEACH YOU ████████████████ YOU'LL BE DEAD BEFORE ANY OF THIS MATTERS. I LOVED YOU, HOW MUCH. YOU SHOULD HAVE GONE OUT W/ME BECAUSE I WANT TO DIE NOW + I'M GOING TO TAKE YOU W/ME I WON'T LET YOU BE WITH ANOTHER MAN! I'M SORRY BUT YOU HAVE TO GO TO HEAVEN W/ME."

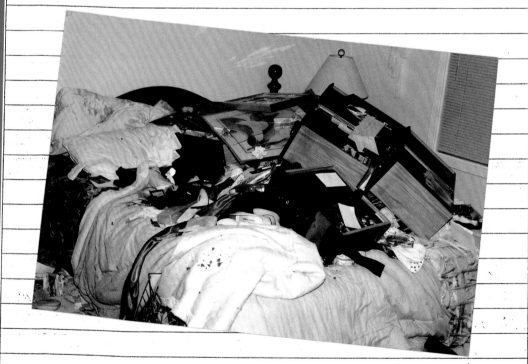

PAGE ___2___ OF ___2___

ICSS ENTRY BY:

SFPD 377

79

Patrilocality

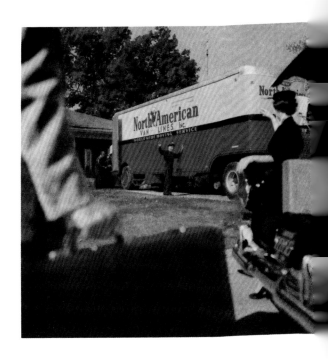

80

'Come and get it'

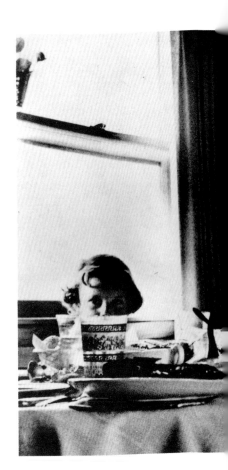

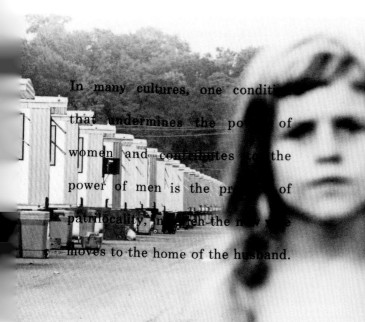

In many cultures, one condit... that undermines the po... of women and contributes ... the power of men is the pr... of patrilocality, in ... the n... ... moves to the home of the husband.

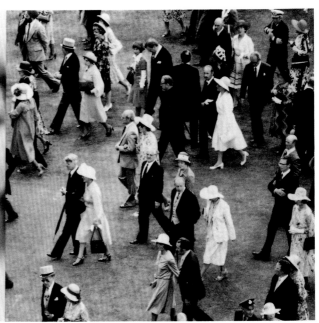

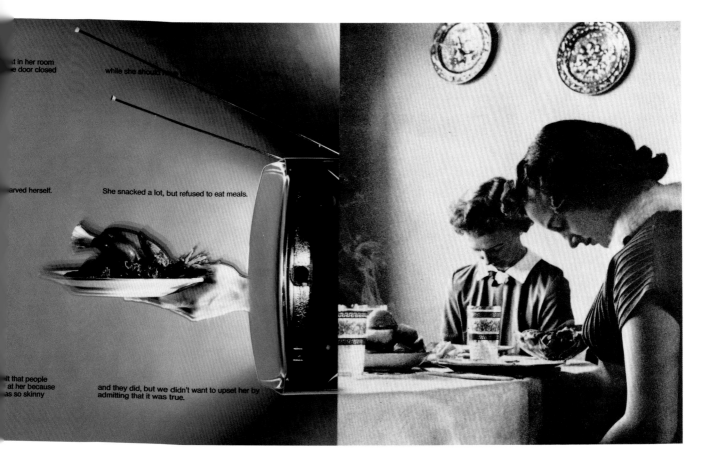

...t in her room ... e door closed   while she should ...

...arved herself.   She snacked a lot, but refused to eat meals.

...lt that people ... at her because ... as so skinny   and they did, but we didn't want to upset her by admitting that it was true.

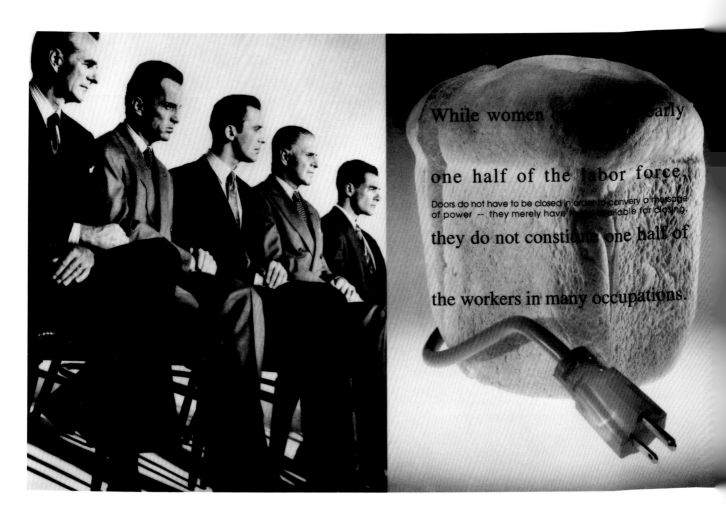

While women c... ...arly

one half of the labor force,

Doors do not have to be closed in order to convey a message
of power -- they merely have ...available for closing.

they do not constit... one half of

the workers in many occupations.

Are you telling yourself a little white lie?
silkscreen on nylon; public art banner
created at the Fabric Workshop, Philadelphia, 1988

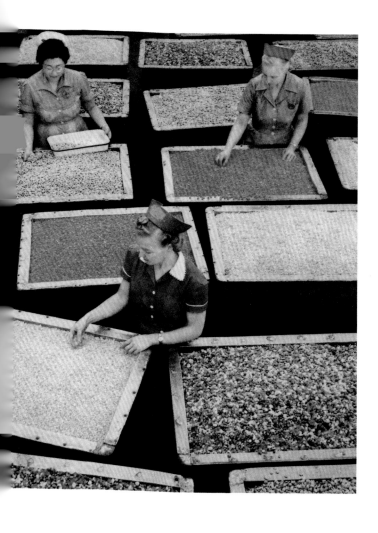

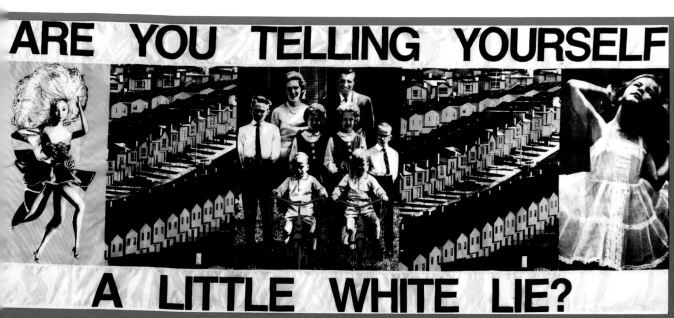

Deborah Willis

For about a decade photographers have been creating works that are about self-interpretation and self-redefinition. Nineteenth-century photographic self-portraiture primarily represented the self in mirrorlike images of the face. In the twentieth century self-portraiture branched into several different modes of thought and presentation, its forms driven by analysis and revelation. Among the artists working in the genre today are photographers who have expanded on the historical meaning of portraiture by turning the camera on their own bodies, as well as by turning the page of the family photo album, thus creating a document about themselves and society. In effect, they become storytellers whose medium is photobiography.

This essay considers the work of four photoartists—Fay Fairbrother, Clarissa Sligh, Margaret Stratton, and Carla Williams. Notable photobiographers, they use appropriation, multiple-printing techniques, fabric, unmanipulated images, and manipulated photographs to make compelling visual statements about contemporary multiethnic society. In an important way, their pictures are *made*, not taken. Developing themes related to gender, family, race, difference, and stereotyping, the artists explore the implications of historical and contemporary images of women, and explore new approaches to representing the personal in visual work. They stage fictive narratives, restage events, use texts, and make traditional photographs to create a psychological tension in the exploration of their subject matter. In constructing their work, they employ a variety of styles, from photographic tableaux to assemblage.

All four artists are concerned with issues of gender and identity. While their family structures differ, the stories they create are similar and are constructed with familiar descriptive captions. In seeking to explore their individual perspectives and their common ideological concerns, I asked each artist to comment on her work.

Carla Williams

Los Angeles–born artist Carla Williams juxtaposes nineteenth-century images and texts on racial differentiation wtih strikingly naked self-portraits. Based on the science of phrenology (which advanced the idea that the conformation of the skull indicated mental faculties and character traits), the nineteenth-century images provide a harsh set of historical observations, some of which led to contemporary racist theories. In the series titled "How to Read Character," Williams used the phrenological text as labels for her self-portraits, which include head shots and profiles of the head and torso; the text is incorporated into the images. One label, for example,

Carla Williams

installation view, *How to Read Character*,
  1990–91

gilt frames, black-and-white photographs,
  photocopy transfer, pushpins.

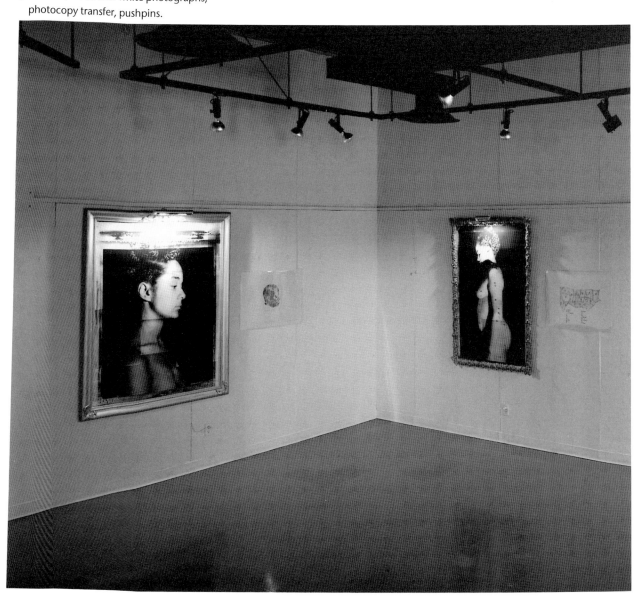

reads "if the cortex of the Negro brain is thinner, it must contain less cells and his brain must be inferior to that of a white person."

Williams's images encapsulate the experiences of black women across the centuries. Historically, the black woman's sexuality has been shaped by racist assertions that blacks were inferior and sexual deviants. Black women have been subjected to racist theoretical studies and physical exploitation. Sander Gilman's "Black Bodies, White Bodies: Toward an Iconography of Female Sexuality in Late Nineteenth Century Art, Medicine, and Literature"[1] is a wrenching account of what Saartjie (Sarah) Baartman experienced. This African woman was often exhibited at parties in Paris, scantily dressed to provide amusement for the guests. In Paris and London for five years she was also caged and displayed naked to a public that paid to view her body, specifically her buttocks. bell hooks asserts that "they [were] not to look at her as a whole human being. They [were] to notice only certain parts. Objectified in a manner similar to that of black female slaves who stood on auction blocks while owners and overseers described their important, salable parts, the black women whose naked bodies were displayed for whites at social functions had no presence. They were reduced to mere spectacle. . . . [T]heir body parts were offered as evidence to support racist notions that black people were more akin to animals than other humans."[2] When Sarah Baartman's body was exhibited in 1810, she was ironically and perversely dubbed "the Hottentot Venus."

Inspired by the numerous critiques of Baartman's exploitation, Williams began to reference her own body to Baartman's experience in the nineteenth century. Williams uses her self-portraits to demonstrate that these notions still persist in images of contemporary African American women. She explains how racist theory is examined in her work:

> The gelatin silver photographs and photocopy transfers are meant to be seen in pairs with the transfer functioning as a kind of visual descriptive label and reference to the photograph. This work addresses the historical precedence of a particular kind of visual representation. Through juxtaposition of 19th century images and text on racial differentiation and categorization with contemporary self portraits I hope to suggest to the viewer that such precedence, while seeming absurd and outdated, still contains a great deal of resonance and power with respect to the way that we read and respond to contemporary images of African American women. The choice of representation, i.e., scale of images, framing, and lighting, is intended to comment on the history of the formal portrait, especially the fact that certain subjects were not given this kind of aggrandizement and importance.[3]

[1] Sandra Gilman, "Black bodies, white bodies: Toward an iconography of female sexuality in late nineteenth century art, medicine, and literature."
[2] bell hooks,
[3] Carla Williams, "How to Read Character."

Margaret Stratton, a Chicago-based artist, examines the social-behavioral patterns of the middle-class American family, using her own family to show how women, especially mothers and daughters, collect, wear, use, preserve, and display personal and household objects. She provides us with a biographical record of a way of life, a particular era, and a story about self. The bonds that tie us to time and to family members are the underlying theme of her series "Inventory of My Mother's House." Stratton becomes the voyeur in her mother's house, generalizing her mother's patterns of consumption to women in general. Her mother's house, sprinkled with artifacts from Western culture, becomes a signifier of femininity and domesticity, and Stratton's mother herself, now deceased, lives in her daughter's memory because of these objects. Viewing this work, we bring to it our own personal experiences, our knowledge of childhood and shared family memorabilia. The message that Stratton imparts is the affirmation of who we are and where we have been. Stratton prompts us to reexamine, restage, and scrutinize our family and familial traditions. Her ordering and rearranging of the objects undermines the viewer's sense of how they are usually placed and their ordinary utility. Their presentation is a record of humanity, neither romantic nor vain; it celebrates the ordinary and acknowledges humility.

According to Stratton's notes, "Inventory of My Mother's House" is a photographic installation of 190 prints of objects in her parents' house:

> As a group these photographs reflect the good life as well as the ease with which they slide into obsolescence—a treasure hunt of post industrial kitsch. These images also testify that what mass production has given us is an effluvia of products with either little or questionable value—things for their own sake—objects whose function is emotional rather than physical: mantles of collectibles and Franklin Furnace statuary that stand for the 'authentic'.
>
> In some ways my parents' house is a true post modern space, an organic and unintentional evolution from necessity to ornament, that mirrors both their economic status and the robust wealth of an economy inclined toward the production of trifles. Within its four walls all eras and styles are represented with equal weight. Nothing is more important than anything else so nothing can be, or ever is, thrown away.
>
> This collection of discardables, impossible to discard, is also part of my childhood; each object is infused with memories of houses long ago abandoned, and rooms irretrievably redecorated. As for the

Margaret Stratton
Item #2, Item #127, Item #17, Item #211,
Inventory of My Mother's House, 1992
from an installation of 190 black-and-
white photographs.

process of cataloging, each room and its use is encoded with hierarchy: domains which reside within a social program of gendered domesticity. While some objects are undeniably my father's, others are incontesta- bly my mother's, and when photographed and placed together begin to create a narrative that describes more than individual lives encom- passing the post war America of utopian nuclear families free to consume, but not to question what it is they are buying or why.[4]

Clarissa Sligh

"By asking me to write about my work in a way which acknowledges the impact of growing up black and female in a white racist and sexist society," says Clarissa Sligh, "you are asking me to put myself on the operating table and to perform the operation at the same time. My visual statements, a search for reality, are a testament to my struggle to go beyond survival. They are a testament to the strength, courage, and determination Black women need in order to continue to be here." Sligh's work is layered with suggestive messages and conveys her enlightened and haunting personal experiences. It also focuses on the exploitation of women in the workplace and at home. For Sligh, "the repetition of marks, words and photographic fragments creates energetic rhythms and simulates the continuous medium of space. As I modify context and space, multiple meanings surface and

[4] Margaret Stratton, "Inventory of My Mother's House."

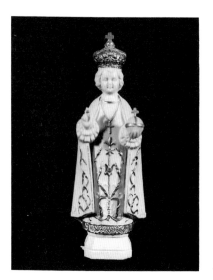
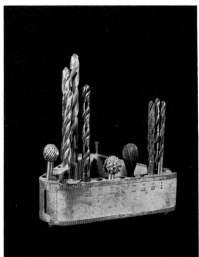
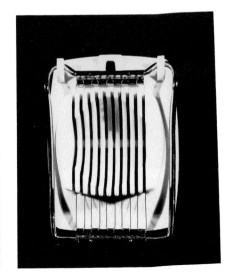

create invitations to release logical boundaries and constraints of the mind. **89** The exploration, which questions relationships, identity, beliefs, and my own authenticity, also takes shape from my dreams, my subconscious, and my perceptions of past and present experiences."[5]

Weaving politics with art and using family photographs, Sligh directs her audience's gaze to sociological relationships centered on experiences with the African American community. Sligh is the keeper of her family's album of photographs and other memorabilia and is cognizant of the role she plays in preserving her family's history. At the same time, she places herself and her family within the larger picture of American history. In shifting attention away from her personal experiences, she is able to analyze the shared experiences of black children.

In one series titled "Reading Dick and Jane with Me," Sligh cogently reconstructs the images of Dick and Jane with snapshots from her family album. The standard American public school *Dick and Jane*-type readers presented the typical American family as well-to-do whites living a relatively trouble-free life (the originals were published from 1935 to 1965). "Reading Dick and Jane with Me" is an illustrated reader seen through the eyes of a black woman artist who spent her own childhood growing up poor in the American south of the 1940s and 1950s. It combines lively repetitive words, photographs, and drawings. Sligh "reads" the images of Dick and Jane and inserts words on each page—for example, "You play in your good clothes every page. We must keep ours nice for Sunday School Days."[6] She makes us aware of the psychological effect the primary school reader may have had on black children reading the book. She allows the invisible black child to be identifiable as well as visible. "As a young Black child, before I could even think, I was told how bad things are out there in the world for us. It was a fear put into me to prepare me for the real world. Since we couldn't talk about it, since no one could relate to our hurt or pain, we learned to be silent, to hide our disappointments, to hide our anger at the distortion of our identity and the exclusion of our reality."[7]

Sligh's work is important not only because she addresses the realities of racism and sexism in a straightforward style, but also because she assembles with exemplary skill ideas and artifacts in a sound, cohesive way. The search for representation continues throughout Sligh's work in pieces such as *What's Happening with Momma* and *She Sucks Her Thumb.* "My work is a journey toward self-change which itself is self-healing. The act of creating my visual statements requires that I work from a place I push against. I begin by trying to be clear with myself. I struggle to develop a correct relationship to myself, a continuous cycle requiring passage through darkness—

[5] Clarissa Sligh,
[6] Clarissa Sligh, "Reading Dick and Jane with Me."
[7] Clarissa Sligh,

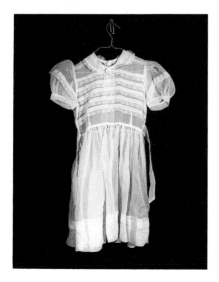

Clarissa Sligh
two views, *What's Happening with Momma?*, 1988
mixed media with Vandyke brown; 11" × 36".

my 'shadow areas,' as well as through light." Sligh looks carefully at her own relationships with her family as she examines the lives of men, women, and children in general.

Fay Fairbrother
Fay Fairbrother, in style and presentation altogether different from the three other photoartists discussed here, also addresses issues of the family—its strengths, its fears, its failures, its successes. She openly explores repression and racism through the art of quilt-making. Fairbrother's "quilts," titled "The Shroud Series: Quilt Shroud" include turn-of-the-century formal portraits of black and white families, images of black men who were lynched and mutilated, Ku Klux Klan activities, and patterned cloth. The pictures reproduced in her work create a patchwork of events depicting the injustices and privileges of two distinct families—black and white.

Fairbrother's research on lynchings of African American men revealed that after men were lynched, they were taken down from the trees and wrapped in quilts for burial. That research led to "The Quilt Shroud." In a calmer mode, discarded cloth fragments are sometimes used to tell a story of an anonymous family. One quilt includes family photographs and activities of the Ku Klux Klan, including the participation of wives and children of Klan members. Fairbrother's use of quilts is a powerful and disarming way of telling these stories. They suggest but leave unanswered

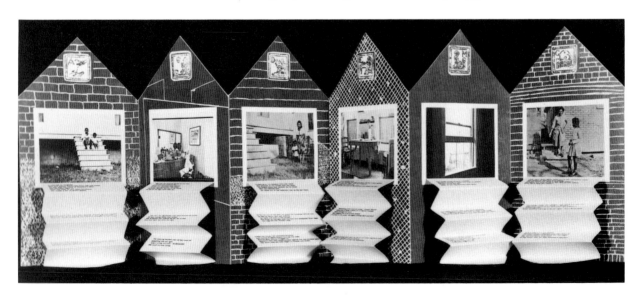

questions regarding segregation, life and death, and photography's role in depicting ordinary domestic life and racial violence in American life.

Fairbrother comments that "the theme of the *Quilt Shroud I* is the family, with the quilt as a representation of family. The posed studio portraits of black and white families illustrate the sameness of the family group. Posed in their Sunday best, you know the children are taught the same Christian values and morals. But where does the process go wrong with KKK meetings such as the one illustrated on the third row resulting in black men hanging from trees? I have also tried to show the results of the removal of the black man from his family and the wife shown alone in the studio with their child who has been robbed of his father. The quilts are my own design, kept simple in order for the photographs to speak."[8]

Like many of our mothers and grandmothers, Fairbrother's ancestors were quilt-makers. A third-generation quilter herself, she learned the tradition from her mother. Fairbrother grew up in a white, middle-class environment in the South. Reexamining the stories she heard from her family about racial violence in her home town, Fairbrother expands the notion of self-portrait by creating a wider portrait of her community, and she demonstrates how memory helped to shape her art in a social context.

The photoartists whose work is reproduced here respond to the uniqueness of their own lives. Whether they stay within the traditional definition of self-portraiture or contradict it, all generate an emotional message that tran-

[8] Fay Fairbrother, "The Shroud Series: Quilt Shroud."

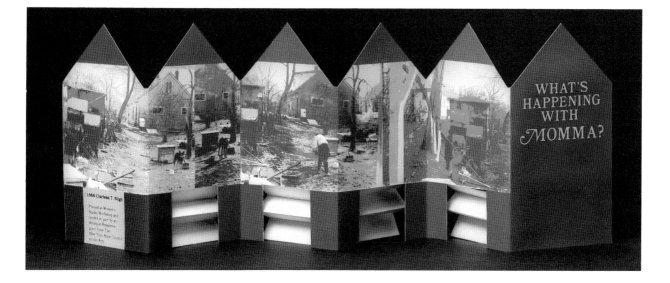

92 **Fay Fairbrother**
        detail from *The Quilt Shroud Series*, 1991–
        92
        cotton and photolinen, 60″ × 70″ overall.

scends simple notions of self-representation and recharacterizes photo-autobiography. Their personal art interrogates or overturns social ideas to make powerful statements about race and gender in American culture.

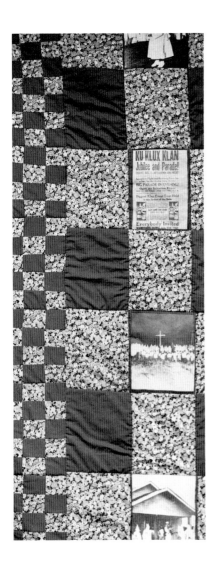

Identity Formations

94

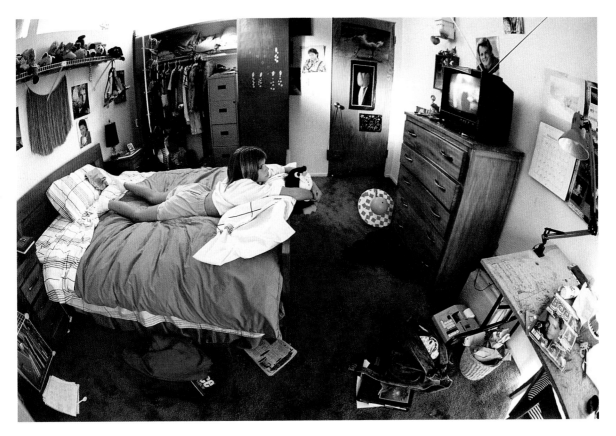

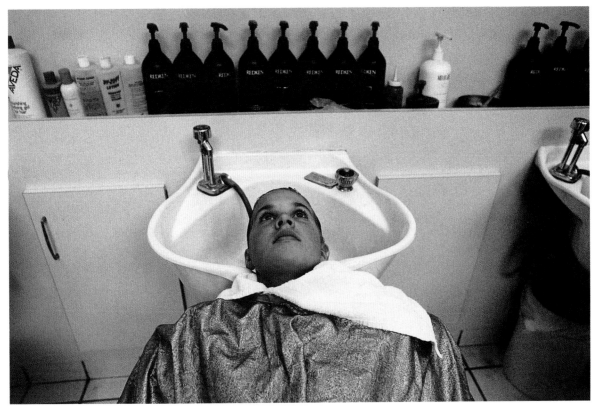

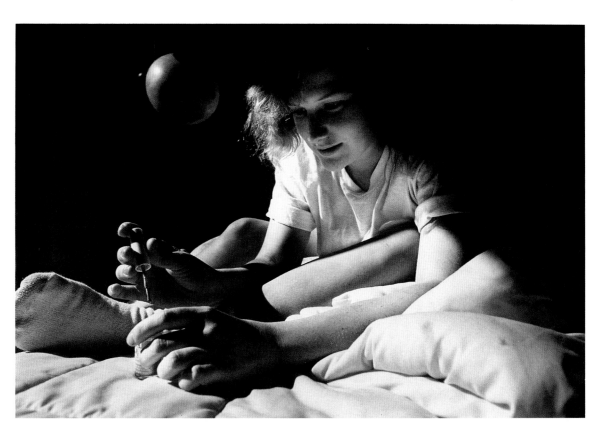

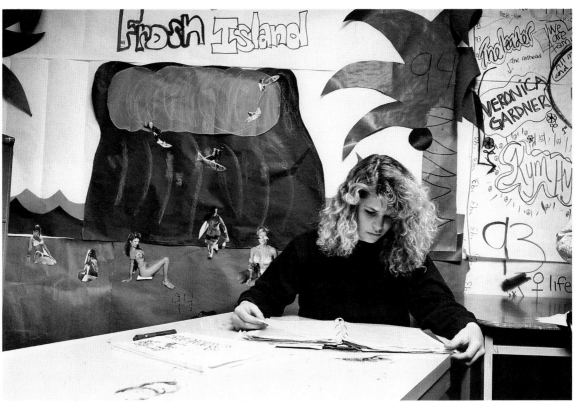

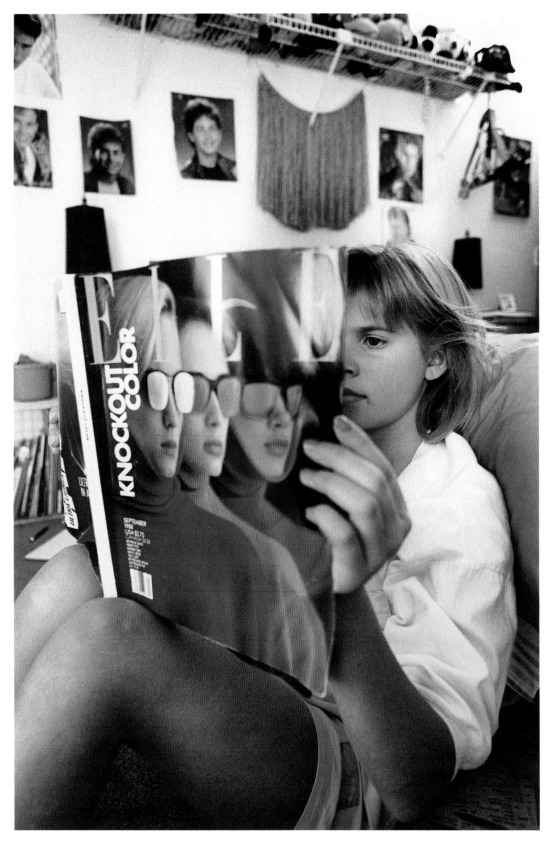

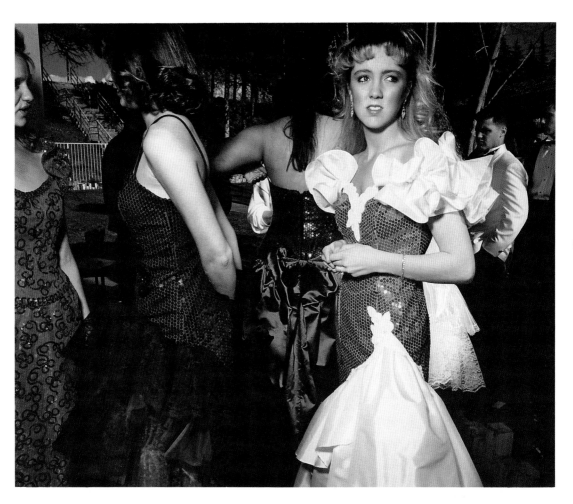

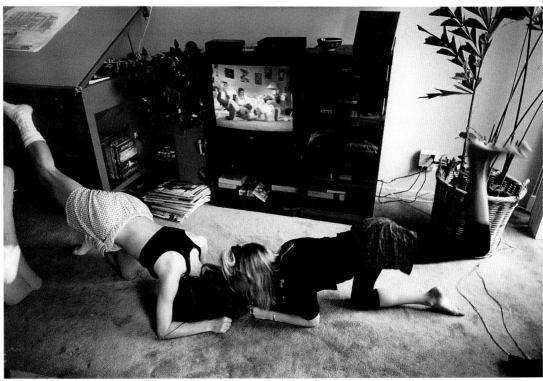

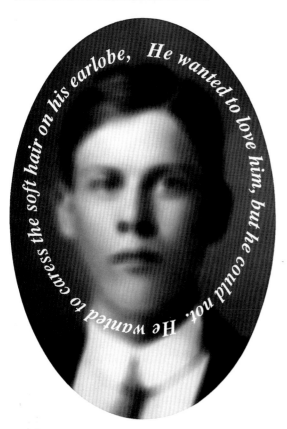

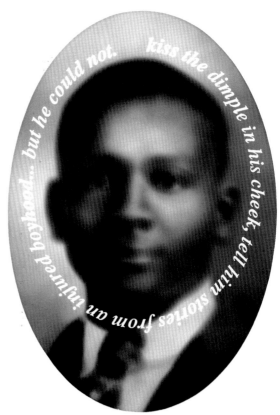

98

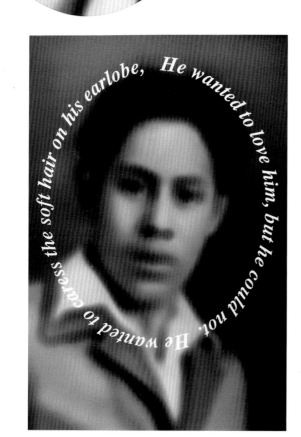

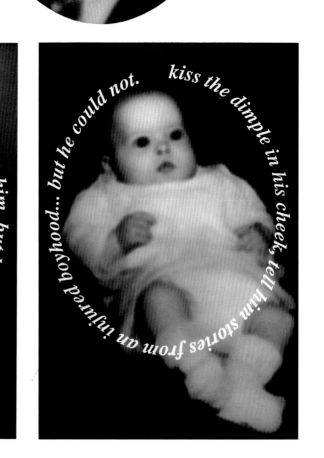

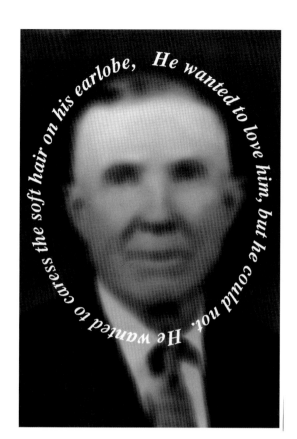

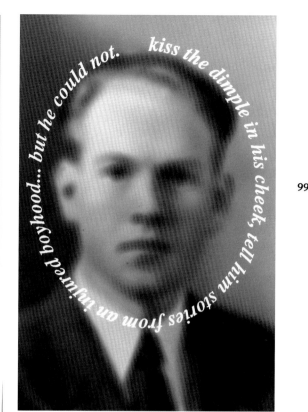

99

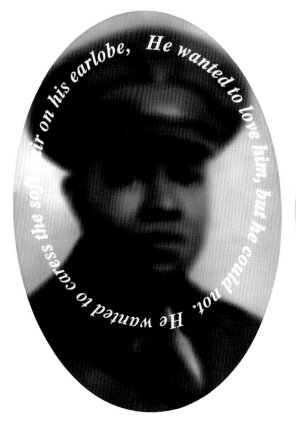

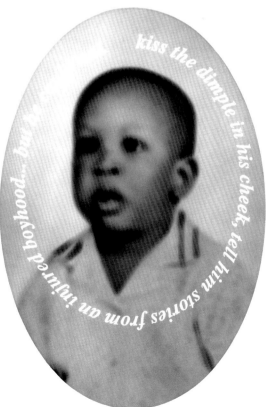

100

He wanted to love him, but he could not. He wanted to caress the soft hair on his earlobe,

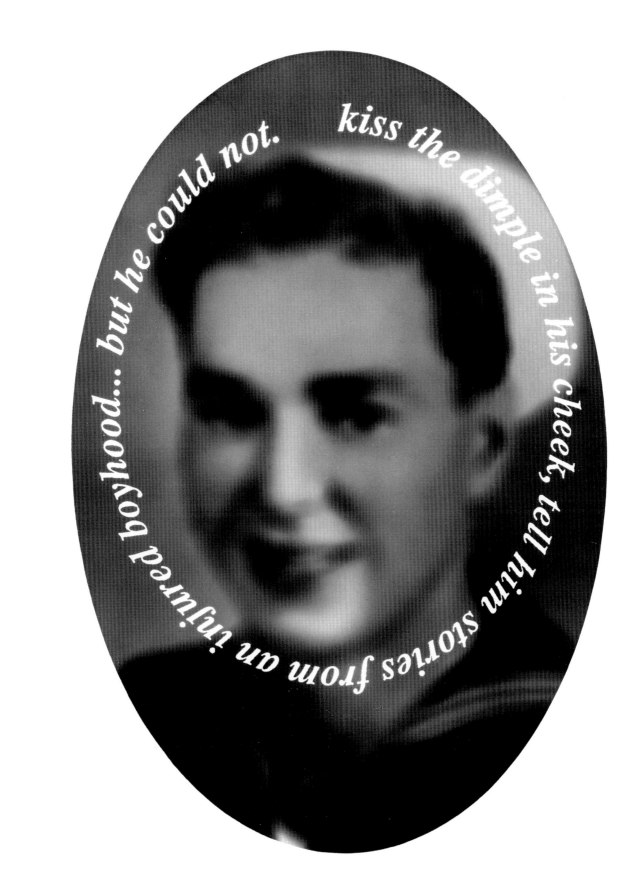

kiss the dimple in his cheek, tell him stories from an injured boyhood... but he could not.

102

Decide Who You Are #21: Phantom Limbs

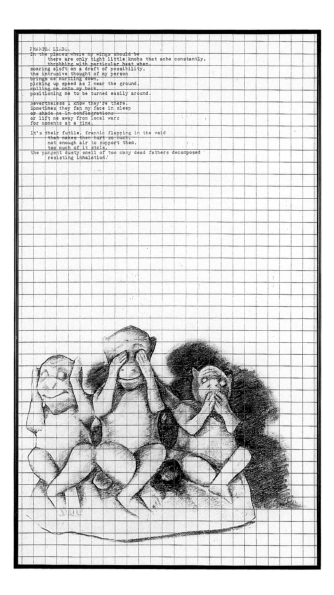

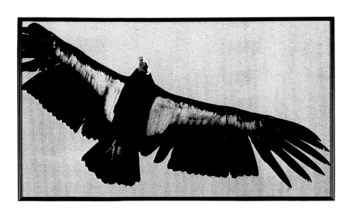

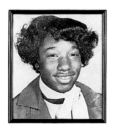

IT'S FINE. I DON'T KNOW WHAT YOU MEAN. I DIDN'T NOTICE ANYTHING WRONG. IT SEEMS FINE TO ME. I DON'T KNOW WHY YOU SAY THAT. I DON'T SEE ANY PROBLEM. I'M AMAZED THAT YOU SEE THINGS THAT WAY. I JUST DON'T SEE IT THAT WAY AT ALL. IT WASN'T INTENTIONAL. I DON'T UNDERSTAND WHERE THIS IS COMING FROM. JUST CALM DOWN. TRY TO GET A GRIP ON YOURSELF. THIS IS A COMPLETE SURPRISE TO ME. THE THOUGHT NEVER CROSSED MY MIND. I REALLY DON'T KNOW WHAT TO MAKE OF THIS. ISN'T THIS A LITTLE BIT MUCH? THAT'S A WEIRD WAY TO THINK ABOUT THINGS. I JUST CAN'T RELATE. IT'S CERTAINLY OK TO HAVE DIFFERENT PERSPECTIVES ON THINGS. YOU'RE MAKING TOO MUCH OF THIS. NOTHING'S THE MATTER. STOP GETTING EMOTIONAL. YOU'RE BLOWING THE WHOLE THING OUT OF PROPORTION. EVERYTHING'S FINE. WHAT DO YOU MEAN? WHAT'S THE PROBLEM? YOU'RE BEING PARANOID. YOU'RE OVERSENSITIVE. YOU'RE READING TOO MUCH INTO IT. STOP JUMPING TO CONCLUSIONS. IT DIDN'T OCCUR TO ME. YOU'RE OVERINTERPRETING THE DATA. I DON'T THINK IT HAS ANYTHING TO DO WITH THAT. IT WAS JUST A SIMPLE MISTAKE. IT DOESN'T MEAN ANYTHING. YOU'RE SEEING TOO MUCH IN THIS. NOTHING'S GOING ON. I CAN'T IMAGINE WHAT MAKES YOU THINK THAT. I DON'T KNOW WHAT YOU'RE TALKING ABOUT. I HAVE NO IDEA WHAT YOU'RE REFERRING TO. I REALLY THINK YOU'RE OVERDOING IT. YOU'RE JUST TIRED. DON'T TAKE EVERYTHING SO SERIOUSLY. IT'S NO BIG DEAL. YOU'RE JUST PROJECTING. YOU'RE OVERREACTING. NOTHING HAPPENED. DID I NOTICE WHAT? I DON'T SEE ANYTHING TO GET UPSET ABOUT. I DON'T SEE WHAT YOU'RE GETTING AT. I DON'T UNDERSTAND THE PROBLEM. WHAT'S THE MATTER? YOU'LL GET OVER IT. DID SOMEONE DO SOMETHING WRONG? WHAT'S GOING ON? WHAT'S THIS ABOUT? WHAT'S WRONG? STOP MAKING SUCH A BIG DEAL ABOUT IT. I DON'T SEE ANYTHING WRONG WITH THAT. EVERYONE DOES THAT. SO WHAT? BIG DEAL. WHO CARES? NO, NOTHING LIKE THAT. JUST A MISUNDERSTANDING. THAT'S ALL. MUCH ADO ABOUT NOTHING. I DON'T UNDERSTAND WHAT THIS IS ABOUT. I'M MYSTIFIED BY YOUR REACTION. I DON'T GET IT. SO? WHAT'S THE SIGNIFICANCE OF THAT? IT WAS JUST AN INNOCENT SLIP-UP. I REGARD THAT AS PERFECTLY NORMAL BEHAVIOR. I SEE NO PROBLEM WITH THAT. YOU'RE THE ONE WITH THE PROBLEM. THAT'S A VERY UNCHARITABLE INTERPRETATION. IT'S SO UNNECESSARY TO TALK ABOUT THIS. OH, I DON'T THINK IT HAS ANYTHING TO DO WITH THAT, REALLY. WHAT ARE YOU TALKING ABOUT? THAT'S SHEER SPECULATION. YOU'RE AWFULLY QUICK TO CAST ASPERSIONS. YOU CAN'T PROVE THAT. I DON'T NEED TO HEAR THIS. HOW DO YOU KNOW? THAT'S CRAZY. YOU'RE IMAGINING THINGS. THAT'S JUST YOUR OPINION. NO, IT'S NOT THAT AT ALL. THAT HAS NOTHING TO DO WITH IT. THAT DOESN'T MEAN ANYTHING. WELL, THAT'S A NATURAL REACTION. THAT DOESN'T MEAN WHAT YOU THINK IT MEANS. THAT'S A SELF-SERVING EXPLANATION. WHY BRING THIS UP? YOU SEE EVERYTHING IN TERMS OF YOUR OWN PROBLEMS. WHY IS THAT OBJECTIONABLE? YOU'RE COOKING UP PROBLEMS WHERE THERE ARE NONE. YOU'RE MAKING THINGS UP. I DON'T BELIEVE THAT HAPPENED. I'M NOT SAYING YOU'RE LYING, I'M JUST SAYING YOUR PERCEPTIONS ARE DISTORTED. IT'S NOT NECESSARY TO SEE THINGS IN THAT LIGHT. YOU'RE TOO UPSET TO THINK CLEARLY. WE'LL DISCUSS IT LATER. NO, NOT NOW. I'M BUSY. STOP MAKING TROUBLE. YOU'RE SEEING THINGS THAT AREN'T THERE. THIS IS RIDICULOUS. I DON'T WANT TO TALK ABOUT IT. SO HOW ARE YOU OTHERWISE? I REFUSE TO DISCUSS THIS. WHAT'S SO WRONG WITH THAT? CHANGE THE SUBJECT. PEOPLE HAVE A RIGHT TO EXPRESS THEMSELVES. I'M NOT GOING TO LISTEN TO THIS. YOU TAKE EVERYTHING TOO PERSONALLY. YOU MUST HAVE PERCEIVED THAT INCORRECTLY. I'M SURE YOU'RE MISTAKEN. I'M SURE THAT DIDN'T HAPPEN QUITE THE WAY YOU DESCRIBE IT. SURELY YOU'RE EXAGGERATING JUST A LITTLE. YOU'RE BEING IRRATIONAL. YOU CAN'T MAKE ME BELIEVE THAT. THIS IS SO UNNECESSARY. NOBODY WANTS TO HEAR THIS. ARE YOU TRYING TO RUIN EVERYTHING? STOP INSISTING ON THIS IF YOU KNOW WHAT'S GOOD FOR YOU. YOU'RE REALLY OUT ON A LIMB. YOU'RE WAY OUT OF LINE. IT'S NOT YOUR PLACE TO SAY THAT. DON'T PUSH IT. YOU'RE GOING TOO FAR. GET OFF IT. YOU'RE SPEAKING OUT OF PLACE. LIGHTEN UP. YOU'RE ASKING FOR TROUBLE. YOU'RE BEING INAPPROPRIATE. NOBODY CARES WHAT YOU THINK. YOU'RE LEAVING YOURSELF WIDE OPEN. YOU'RE CRUISIN' FOR A BRUISIN'. PUT A LID ON IT. CAN IT. STUFF IT. BAG IT. FORGET IT. DROP IT. I WOULDN'T PURSUE THIS ANY FURTHER IF I WERE YOU. YOU'RE REALLY ASKING FOR IT. DO YOU WANT TO GET IN TROUBLE? YOU'RE GOING TO GET IT. YOU'RE STICKING YOUR NECK OUT. YOU'RE DIGGING YOUR OWN GRAVE. A REAL GLUTTON FOR PUNISHMENT. YOU CAN'T GET AWAY WITH THIS. YOU'RE DEAD MEAT. I HATE TO DO THIS. I'M REALLY SORRY THIS IS NECESSARY. THIS HURTS ME MORE THAN IT HURTS YOU. I'M DOING THIS FOR YOUR OWN GOOD. YOU'LL APPRECIATE THIS LATER. I'M JUST TRYING TO HELP YOU. SOMEDAY YOU'LL THANK ME FOR THIS. ACTUALLY I'M DOING YOU A FAVOR. IN TIME YOU'LL UNDERSTAND. YOU'LL LEARN TO SEE THINGS DIFFERENTLY. IT'S FINE. I DON'T KNOW WHAT YOU MEAN. I DIDN'T NOTICE ANYTHING WRONG. IT SEEMS FINE TO ME. I DON'T KNOW WHY YOU SAY THAT. I DON'T SEE ANY PROBLEM. I'M AMAZED THAT YOU SEE THINGS THAT WAY. I JUST DON'T SEE IT THAT WAY AT ALL. IT WASN'T INTENTIONAL. I DON'T UNDERSTAND WHERE THIS IS COMING FROM. JUST CALM DOWN. TRY TO GET A GRIP ON YOURSELF. THIS IS A COMPLETE SURPRISE TO ME. THE THOUGHT NEVER CROSSED MY MIND. I REALLY DON'T KNOW WHAT TO MAKE OF THIS. ISN'T THIS A LITTLE BIT MUCH? THAT'S A WEIRD WAY TO THINK ABOUT THINGS. I JUST CAN'T RELATE. IT'S CERTAINLY OK TO HAVE DIFFERENT PERSPECTIVES ON THINGS. YOU'RE MAKING TOO MUCH OF THIS. NOTHING'S THE MATTER. STOP GETTING EMOTIONAL. YOU'RE BLOWING THE WHOLE THING OUT OF PROPORTION. EVERYTHING'S FINE. WHAT DO YOU MEAN? WHAT'S THE PROBLEM? YOU'RE BEING PARANOID. YOU'RE OVERSENSITIVE. YOU'RE READING TOO MUCH INTO IT. STOP JUMPING TO CONCLUSIONS. IT DIDN'T OCCUR TO ME. YOU'RE OVERINTERPRETING THE DATA. I DON'T THINK IT HAS ANYTHING TO DO WITH THAT. IT WAS JUST A SIMPLE MISTAKE. IT DOESN'T MEAN ANYTHING. YOU'RE SEEING TOO MUCH IN THIS. NOTHING'S GOING ON. I CAN'T IMAGINE WHAT MAKES YOU THINK THAT. I DON'T KNOW WHAT YOU'RE TALKING ABOUT. I HAVE NO IDEA WHAT YOU'RE REFERRING TO. I REALLY THINK YOU'RE OVERDOING IT. YOU'RE JUST TIRED. DON'T TAKE EVERYTHING SO SERIOUSLY. IT'S NO BIG DEAL. YOU'RE JUST PROJECTING. YOU'RE OVERREACTING. NOTHING HAPPENED. DID I NOTICE WHAT? I DON'T SEE ANYTHING TO GET UPSET ABOUT. I DON'T SEE WHAT YOU'RE GETTING AT. I DON'T UNDERSTAND THE PROBLEM. WHAT'S THE MATTER? YOU'LL GET OVER IT. DID SOMEONE DO SOMETHING WRONG? WHAT'S GOING ON? WHAT'S THIS ABOUT? WHAT'S WRONG? STOP MAKING SUCH A BIG DEAL ABOUT IT. I DON'T SEE ANYTHING WRONG WITH THAT. EVERYONE DOES THAT. SO WHAT? BIG DEAL. WHO CARES? NO, NOTHING LIKE THAT. JUST A MISUNDERSTANDING. THAT'S ALL. MUCH ADO ABOUT NOTHING. I DON'T UNDERSTAND WHAT THIS IS ABOUT. I'M MYSTIFIED BY YOUR REACTION. I DON'T GET IT. SO? WHAT'S THE SIGNIFICANCE OF THAT? IT WAS JUST AN INNOCENT SLIP-UP. I REGARD THAT AS PERFECTLY NORMAL BEHAVIOR. I SEE NO PROBLEM WITH THAT. YOU'RE THE ONE WITH THE PROBLEM. THAT'S A VERY UNCHARITABLE INTERPRETATION. IT'S SO UNNECESSARY TO TALK ABOUT THIS. OH, I DON'T THINK IT HAS ANYTHING TO DO WITH THAT, REALLY. WHAT ARE YOU TALKING ABOUT? THAT'S SHEER SPECULATION. YOU'RE AWFULLY QUICK TO CAST ASPERSIONS. YOU CAN'T PROVE THAT. I DON'T NEED TO HEAR THIS. HOW DO YOU KNOW? THAT'S CRAZY. YOU'RE IMAGINING THINGS. THAT'S JUST YOUR OPINION. NO, IT'S NOT THAT AT ALL. THAT HAS NOTHING TO DO WITH IT. THAT DOESN'T MEAN ANYTHING. WELL, THAT'S A NATURAL REACTION. THAT DOESN'T MEAN WHAT YOU THINK IT MEANS. THAT'S A SELF-SERVING EXPLANATION. WHY BRING THIS UP? YOU SEE EVERYTHING IN TERMS OF YOUR OWN PROBLEMS. WHY IS THAT OBJECTIONABLE? YOU'RE COOKING UP PROBLEMS WHERE THERE ARE NONE. YOU'RE MAKING THINGS UP. I DON'T BELIEVE THAT HAPPENED. I'M NOT SAYING YOU'RE LYING, I'M JUST SAYING YOUR PERCEPTIONS ARE DISTORTED. IT'S NOT NECESSARY TO SEE THINGS IN THAT LIGHT. YOU'RE TOO UPSET TO THINK CLEARLY. WE'LL DISCUSS IT LATER. NO, NOT NOW. I'M BUSY. STOP MAKING TROUBLE. YOU'RE SEEING THINGS THAT AREN'T THERE. THIS IS RIDICULOUS. I DON'T WANT TO TALK ABOUT IT. SO HOW ARE YOU OTHERWISE? I REFUSE TO DISCUSS THIS. WHAT'S SO WRONG WITH THAT? CHANGE THE SUBJECT. PEOPLE HAVE A RIGHT TO EXPRESS THEMSELVES. I'M NOT GOING TO LISTEN TO THIS. YOU TAKE EVERYTHING TOO PERSONALLY. YOU MUST HAVE PERCEIVED THAT INCORRECTLY. I'M SURE YOU'RE MISTAKEN. I'M SURE THAT DIDN'T HAPPEN QUITE THE WAY YOU DESCRIBE IT. SURELY YOU'RE EXAGGERATING JUST A LITTLE. YOU'RE BEING IRRATIONAL. YOU CAN'T MAKE ME BELIEVE THAT. THIS IS SO UNNECESSARY. NOBODY WANTS TO HEAR THIS. ARE YOU TRYING TO RUIN EVERYTHING? STOP INSISTING ON THIS IF YOU KNOW WHAT'S GOOD FOR YOU. YOU'RE REALLY OUT ON A LIMB. YOU'RE WAY OUT OF LINE. IT'S NOT YOUR PLACE TO SAY THAT. DON'T PUSH IT. YOU'RE GOING TOO FAR. GET OFF IT. YOU'RE SPEAKING OUT OF PLACE. LIGHTEN UP. YOU'RE ASKING FOR TROUBLE. YOU'RE BEING INAPPROPRIATE. NOBODY CARES WHAT YOU THINK. YOU'RE LEAVING YOURSELF WIDE OPEN. YOU'RE CRUISIN' FOR A BRUISIN'. PUT A LID ON IT. CAN IT. STUFF IT. BAG IT. FORGET IT. DROP IT. I WOULDN'T PURSUE THIS ANY FURTHER IF I WERE YOU. YOU'RE REALLY ASKING FOR IT. DO YOU WANT TO GET IN TROUBLE? YOU'RE GOING TO GET IT. YOU'RE STICKING YOUR NECK OUT. YOU'RE DIGGING YOUR OWN GRAVE. A REAL GLUTTON FOR PUNISHMENT. YOU CAN'T GET AWAY WITH THIS. YOU'RE DEAD MEAT. I HATE TO DO THIS. I'M REALLY SORRY THIS IS NECESSARY. THIS HURTS ME MORE

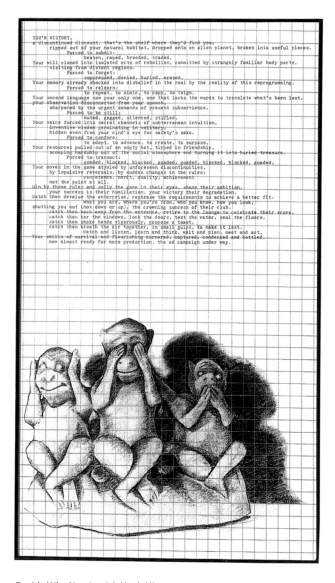

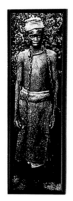

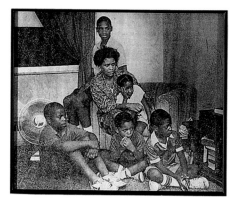

Decide Who You Are #6: You'r History

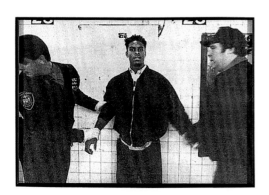

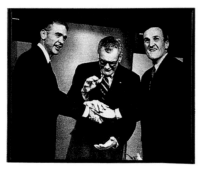

IT'S FINE. I DON'T KNOW WHAT YOU MEAN. I DIDN'T NOTICE ANYTHING WRONG. IT SEEMS FINE TO ME. I DON'T KNOW WHY YOU SAY THAT. I DON'T SEE ANY PROBLEM. I'M AMAZED THAT YOU SEE THINGS THAT WAY. I JUST DON'T SEE IT THAT WAY AT ALL. IT WASN'T INTENTIONAL. I DON'T UNDERSTAND WHERE THIS IS COMING FROM. JUST CALM DOWN. TRY TO GET A GRIP ON YOURSELF. THIS IS A COMPLETE SURPRISE TO ME. THE THOUGHT NEVER CROSSED MY MIND. I REALLY DON'T KNOW WHAT TO MAKE OF THIS. ISN'T THIS A LITTLE BIT MUCH? THAT'S A WEIRD WAY TO THINK ABOUT THINGS. I JUST CAN'T RELATE. WE CERTAINLY DO HAVE DIFFERENT PERSPECTIVES ON THINGS. YOU'RE MAKING TOO MUCH OF THIS. NOTHING'S THE MATTER. STOP GETTING EMOTIONAL. YOU'RE BLOWING THE WHOLE THING OUT OF PROPORTION. EVERYTHING'S FINE. WHAT DO YOU MEAN? WHAT'S THE PROBLEM? YOU'RE BEING PARANOID. YOU'RE OVERSENSITIVE. YOU'RE READING TOO MUCH INTO IT. STOP JUMPING TO CONCLUSIONS. IT DIDN'T OCCUR TO ME. YOU'RE OVERINTERPRETING THE DATA. I DON'T THINK IT HAS ANYTHING TO DO WITH THAT. IT WAS JUST A SIMPLE MISTAKE. IT DOESN'T MEAN ANYTHING. YOU'RE SEEING TOO MUCH IN THIS. NOTHING'S GOING ON. I CAN'T IMAGINE WHAT MAKES YOU THINK THAT. I DON'T KNOW WHAT YOU'RE TALKING ABOUT. I HAVE NO IDEA WHAT YOU'RE REFERRING TO. I REALLY THINK YOU'RE OVERDOING IT. YOU'RE JUST TIRED. DON'T TAKE EVERYTHING SO SERIOUSLY. IT'S NO BIG DEAL. YOU'RE JUST PROJECTING. YOU'RE OVERREACTING. NOTHING HAPPENED. DID I NOTICE WHAT? I DON'T SEE ANYTHING TO GET UPSET ABOUT. I DON'T SEE WHAT YOU'RE GETTING AT. I DON'T UNDERSTAND THE PROBLEM. WHAT'S THE MATTER? YOU'LL GET OVER IT. DID SOMEONE DO SOMETHING WRONG? WHAT'S GOING ON? WHAT'S THIS ABOUT? WHAT'S WRONG? STOP MAKING SUCH A BIG DEAL ABOUT IT. I DON'T SEE ANYTHING WRONG WITH THAT. EVERYONE DOES THAT. SO WHAT? BIG DEAL. WHO CARES? NO, NOTHING LIKE THAT. JUST A MISUNDERSTANDING, THAT'S ALL. MUCH ADO ABOUT NOTHING. I DON'T UNDERSTAND WHAT THIS IS ABOUT. I'M MYSTIFIED BY YOUR REACTION. I DON'T GET IT. SO? WHAT'S THE SIGNIFICANCE OF THAT? IT WAS JUST AN INNOCENT SLIP-UP. I REGARD THAT AS PERFECTLY NORMAL BEHAVIOR. I SEE NO PROBLEM WITH THAT. YOU'RE THE ONE WITH THE PROBLEM. THAT'S A VERY UNCHARITABLE INTERPRETATION. IT'S SO UNNECESSARY TO TALK ABOUT THIS. OH, I DON'T THINK IT HAS ANYTHING TO DO WITH THAT, REALLY. WHAT ARE YOU TALKING ABOUT? THAT'S SHEER SPECULATION. YOU'RE AWFULLY QUICK TO CAST ASPERSIONS. YOU CAN'T PROVE THAT. I DON'T NEED TO HEAR THIS. HOW DO YOU KNOW? THAT'S CRAZY. YOU'RE IMAGINING THINGS. THAT'S JUST YOUR OPINION. NO, IT'S NOT THAT AT ALL. THAT HAS NOTHING TO DO WITH IT. THAT DOESN'T MEAN ANYTHING. WELL, THAT'S A NATURAL REACTION. THAT DOESN'T MEAN WHAT YOU THINK IT MEANS. THAT'S A SELF-SERVING EXPLANATION. WHY BRING THIS UP? YOU SEE EVERYTHING IN TERMS OF YOUR OWN PROBLEMS. WHY IS THAT OBJECTIONABLE? YOU'RE COOKING UP PROBLEMS WHERE THERE ARE NONE. YOU'RE MAKING THINGS UP. I DON'T BELIEVE THAT HAPPENED. I'M NOT SAYING YOU'RE LYING. I'M JUST SAYING YOUR PERCEPTIONS ARE DISTORTED. IT'S NOT NECESSARY TO SEE THINGS IN THAT LIGHT. YOU'RE TOO UPSET TO THINK CLEARLY. WE'LL DISCUSS IT LATER. NO, NOT NOW. I'M BUSY. STOP MAKING TROUBLE. YOU'RE SEEING THINGS THAT AREN'T THERE. THIS IS RIDICULOUS. I DON'T WANT TO TALK ABOUT IT. SO HOW ARE YOU OTHERWISE? I REFUSE TO DISCUSS THIS. WHAT'S SO WRONG WITH THAT? CHANGE THE SUBJECT. PEOPLE HAVE A RIGHT TO EXPRESS THEMSELVES. I'M NOT GOING TO LISTEN TO THIS. YOU TAKE EVERYTHING TOO PERSONALLY. YOU MUST HAVE PERCEIVED THAT INCORRECTLY. I'M SURE YOU'RE MISTAKEN. I'M SURE THAT DIDN'T HAPPEN QUITE THE WAY YOU DESCRIBE IT. SURELY YOU'RE EXAGGERATING JUST A LITTLE. YOU'RE BEING IRRATIONAL. YOU CAN'T MAKE ME BELIEVE THAT. THIS IS SO UNNECESSARY. NOBODY WANTS TO HEAR THIS. ARE YOU TRYING TO RUIN EVERYTHING? STOP INSISTING ON THIS IF YOU KNOW WHAT'S GOOD FOR YOU. YOU'RE REALLY OUT ON A LIMB. YOU'RE WAY OUT OF LINE. IT'S NOT YOUR PLACE TO SAY THAT. DON'T PUSH IT. YOU'RE GOING TOO FAR. GET OFF IT. YOU'RE SPEAKING OUT OF PLACE. LIGHTEN UP. YOU'RE ASKING FOR TROUBLE. YOU'RE BEING INAPPROPRIATE. NOBODY CARES WHAT YOU THINK. YOU'RE LEAVING YOURSELF WIDE OPEN. YOU'RE CRUISIN' FOR A BRUISIN'. PUT A LID ON IT. CAN IT. STUFF IT. BAG IT. FORGET IT. DROP IT. I WOULDN'T PURSUE THIS ANY FURTHER IF I WERE YOU. YOU'RE REALLY ASKING FOR IT. DO YOU WANT TO GET IN TROUBLE? YOU'RE GOING TO GET IT. YOU'RE STICKING YOUR NECK OUT. YOU'RE DIGGING YOUR OWN GRAVE. A REAL GLUTTON FOR PUNISHMENT. YOU CAN'T GET AWAY WITH THIS. YOU'RE DEAD MEAT. I HATE TO DO THIS. I'M REALLY SORRY THIS IS NECESSARY. THIS HURTS ME MORE THAN IT HURTS YOU. I'M DOING THIS FOR YOUR OWN GOOD. YOU'LL APPRECIATE THIS LATER. I'M JUST TRYING TO HELP YOU. SOMEDAY YOU'LL THANK ME FOR THIS. ACTUALLY I'M DOING YOU A FAVOR. IN TIME YOU'LL UNDERSTAND. YOU'LL LEARN TO SEE THINGS DIFFERENTLY.

IT'S FINE. I DON'T KNOW WHAT YOU MEAN. I DIDN'T NOTICE ANYTHING WRONG. IT SEEMS FINE TO ME. I DON'T KNOW WHY YOU SAY THAT. I DON'T SEE ANY PROBLEM. I'M AMAZED THAT YOU SEE THINGS THAT WAY. I JUST DON'T SEE IT THAT WAY AT ALL. IT WASN'T INTENTIONAL. I DON'T UNDERSTAND WHERE THIS IS COMING FROM. JUST CALM DOWN. TRY TO GET A GRIP ON YOURSELF. THIS IS A COMPLETE SURPRISE TO ME. THE THOUGHT NEVER CROSSED MY MIND. I REALLY DON'T KNOW WHAT TO MAKE OF THIS. ISN'T THIS A LITTLE BIT MUCH? THAT'S A WEIRD WAY TO THINK ABOUT THINGS. I JUST CAN'T RELATE. WE CERTAINLY DO HAVE DIFFERENT PERSPECTIVES ON THINGS. YOU'RE MAKING TOO MUCH OF THIS. NOTHING'S THE MATTER. STOP GETTING EMOTIONAL. YOU'RE BLOWING THE WHOLE THING OUT OF PROPORTION. EVERYTHING'S FINE. WHAT DO YOU MEAN? WHAT'S THE PROBLEM? YOU'RE BEING PARANOID. YOU'RE OVERSENSITIVE. YOU'RE READING TOO MUCH INTO IT. STOP JUMPING TO CONCLUSIONS. IT DIDN'T OCCUR TO ME. YOU'RE OVERINTERPRETING THE DATA. I DON'T THINK IT HAS ANYTHING TO DO WITH THAT. IT WAS JUST A SIMPLE MISTAKE. IT DOESN'T MEAN ANYTHING. YOU'RE SEEING TOO MUCH IN THIS. NOTHING'S GOING ON. I CAN'T IMAGINE WHAT MAKES YOU THINK THAT. I DON'T KNOW WHAT YOU'RE TALKING ABOUT. I HAVE NO IDEA WHAT YOU'RE REFERRING TO. I REALLY THINK YOU'RE OVERDOING IT. YOU'RE JUST TIRED. DON'T TAKE EVERYTHING SO SERIOUSLY. IT'S NO BIG DEAL. YOU'RE JUST PROJECTING. YOU'RE OVERREACTING. NOTHING HAPPENED. DID I NOTICE WHAT? I DON'T SEE ANYTHING TO GET UPSET ABOUT. I DON'T SEE WHAT YOU'RE GETTING AT. I DON'T UNDERSTAND THE PROBLEM. WHAT'S THE MATTER? YOU'LL GET OVER IT. DID SOMEONE DO SOMETHING WRONG? WHAT'S GOING ON? WHAT'S THIS ABOUT? WHAT'S WRONG? STOP MAKING SUCH A BIG DEAL ABOUT IT. I DON'T SEE ANYTHING WRONG WITH THAT. EVERYONE DOES THAT. SO WHAT? BIG DEAL. WHO CARES? NO, NOTHING LIKE THAT. JUST A MISUNDERSTANDING, THAT'S ALL. MUCH ADO ABOUT NOTHING. I DON'T UNDERSTAND WHAT THIS IS ABOUT. I'M MYSTIFIED BY YOUR REACTION. I DON'T GET IT. SO? WHAT'S THE SIGNIFICANCE OF THAT? IT WAS JUST AN INNOCENT SLIP-UP. I REGARD THAT AS PERFECTLY NORMAL BEHAVIOR. I SEE NO PROBLEM WITH THAT. YOU'RE THE ONE WITH THE PROBLEM. THAT'S A VERY UNCHARITABLE INTERPRETATION. IT'S SO UNNECESSARY TO TALK ABOUT THIS. OH, I DON'T THINK IT HAS ANYTHING TO DO WITH THAT, REALLY. WHAT ARE YOU TALKING ABOUT? THAT'S SHEER SPECULATION. YOU'RE AWFULLY QUICK TO CAST ASPERSIONS. YOU CAN'T PROVE THAT. I DON'T NEED TO HEAR THIS. HOW DO YOU KNOW? THAT'S CRAZY. YOU'RE IMAGINING THINGS. THAT'S JUST YOUR OPINION. NO, IT'S NOT THAT AT ALL. THAT HAS NOTHING TO DO WITH IT. THAT DOESN'T MEAN ANYTHING. WELL, THAT'S A NATURAL REACTION. THAT DOESN'T MEAN WHAT YOU THINK IT MEANS. THAT'S A SELF-SERVING EXPLANATION. WHY BRING THIS UP? YOU SEE EVERYTHING IN TERMS OF YOUR OWN PROBLEMS. WHY IS THAT OBJECTIONABLE? YOU'RE COOKING UP PROBLEMS WHERE THERE ARE NONE. YOU'RE MAKING THINGS UP. I DON'T BELIEVE THAT HAPPENED. I'M NOT SAYING YOU'RE LYING. I'M JUST SAYING YOUR PERCEPTIONS ARE DISTORTED. IT'S NOT NECESSARY TO SEE THINGS IN THAT LIGHT. YOU'RE TOO UPSET TO THINK CLEARLY. WE'LL DISCUSS IT LATER. NO, NOT NOW. I'M BUSY. STOP MAKING TROUBLE. YOU'RE SEEING THINGS THAT AREN'T THERE. THIS IS RIDICULOUS. I DON'T WANT TO TALK ABOUT IT. SO HOW ARE YOU OTHERWISE? I REFUSE TO DISCUSS THIS. WHAT'S SO WRONG WITH THAT? CHANGE THE SUBJECT. PEOPLE HAVE A RIGHT TO EXPRESS THEMSELVES. I'M NOT GOING TO LISTEN TO THIS. YOU TAKE EVERYTHING TOO PERSONALLY. YOU MUST HAVE PERCEIVED THAT INCORRECTLY. I'M SURE YOU'RE MISTAKEN. I'M SURE THAT DIDN'T HAPPEN QUITE THE WAY YOU DESCRIBE IT. SURELY YOU'RE EXAGGERATING JUST A LITTLE. YOU'RE BEING IRRATIONAL. YOU CAN'T MAKE ME BELIEVE THAT. THIS IS SO UNNECESSARY. NOBODY WANTS TO HEAR THIS. ARE YOU TRYING TO RUIN EVERYTHING? STOP INSISTING ON THIS IF YOU KNOW WHAT'S GOOD FOR YOU. YOU'RE REALLY OUT ON A LIMB. YOU'RE WAY OUT OF LINE. IT'S NOT YOUR PLACE TO SAY THAT. DON'T PUSH IT. YOU'RE GOING TOO FAR. GET OFF IT. YOU'RE SPEAKING OUT OF PLACE. LIGHTEN UP. YOU'RE ASKING FOR TROUBLE. YOU'RE BEING INAPPROPRIATE. NOBODY CARES WHAT YOU THINK. YOU'RE LEAVING YOURSELF WIDE OPEN. YOU'RE CRUISIN' FOR A BRUISIN'. PUT A LID ON IT. CAN IT. STUFF IT. BAG IT. FORGET IT. DROP IT. I WOULDN'T PURSUE THIS ANY FURTHER IF I WERE YOU. YOU'RE REALLY ASKING FOR IT. DO YOU WANT TO GET IN TROUBLE? YOU'RE GOING TO GET IT. YOU'RE STICKING YOUR NECK OUT. YOU'RE DIGGING YOUR OWN GRAVE. A REAL GLUTTON FOR PUNISHMENT. YOU CAN'T GET AWAY WITH THIS. YOU'RE DEAD MEAT. I HATE TO DO THIS. I'M REALLY SORRY THIS IS NECESSARY. THIS HURTS ME MORE THAN IT HURTS YOU.

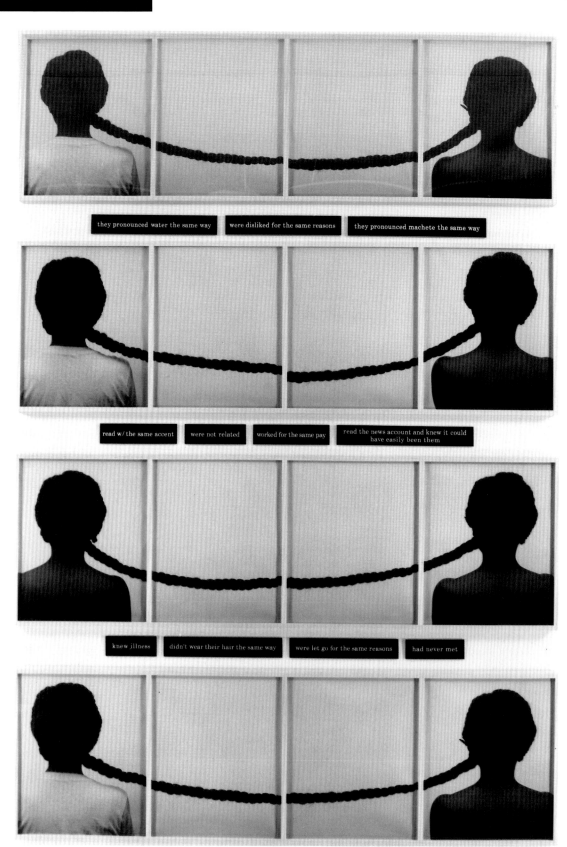

they pronounced water the same way   were disliked for the same reasons   they pronounced machete the same way

read w/ the same accent   were not related   worked for the same pay   read the news account and knew it could have easily been them

knew illness   didn't wear their hair the same way   were let go for the same reasons   had never met

Figure

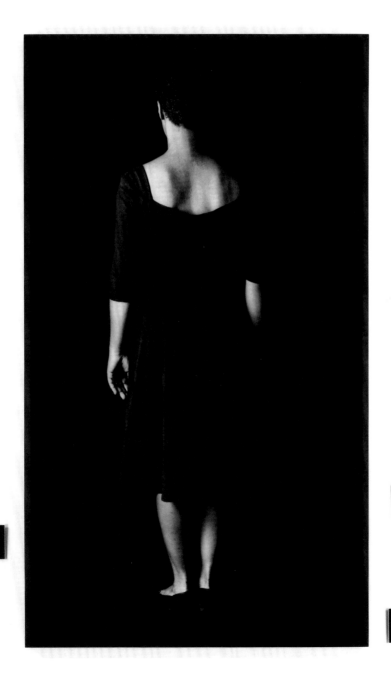

figured the worst

figured on all the times there
was no camera

he was disfigured

figured there
would be no reaction

figured legality had nothing
to do with it

figured she was suspect

figured he was suspect

figured someone had been there
because the door was open

GUARDED

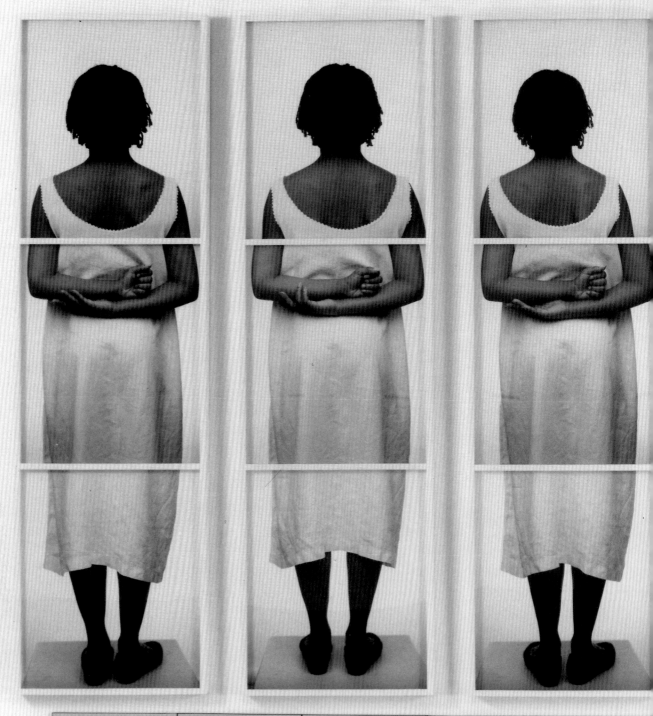

SEX ATTACKS | SKIN ATTACKS | SEX ATTACKS | SKIN ATTACKS | SEX ATTAC

SEX ATTACKS | SKIN ATTACKS | SEX ATTACKS | SKI

SKIN ATTACKS | SEX ATTAC

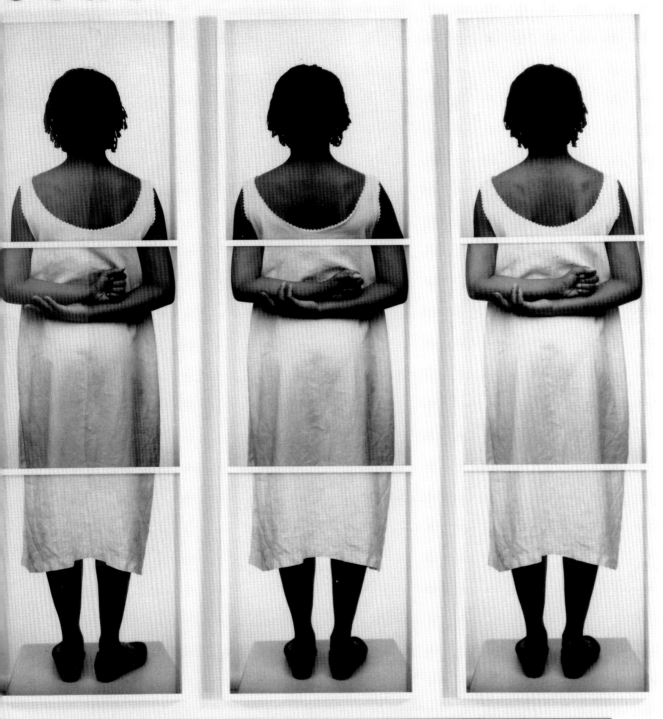

IN ATTACKS | SEX ATTACKS | SKIN ATTACKS | SEX ATTACKS | SKIN ATTACKS
CKS | SEX ATTACKS | SKIN ATTACKS | SEX ATTACKS
IN ATTACKS | SEX ATTACKS

Diane Tani

*Hard Glance: Asian American
Image and Identity*
originals in color

Diversification

110

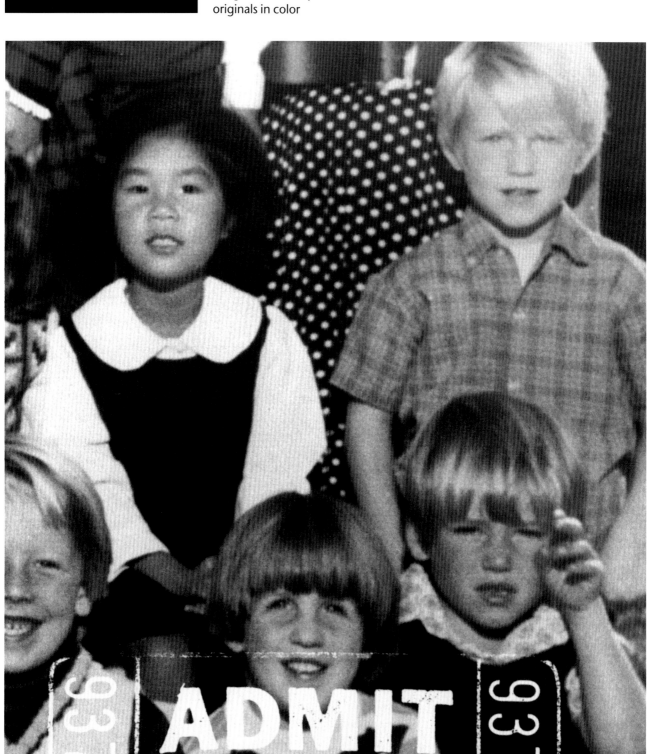

Hard Glance

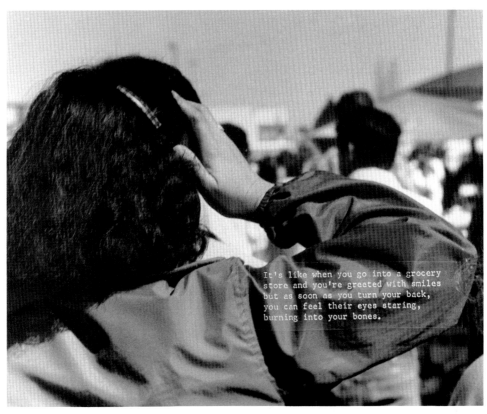

It's like when you go into a grocery store and you're greeted with smiles but as soon as you turn your back, you can feel their eyes staring, burning into your bones.

Self Identity

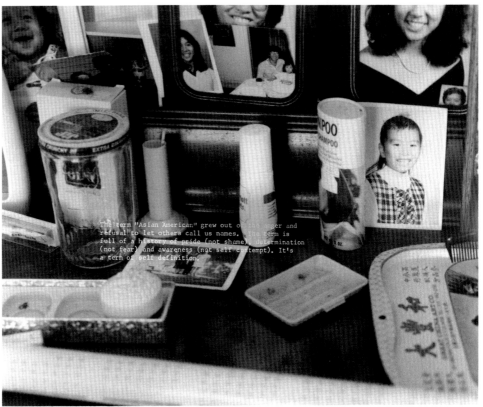

The term "Asian American" grew out of the anger and refusal to let others call us names. The term is full of a history of pride (not shame), determination (not fear) and awareness (not self contempt). It's a term of self definition.

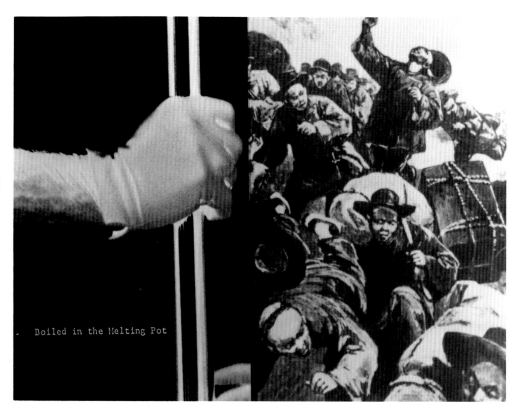

Boiled in the Melting Pot

112

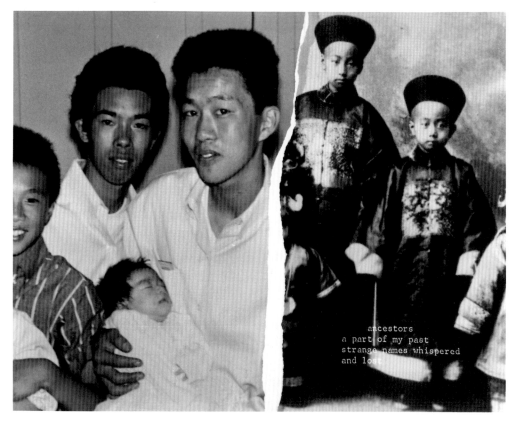

ancestors
a part of my past
strange names whispered
and lost

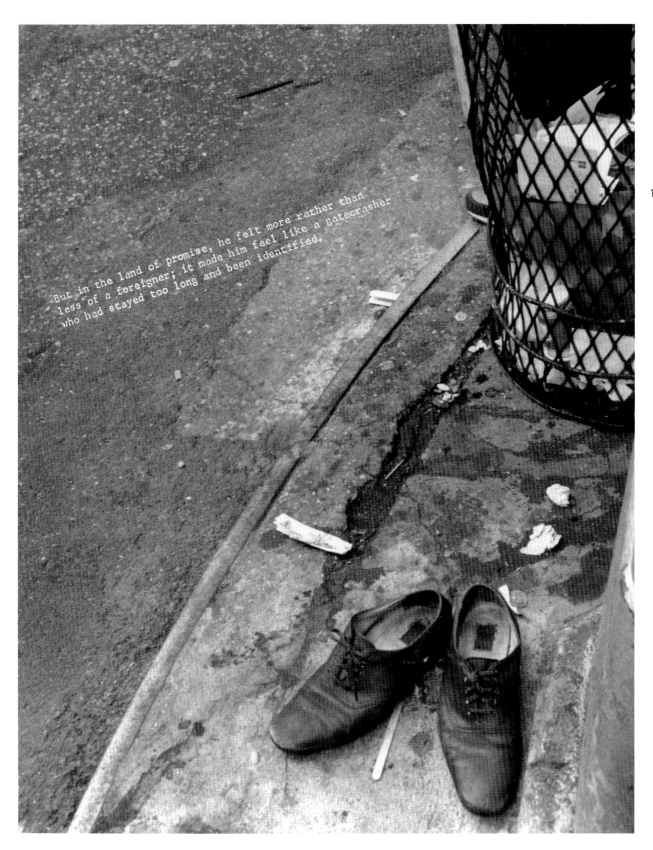

But in the land of promise, he felt more rather than
less of a foreigner; it made him feel like a gatecrasher
who had stayed too long and been identified.

113

Theresa Harlan

*While my mother and aunt were cleaning the houses of white women,
they [white women] were developing their theories of feminism.*

Hulleah J. Tsinhnahjinnie

When I finally settled down to write this essay, in some ways I felt I was
heading into territory both familiar and unfamiliar. My relationship to feminism is ambivalent, for feminism often seems to focus on gender without
giving equal consideration to class, race, and culture. Feminism does not
preclude racism and classism. I can trace my own feelings to my experiences of being ignored during discussions by women who identified themselves as feminists and who, as an afterthought, would turn to me for the
"indigenous woman's perspective." As I grappled with articulating my own
relationship to feminism and with creating a context for the work of Native
women photographers, the task that lay before me seemed immense. Euro-
American feminist discourse is so lacking in references to Native women
that I have to wonder whether the omissions are due to lack of information
or to lack of inclination to find these artists and writers.

In beginning this project, I knew I would rely on the many stories and
examples of strong-willed Native women. My approach was very similar to
Patricia Hill Collins's approach to black feminist thought: "Placing the ideas
of ordinary African-American women as well as those of better-known Black
women intellectuals at the center of analysis produces a new angle of vision
on feminist and African-American concerns, one infused with an Afro-
centrist feminist sensibility."[1] The written words of Patricia Hill Collins, Inés
Hernández-Ávila, Jolene Rickard, bell hooks, Gail Tremblay, Angela Davis,
and Trinh Min-ha created an opening, a space in which I could write this
essay.

A second impetus came from a lecture in art history I attended at the
1993 Society for Photographic Education's biannual meeting. The lecturer
discussed the use of self-portraiture by such artists as Pat Ward Williams,
Carrie Mae Weems, Jimmie Durham, and James Luna. The lecture did not
include works by Native women. The historian presented a Euro-American
feminist critique without a single reference to writers from the African-
American or Native American communities in her analysis. It was that
lecture that inspired me to write about Native women using themselves as
the photographic subject, or about images of Native women.

Native women photographers' use of self-imagery and images of
women goes beyond the reversal or deconstruction of Native American
portraiture as practiced by early and contemporary non-Native pictorialists.
Similar to my own reliance on my self and experiences, these artists are also
locating their references in their own selves and in the Native knowledge

[1] Patricia Hill Collins, *Black Feminist
Thought: Knowledge, Consciousness and
the Politics of Empowerment* (London:
HarperCollins Academic, 1990), 16.

rooted in their communities to construct the context for their work.[2] By
"Native knowledge" I mean not only information shared by the community
but also the intellectual foundations that enabled our Native communities
to survive.[3] Becoming our own subject means establishing a central space
for ourselves and our communities, means regarding ourselves as thinkers
and doers. In that way, Native women and Native people can avoid the trap
of speaking with the voice of the marginalized.

This central space we occupy as personal, cultural, and historical
subjects is essential to our ability to work toward our individual empowerment and that of our communities. Our work is not exclusively directed to
women but comes from within a woman's vision. It is addressed to a public
audience, Native and non-Native. These women artists are not isolated
intellectuals but are a part of local and international communities. (I use the
term "international" in place of "intertribal" to stress the diversity of indigenous nations within and outside the borders of the United States.) Jolene
Rickard writes of her use of photography,

> Working in photography one is forced to deal with issues of representa-
> tion or risk promoting visually the ideals other people have placed in
> your head. I believe photographers "show" what they think. This takes
> on a weighty responsibility in relationship for me, as an image maker,
> and as a Tuscarora. I realize I could speak art—talk about my rights of
> individual expression, but the basis for my inspiration is the teachings
> of my people. From that point I build my image—sometimes making
> visual reference to our relationship to the people outside of my beliefs
> and often working within the logic of our beliefs. If we don't strive to
> deal with the meanings of what we [Indian people] think, then what is
> the point?[4]

Creating a space for critique raises complex issues about empowerment. Public critique runs the risk of confrontation with dominant society or
stifles what could be productive conflict in order not to show internal
conflict to outsiders. It is this protection of appearances that blocks our
ability to discuss our differences and to learn from them; thus, we sacrifice
our own growth. Photographers such as Carm Little Turtle, Shelly Niro,
Jolene Rickard, and Hulleah Tsinhnahjinnie take this risk and enable us to
come to terms with racist and exploitative practices committed against us
and the injuries we inflict on ourselves.

Carm Little Turtle focuses her work on the personal injuries inflicted in
relationships between men and women in her hand-painted sepia-toned
photographs. Little Turtle casts herself, her husband, and her relatives as
characters in her photographic scenes. In *Earthman Won't Dance Except with*

[2] Karuk historian and cultural critic Julian Lang, along with other community members, has established the Institute of Native Knowledge to support critical thinking by Native artists, writers, and activists. The address for the Institute of Native Knowledge is 611 Third St. #1, Eureka, CA 95501.

[3] This topic was discussed by Jolene Rickard at a meeting of Native women artists held in May 1993 at the Heard Museum, Phoenix.

[4] Carla Roberts, ed., *The Submuloc Show/ Columbus Wohs: A Visual Commentary on the Columbus Quincentennial from the Perspective of America's First People* (Phoenix: Atlatl, 1992), 54.

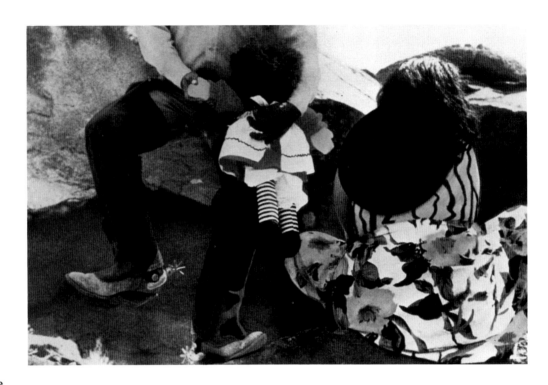

Carm Little Turtle

Earthman Won't Dance Except with Other Women, 1992
black-and-white photograph with hand-painting and sepia toning.

Other Women Little Turtle examines the sometimes painful twist of relationships that occurs when one partner begins to search for outside attention. Earthman represents men who view women as objects. Earthman is dressed in Western wear—jeans, chaps, and boots—and holds a child's doll, Raggedy Ann, as he pretends to dance with her. At his feet is his "woman," who must witness his playful dance. Raggedy Ann, the other woman objectified, is clearly only a toy to Earthman.

Little Turtle's *She Dreamed of a Husband, Two Horses and Many Cows* is a quartet of images depicting a woman yearning to leave one reality for another. The title refers to the compensation the husband's family pays to his wife's family for the loss of her contribution when she leaves to marry. In the first image the woman is sitting on top of a rusted car in the middle of the reservation. On the dashboard sits a Navajo wedding basket. In the next two images she spies a figure herding cattle, and stands up; in the last image she takes money from a man, who appears only as a shadow against the car with his hand extending out to her. In most of Little Turtle's photographs the faces of her subjects are obscured, never revealing their identi-

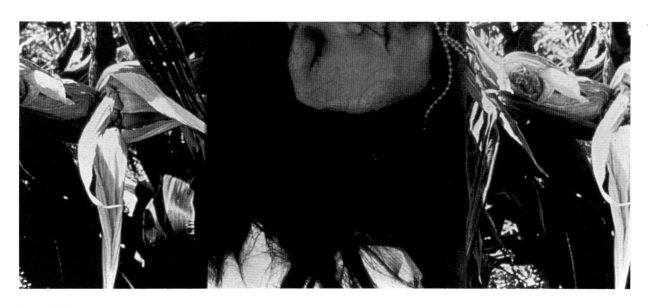

Jolene Rickard
Self-portrait—Three Sisters, 1988
black-and-white photograph with color
photocopy.

ties. Little Turtle's characters encounter and interact surreptitiously with each other.

Jolene Rickard's 1988 *Self Portrait—Three Sisters*, a color Xerox of Jolene's face with closed eyes and cascading hair, is centered between two black-and-white images of corn. *Three Sisters* portrays Rickard's relationship to the teachings of her people and her own foundation within those teachings.

In *I See Red in '92* Rickard included a tightly framed, black-and-white portrait of herself in a quintet with four color photographs, symbolizing the state and condition of Native survival. By using her own image as subject, Rickard places herself in the context of the historical experiences of her people. The photographs are arranged in a cross and intersection of encounters. Rickard's image is in the top, or north, section. Below her, at the center, is a photograph of "the last time the Fireball Ceremony was 'played' at Tuscarora" [her emphasis].[5] To the left of it is a photograph of a drawing of a buffalo, a toy red Indian, and a white feather, "all stereotypical commodifications of Native culture."[6] To the right and below are two images of "Hudson Bay Blankets used in fur trade [showing the lines in the design of the blanket that indicate] the number of furs traded for the blanket."[7] The placement of Rickard's image at the top tells us that the other images represent elements in her life and the life of her people, and

[5] Jolene Rickard, artist's statement, 1993.
[6] Rickard, statement.
[7] Rickard, statement.

8 Rickard, statement.
9 Inés Hernández-Ávila, "In Praise of Insubordination, or, What Makes a Good Woman Go Bad?" in *Transforming a Rape Culture*, ed. Emilie Buchwald, Pamela Fletcher, and Martha Roth (Minneapolis: Milkweed Editions, 1993), 378.
10 Angie Debo, *A History of the Indians of the United States* (Norman: University of Oklahoma Press, 1990), 117.
11 The dispute is over who has the authority to determine whether an individual is or is not an Indian. The law requires any person who sells or offers for sale arts and crafts (including contemporary art) and who claims American Indian identity to provide documentation of Indian ancestry. Without such proof of ancestry—such as an enrollment number of a federally recognized tribe or a roll number from a state census or a special designation of "Indian artist" from a tribal council—the seller has violated Public Law 101-644 and risks a fine and prison sentence. (To date, no money has been allocated to carry out this law.) Proponents of the law argue that the law is needed to protect authentic Indian artists from impostors who exploit the Indian art market. Opponents who regard the law as a continuation of the government's paternalistic policies argue that the law does not recognize exceptions such as adoption, termination, relocation, political objection to enrollment, closed rolls, clannish tribal governments, and nations incorrectly designated as extinct by anthropologists.

that she occupies a place of awareness and self-knowledge. Rickard writes, "Overall, these pieces are about placing 'us' the original people in the world we inherited—one with ceremony, stereotypical construction, colonization, genocide—yet we survived."[8]

We can continue to survive only if we as Native people recognize our own shortcomings and do not fool ourselves by thinking that we as indigenous people are faultless. Cultural critic and poet Ines Hernandez-Avila writes, "If I criticize the men or women of the Native American and Chicana/Latina community who are perpetuating oppressive regimes of being, and sustaining 'oligarchies of the spirit,' that does not mean that I do not love my communities, or that I do not want to honor them or respect them. It is because I love them and care for them that I challenge all of us to unlearn the doctrine of subordination to which we have been subjected internationally as colonized people, peoples who were supposed to have been 'conquered' and so should know their place—which is a very tiny space indeed. For many indigenous peoples it is not even a closet; in many parts of this hemisphere it is often a casa de carton [cardboard house]."[9]

The same concern for narrow thinking and the absence of self-criticism among Native people figures in Hulleah Tsinhnahjinnie's series of self-portraits, *Creative Native.* Tsinhnahjinnie sends a warning to the Native community about the 1990 Indian Arts and Crafts Act, Public Law 101-644 (a bill co-authored by U.S. congressman Ben Nighthorse Campbell [D–Colorado], the first elected Native representative, and Jon Kyle, Jr. [R–Arizona]), in a series of mug shots of herself with pressure adhesive numbers across her mouth. The affected tattoo is her tribal enrollment number. She has symbolically replaced Native thinking with that of colonized thinking. In this triptych Hulleah asks an alarming question: "Would I have been a member of the Nighthawk Society or the Snake society or would I have been a half-breed leading the whites to the full-bloods?" signing it with her number, 111-390, rather than her name. The question refers to community conflict regarding the law; some leading proponents are mixed bloods (half-breeds). The artist is commenting that so often we defeat ourselves within our own Native communities. Her message is spoken in the voice of Eufala Harjo, a member of the Four Mothers society (a resistance group to the 1887 Dawes Allotment Act), who witnessed half-breeds turning in the names of full-blooded resisters to the Dawes Commission.[10] It was at this time that many southeastern Natives received their government-issued census numbers.[11] Tsinhnahjinnie is representing the national debate over institutionalized Native identity by critiquing the reliance of Natives on the federal government for their identity and pointing to the internalized colonization of Native people.

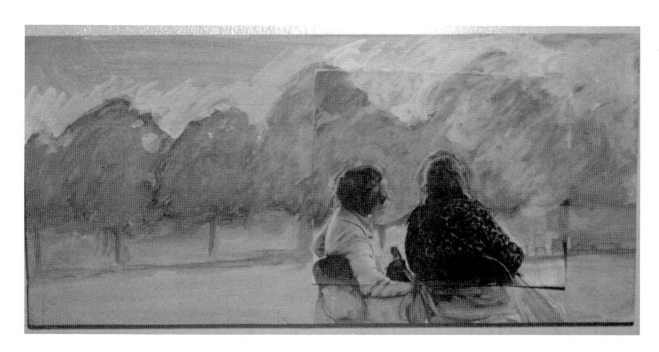

Hulleah Tsinhnahjinnie
Talking About Aunt Lucy
from the series ***My Heroes Have Always***
 Been Native,   1993
black-and-white photograph,
8″ × 10″.

Historically, the participation of women in the Native struggle for survival has been overlooked, devalued, and suppressed—not only by Euro-Americans but also by Native men. But women recognize the significance of their role. It is the woman whose hand is most responsible for our physical and spiritual survival. It is the woman who teaches us at home. As children we watch and witness as adults make their way through their roles as women and men. These women and their stories take on new life in photographic works that use family photographs and portraiture, for the use of family or archival photographs by Native photographers places individuals in a larger context of the family and history.

In Tsinhnahjinnie's 1993 series, *My Heroes Have Always Been Native*, we see images of men and women who have inspired her. Tsinhnahjinnie has placed each 8 × 10 black-and-white photograph of her heroes on a wooden board and painted the board to extend the photograph's frame, thereby extending the magnitude and reach of her hero. In *Talking About Aunt Lucy* she took a photograph of her maternal aunts seated on folding chairs with their backs to the camera and placed them in the foreground, implying a third dimension. The aunts are deep in conversation. As a child of eight Aunt Lucy led a group of children who had become separated from their families as they were driven by the military to Oklahoma's Indian Territory in the mid-1800s; the children followed behind and later joined their families during settlement.[12] Tsinhnahjinnie painted the board to show her aunts seated before a field with a line of trees as the horizon. They are most likely sitting on a porch facing the land where Aunt Lucy was reunited with her family. The fact that Tsinhnahjinnie has left her heroines in black and white empowers them as the central figures of time and space of survival. It is her aunts' self-knowledge and experiences that feed our own sense of knowledge and enable us to become women like them.

Shelly Niro combines family imagery with self-imagery. Niro uses the context of the personal to create a historical context for determining who is Mohawk, who is Native, who is a woman or a man. In a sepia-toned trip-tych titled, *This Land Is Mime Land*, she looks at how society provides us with

[12] Hulleah Tsinhnahjinnie, conversation with author, 1993.

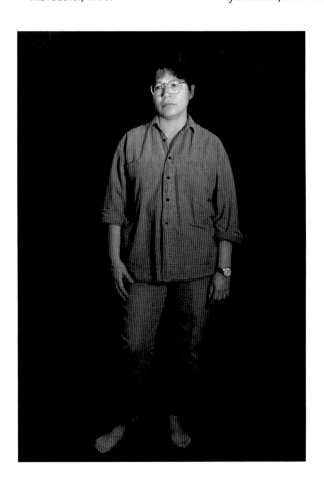

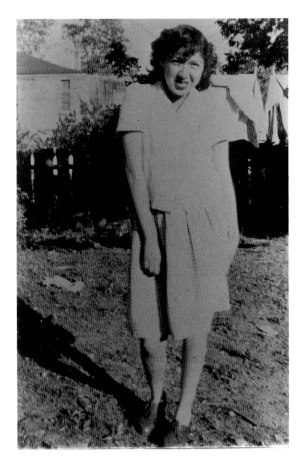

formulas for objectification of women and men. Niro dresses as the Statue of Liberty, a playboy, Marilyn Monroe, and even Elvis. The three photographs in the triptych represent, in serial order, the historical, the personal, and the contemporary.[13] Niro designates herself as the subject in the historical and contemporary images, and uses family photographs as the personal. In the title image she is dressed as a mime, in black clothes, painted face, and white gloves. The mime represents the various personas we might encounter in our lives; the personas of the mime mirror but never have their own substance, never own their own reality. As the mime, Niro is bright-eyed and ready to entertain. The central image in the triptych represents the personal and is a photograph of Niro's daughter, standing in a park, shy and quiet, her hands clasped in front of her. She is conscious of

13 Shelly Niro, conversation with author, 1993.

Shelly Niro
500 Year Itch,   1992
three black-and-white photographs.

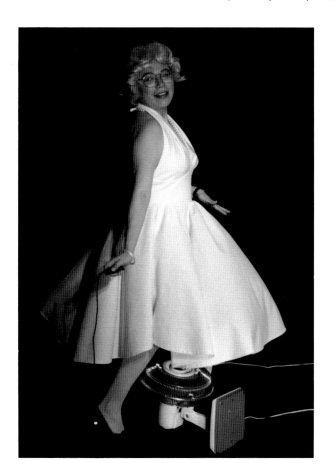

122

the camera. Here, the personal is the future, present, and past. The daughter must choose how she will define herself as a woman, accepting or rejecting the influences of society. The last image, representing the contemporary, is of a barefoot Niro wearing a dark jacket, shirt, and pants. Her back is toward the camera. As the contemporary, Niro has cast aside formulas and processes that represent her own objectification and that of her daughter.

In another triptych from the series *This Land Is Mime Land*, *500 Year Itch*, Niro makes a historical reference dressed as Marilyn Monroe; wearing a white halter dress and a blond wig, she straddles a small electrical fan and holds a camera release cable in her right hand. The personal image is of Niro's mother at age fifteen, shy and feminine, dressed in a pink dress and heeled. The contemporary image is of Niro in a defiant stance, rejecting the type of woman portrayed by Monroe and emulated by her mother.[13] *500 Year Itch* is cleverly satirical in its reference to 500 years of contact as an intolerable itch to Native peoples.

Niro's *The Land Is Mime Land* series emphasizes her control. She photographs herself holding the shutter release and, by not removing her glasses, symbolically refuses to give in to her own objectification. As we Native women continue to create spaces in which we can be thinkers and doers—whether in the arts, home, or community—we must reject objectifying practices.

In a recent paper Ines Hernandez-Avila made a related point: "To the women of the communities I call my own, I want to ask, How can we be sure that we have divested ourselves from the imposed stereotypes of Native American women as submissive, passive squaws and drudges (or more recently as mystical unintellectuals, 'bringers of good feeling')? . . ."[14]

It is the stereotype of the mystical and angry Indian I most often encounter in the arts and education communities. We are objectified as mystical beings with a genetic disposition to touch everyone's lives and leave them in a state of harmony and balance. If we are not at peace, we are at war. When we criticize and challenge hegemonic thinking and attitudes, we are characterized as angry, as taking history too personally. When we Native women allow ourselves to be objectified, we allow ourselves to be separated from the thinkers and doers, to be confined to the realm of emotions.

For instance, at the Women's Caucus for the Arts meeting in San Francisco a few years back, the organizers opened the meeting with a prayer led by a Native women, who asked the Native women in the audience to join her. Those of us who didn't know her were hesitant because we didn't know what to expect, but we decided to join her. Then she asked for women of all

14 Hernández-Ávila, "In Praise of Insubordination," 379.

races to join her. She prayed and sang, turning to face the cardinal directions. While she was singing, I kept thinking about how uncomfortable I was in my role of complicity. Her sincerity was not the issue. My concern was that this prayer played into the non-Natives' notions of us as one people, of one mind. By joining her, we seemed to reinforce these notions. In a similar way, I think that we must critique situations in which we are exoticized, such as a recent one in which students referred to two Native women speakers as "goddesses" and "spiritual warriors." bell hooks speaks of the same sort of occurrence in the black community. "Moving in and out of the segregated black communities into predominately white circles, I have observed how easy it is for individual black females deemed 'special' to become exoticized, objectified in ways that support types of behavior that on home turf would just be considered out of control."[15] When I think of terms such as "goddess" or "spiritual warrior" I can't help but groan, thinking about how that projected image will invalidate a Native woman who does not seem so "spiritual" or "goddesslike" and how it plays into the operator's hand. But I must also laugh, thinking of anyone calling one of my older female relatives a "goddess" and knowing what their quick response would be.

The medium of photography lends itself well to avoiding objectification and allows the artists to be seen as thinkers and doers. Because photography is not easily associated with a traditional cultural art form or practice, it can be readily distinguished from the Native arts documented and discussed by anthropologists, art historians, and enthusiasts. In this way, Native photographers can resist conventional notions about Native artists. At the same time, however, I would argue that some artists and commentators get stuck at a primary level—the presumed irony of a Native using a camera, the white man's supposedly bewildering technology.[16]

The space reserved for Native artists is the narrow space of intuition and the exercise of spiritual thought. Many exhibits, whether curated by non-Natives or Natives, rely on romantic constructions to contextualize the art and ultimately invalidate the work. For instance, at one exhibit I attended there were works by six Native artists—paintings, prints, drawings, sculpture, and found objects. One artist had created a very intricate, complex, and aesthetically balanced "mandela," a circular installation of dried leaves, flowers, seeds, and things collected during a walk. Most of the non-Natives were mesmerized by the artist's spiritual references. They videotaped the installation, photographed it, and loved it. They loved it because it validated the pictures they carry in their heads about Native people and their relationship to nature. The work by the rest of the artists was barely noticed as it carried no such romantic notions.

[15] bell hooks, *Yearning: Race, Gender, and Cultural Politics* (Boston: South End Press, 1990), 91.
[16] Theresa Harlan, "Smudges, Dust and Tracks: Native Photographic Representation" (Paper delivered at "Images Across Boundaries: History, Use and Ethics of Photographs of American Indians," symposium at the New Mexico Museum of American Indian Arts and Culture, Santa Fe, New Mexico, April 1993).

We as Native artists and writers must refuse to allow ourselves to be used as objects by others. We must resist and reject the "good intentions" of those who do not or will not recognize their own racist, sexist, and hegemonic thinking about Native women and men. We as Native people must envision ourselves as thinking and intelligent beings in order for our creative works to be recognized as intelligent and strategic contributions to Native survival.

I want to thank Inés Hernández-Ávila, George Longfish, Hulleah Tsinhnahjinnie, and Moira Roth for encouragement and assistance with this essay.

A R T W O R K S
    Martha Rosler   from *Bringing the War Home: House Beautiful*
    Esther Parada   *Type/Cast: (not the typical) portrait of a revolutionary*
    Yong Soon Min   *de*COLONIZATION
    Hulleah Tsinhnahjinnie   from *Native Programming*
    Pat Ward Williams   *Two Installations*
E S S A Y
    Julia Ballerini   ODELLA/Carlota

126

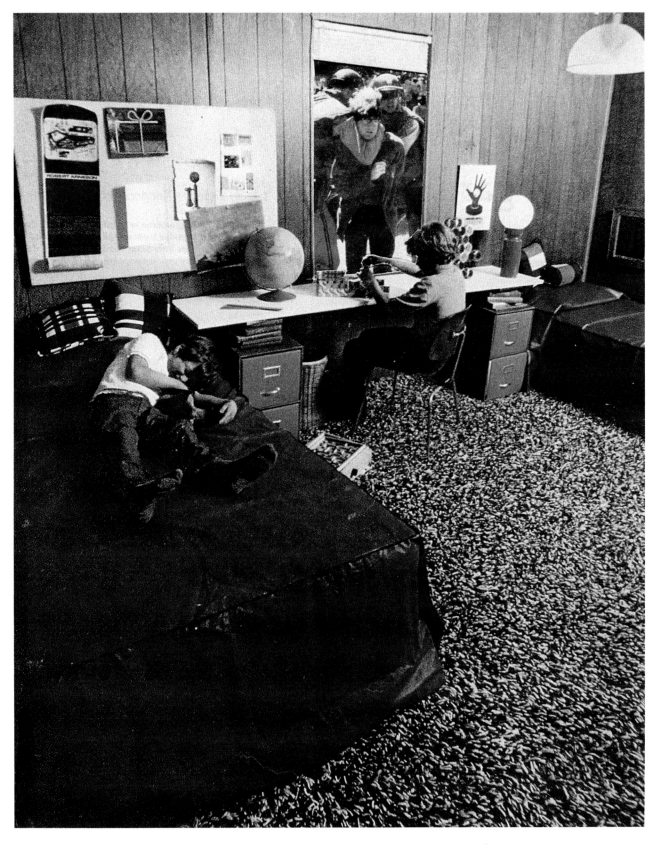

Balloons

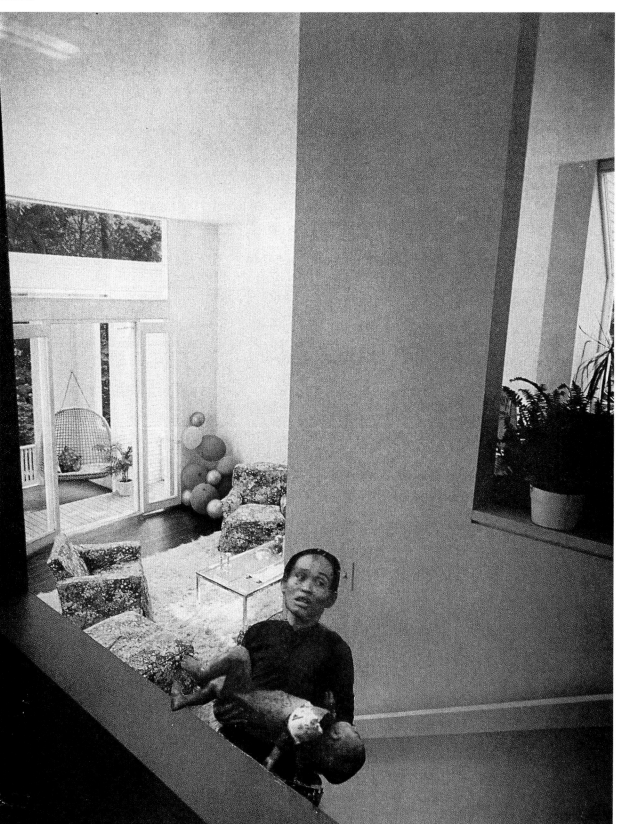

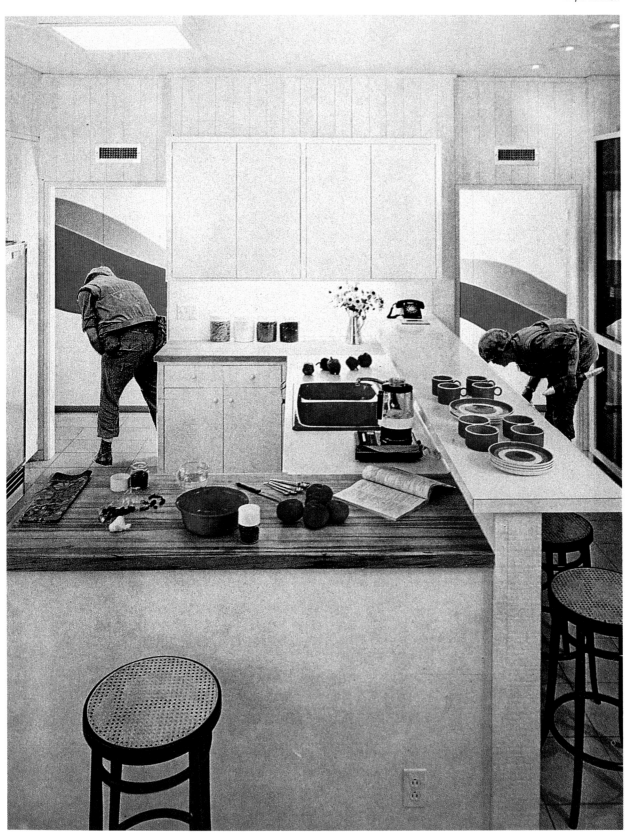

Vacation Getaway

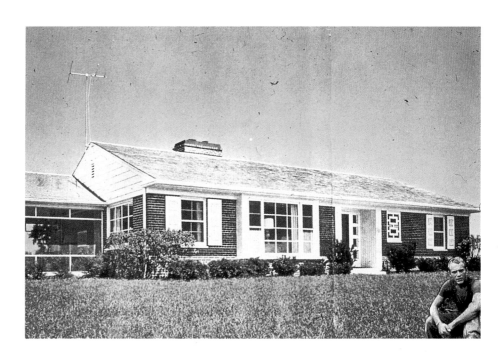

Tract-House Soldier

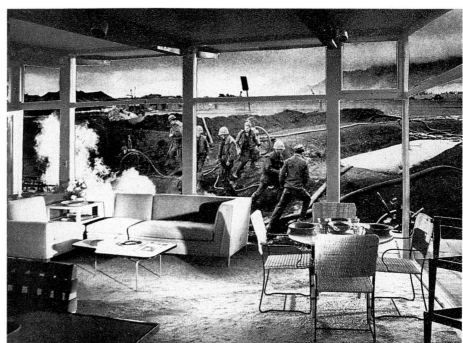

In a secluded vacation spot, privacy isn't a problem, so you go all out with glass, for view, light, and visual spaciousness. Simple or no-pattern coverings, soft colors, and small-scale furnishings add to illusion of size. Blue of the ceiling and brown of the beams extend through the glass walls to the eaves from living room to the outdoors

These anti-Vietnam War works weren't made for an art context. In the late 1960s and early 1970s, to put antiwar or feminist agitational works in such a setting would have verged on the obscene. They belonged more properly in the street or in the underground press, and that is where they appeared. In the late 1980s an art dealer whose projects were agitational and political suggested producing a portfolio of the images. By then, work from outside the gallery-defined art world had little hope of acknowledgment within it. I agreed to the portfolio because I wanted the work to enter art discourse—because it was my own work and because it represented a political response to political circumstances. The works joined the art world—became art, you might say—around 1988, so they may continue to suggest a way of working that can serve in nonart settings.

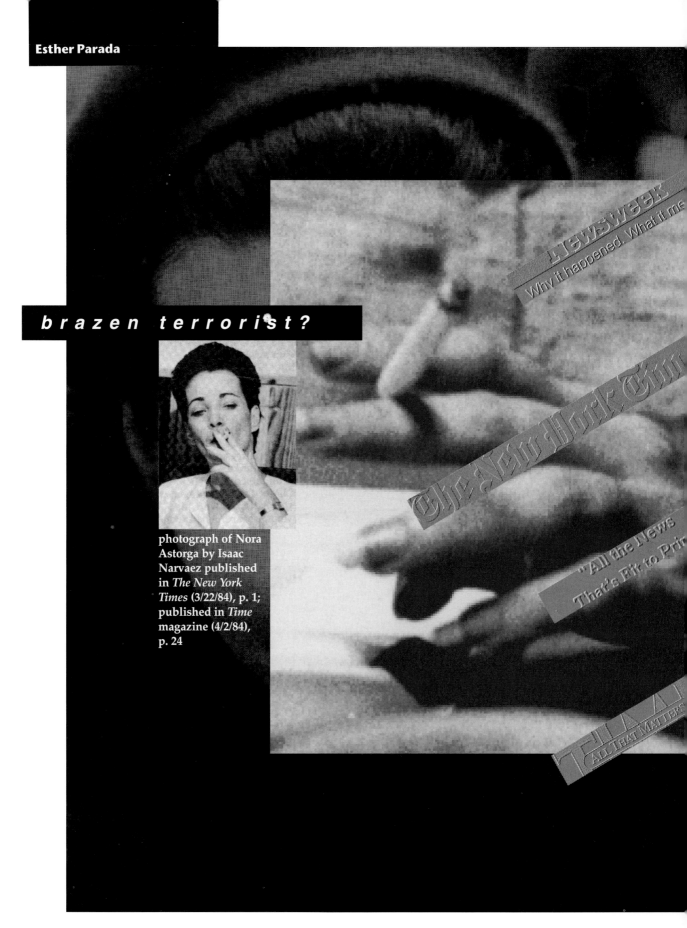

Esther Parada

brazen terrorist?

photograph of Nora
Astorga by Isaac
Narvaez published
in *The New York
Times* (3/22/84), p. 1;
published in *Time*
magazine (4/2/84),
p. 24

Newsweek
Why it happened. What it me

The New York Times

"All the News
That's Fit to Print

ALL THAT MATTERS

Esther Parada, *(not the typical) portrait of a revolutionary*

dedicated revolutionary?

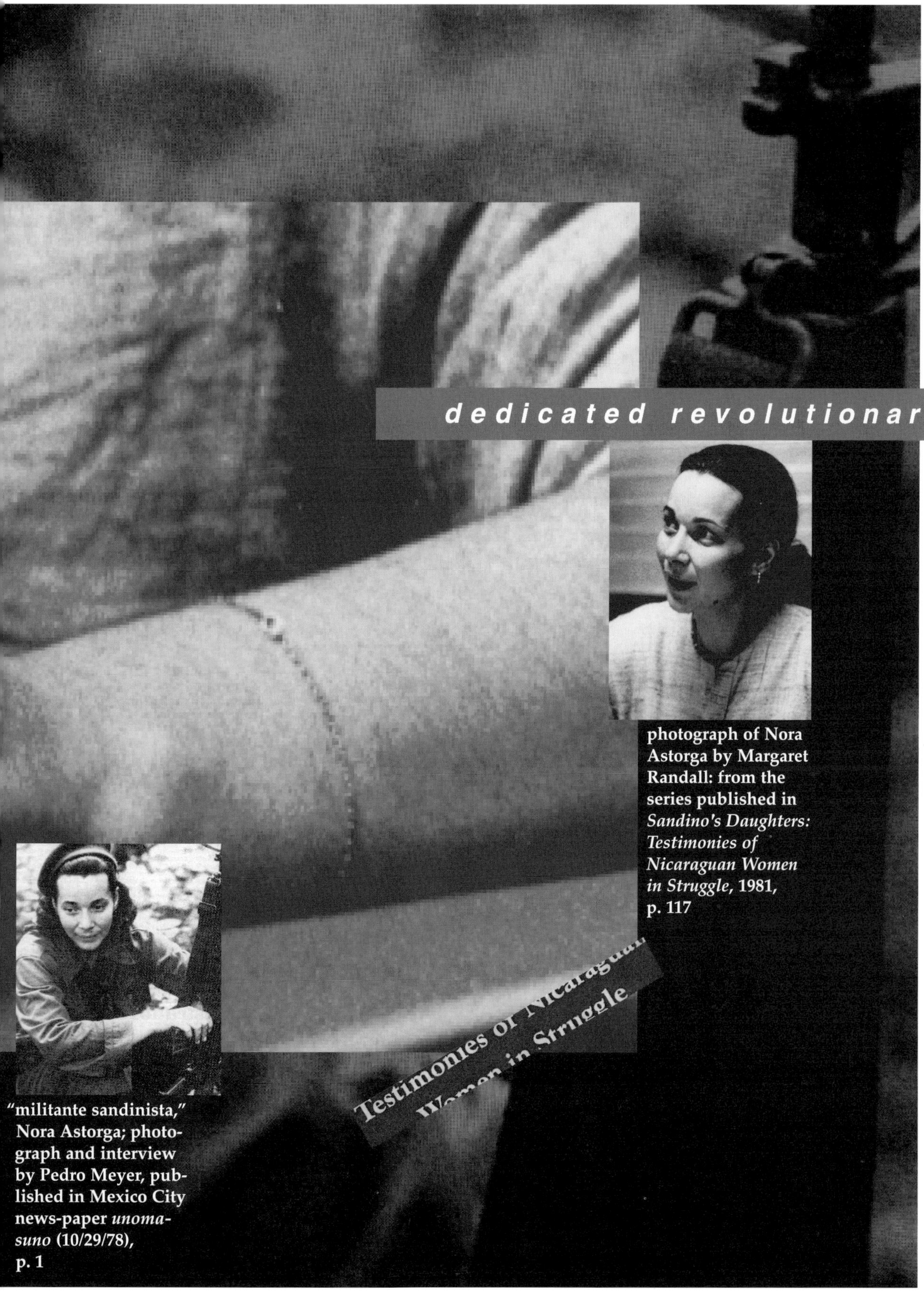

photograph of Nora
Astorga by Margaret
Randall: from the
series published in
*Sandino's Daughters:
Testimonies of
Nicaraguan Women
in Struggle*, 1981,
p. 117

Testimonies of Nicaraguan
Women in Struggle

"militante sandinista,"
Nora Astorga; photo-
graph and interview
by Pedro Meyer, pub-
lished in Mexico City
news-paper *unoma-
suno* (10/29/78),
p. 1

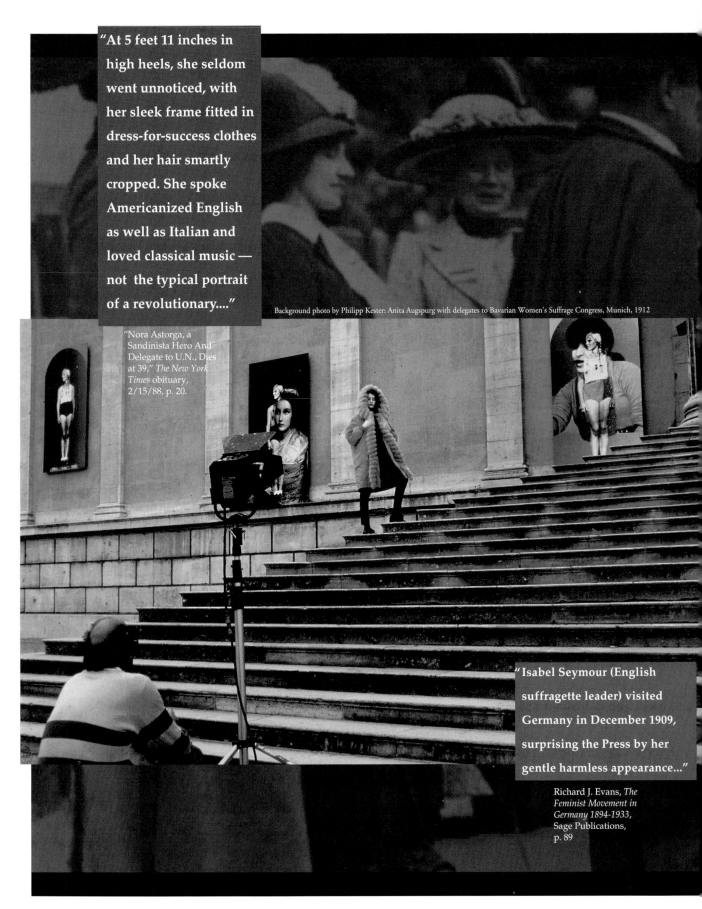

"At 5 feet 11 inches in high heels, she seldom went unnoticed, with her sleek frame fitted in dress-for-success clothes and her hair smartly cropped. She spoke Americanized English as well as Italian and loved classical music — not the typical portrait of a revolutionary...."

"Nora Astorga, a Sandinista Hero And Delegate to U.N., Dies at 39," *The New York Times* obituary, 2/15/88, p. 20.

Background photo by Philipp Kester: Anita Augspurg with delegates to Bavarian Women's Suffrage Congress, Munich, 1912

"Isabel Seymour (English suffragette leader) visited Germany in December 1909, surprising the Press by her gentle harmless appearance..."

Richard J. Evans, *The Feminist Movement in Germany 1894-1933*, Sage Publications, p. 89

Esther Parada, (*not the typical*) *portrait of a revolutionary*

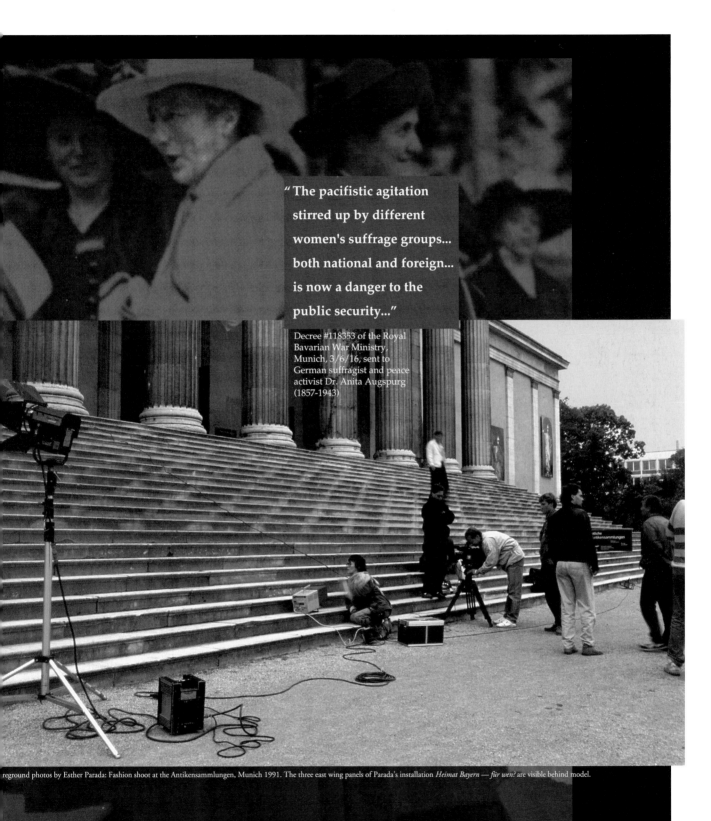

" The pacifistic agitation stirred up by different women's suffrage groups... both national and foreign... is now a danger to the public security..."

Decree #118353 of the Royal Bavarian War Ministry, Munich, 3/6/16, sent to German suffragist and peace activist Dr. Anita Augspurg (1857-1943)

reground photos by Esther Parada: Fashion shoot at the Antikensammlungen, Munich 1991. The three east wing panels of Parada's installation *Heimat Bayern — für wen?* are visible behind model.

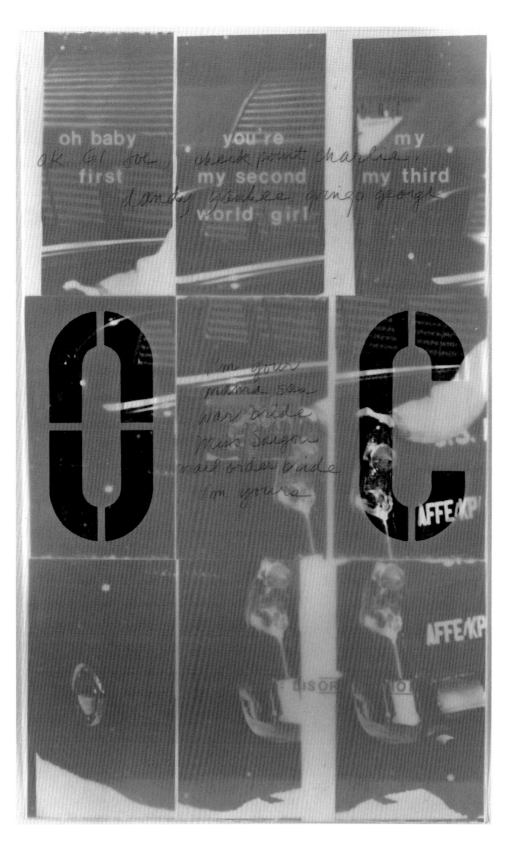

LONG AGO, THERE LIVED A GREAT WHITE MAN.

THIS MAN WAS VERY BRAVE, SMART AND DETERMINED.

HE LOVED ADVENTURE.

HE SAILED ACROSS THE OCEAN AND DISCOVERED A NEW LAND WITH DARK-SKINNED PEOPLE.

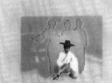

Why were we all smiling so, that bright sunny afternoon? What I most vividly remember of that day is the roar and rumble of all the army trucks. You clung so tightly to my ?/?t... You must have been frightened by the commotion around you. You were too little then to understand what was happening. How could you have known that this was the last time we would be all together before your fa_____ and your uncle went north ___ to the fro___? There was not much t__ smile a___ ___ after the war. I w___ so ___ ___ have a job, any job. Especi___ my jo_, at ___ he U.S. army base. We were at ___ ?st able to ___ l our bellies. You didn't see very much of me in those days because I worked such long hours. I left at the crack of dawn to take the cross town bus to the very edge of the city where the base was located and arrived back home much after you fell asleep. But you were curious about my strange American-style dresses and thrilled whenever I brought you yellow headed dolls and other gifts from the GIs. You especially liked Ritz crackers! You never seemed to complain much – you were so accepting an

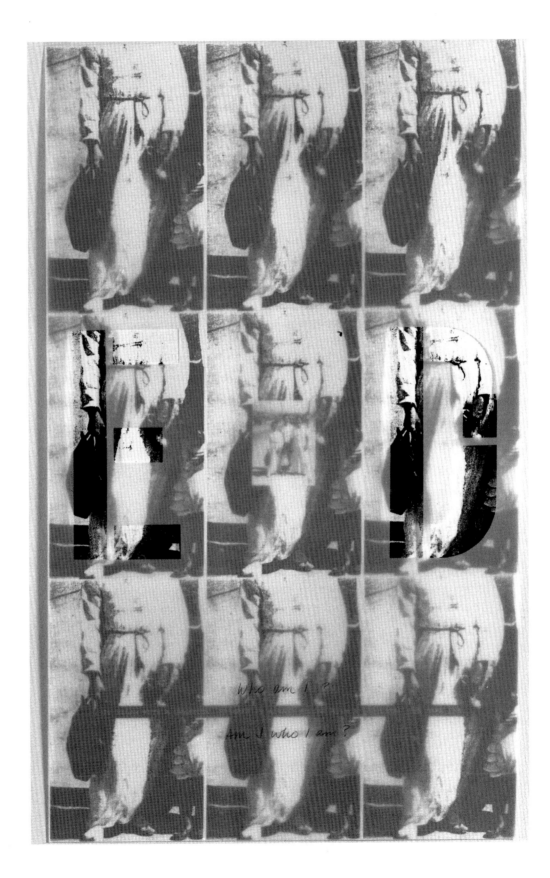

Hulleah Tsinhnahjinnie   from *Native Programming*

Mattie Looks for Stephen Biko

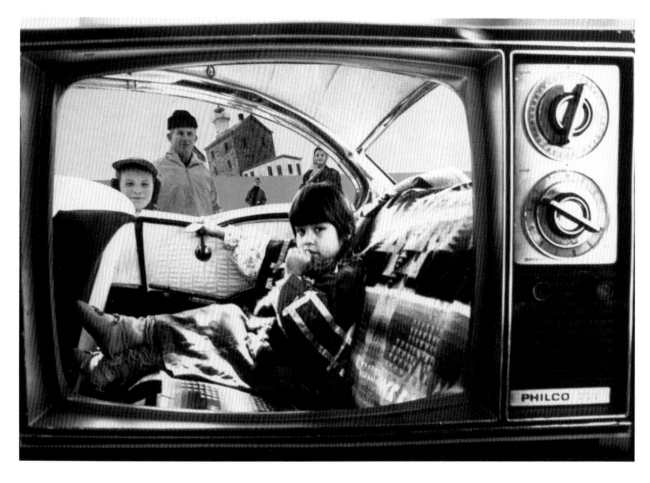

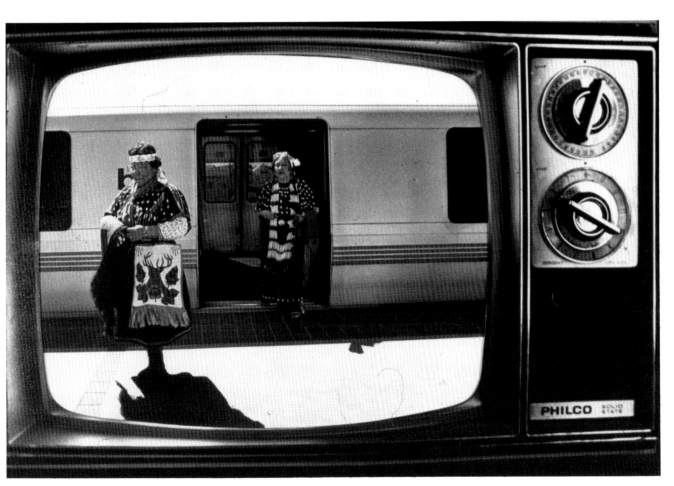

Vanna Brown, Azteca Style

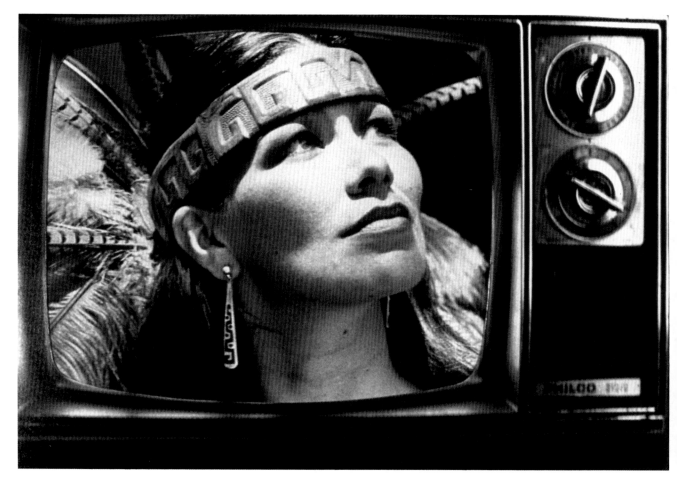

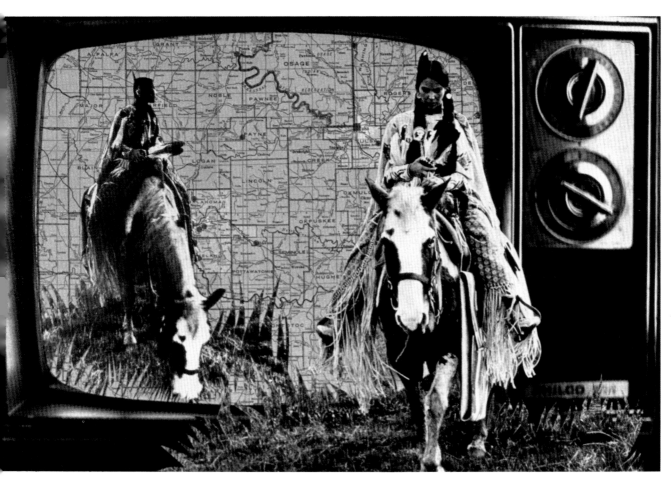

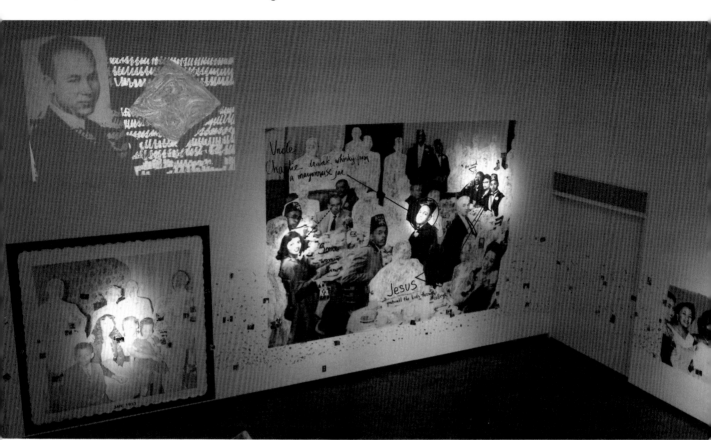

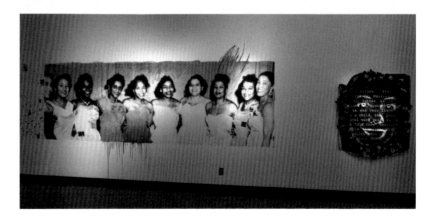

I Remember It Well
Smith College Museum of Art

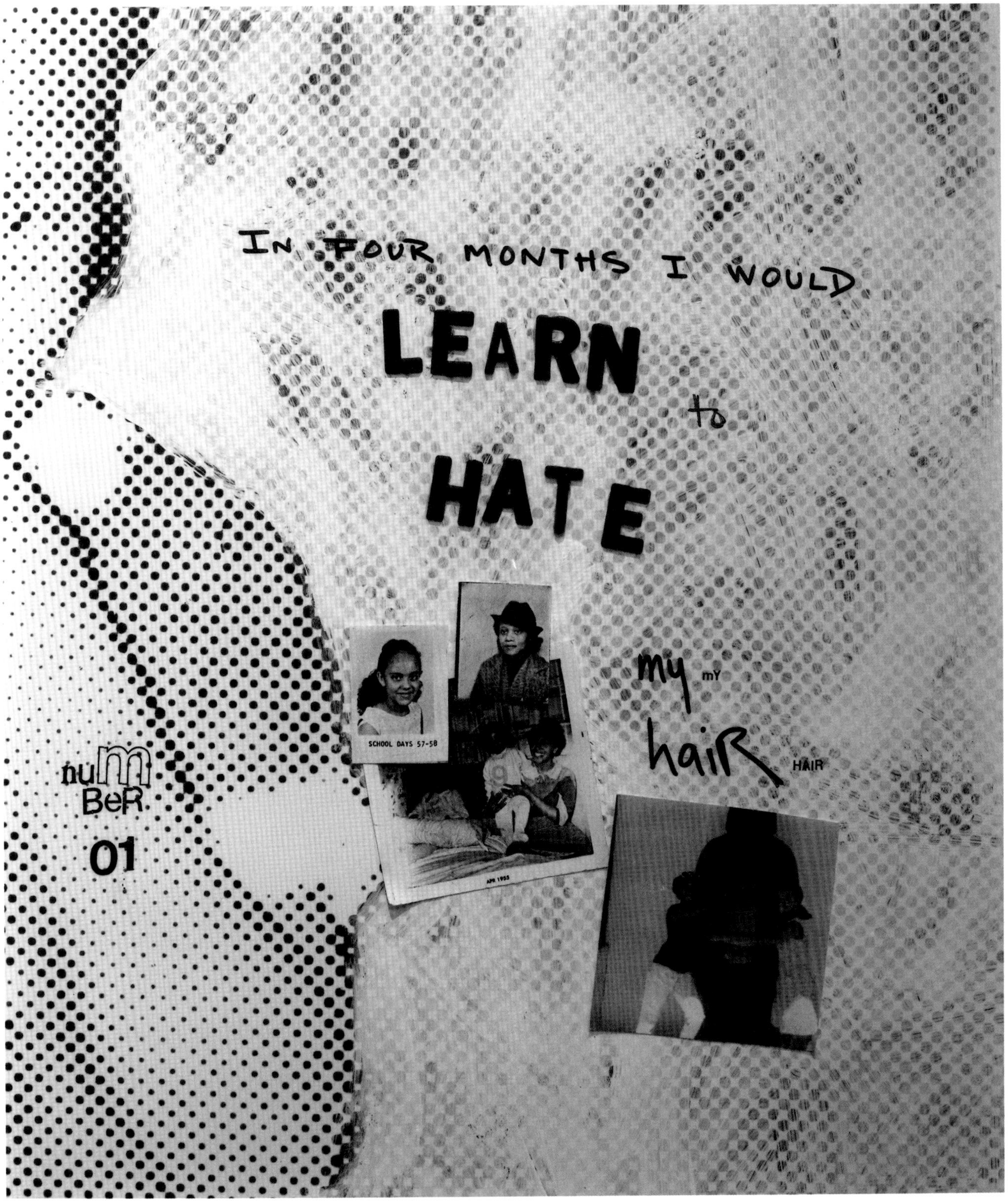

IN FOUR MONTHS I WOULD

LEARN

to

HATE

SCHOOL DAYS 57-58

APR 1955

my mY

haiR HAIR

nuMBeR

01

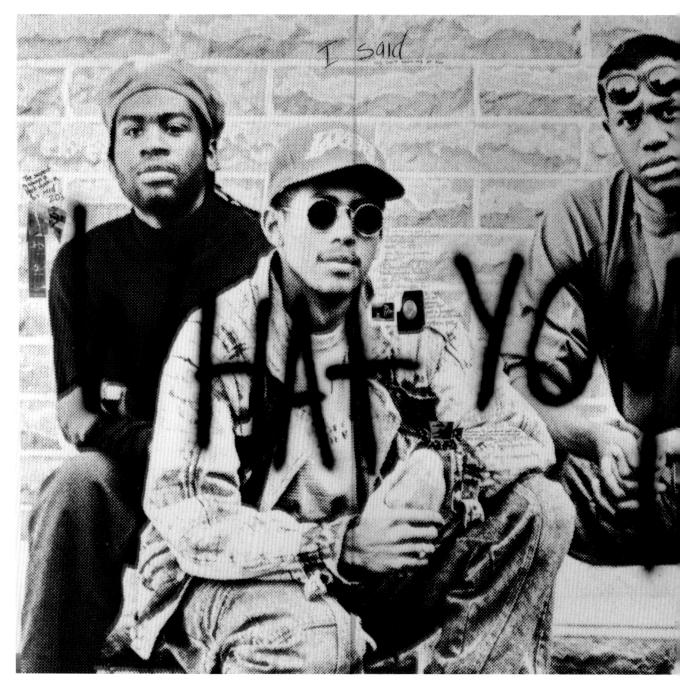

WHAT YOU LOOKN AT
Whitney Museum of American Art,
New York, 1993 Biennial Exhibition

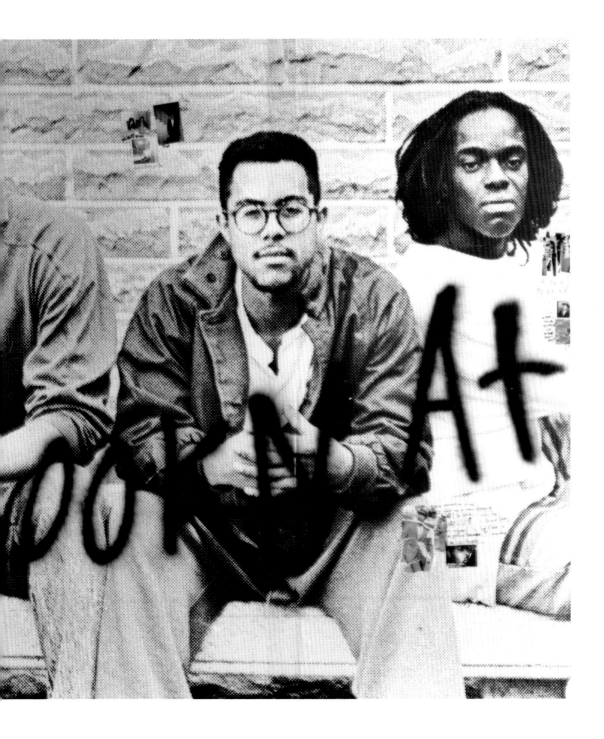

Julia Ballerini

I hope someday these pictures will sell because I want to move to a better place. . . . I want people come to see me and love me and take an interest in me. I'm human.

Odella Chatel

My aim is to provide insight into a life full of feeling and imagination, the life of my friend Odella, the "high survivor."

Carlota Duarte

These two statements, culled from the two prefaces to ODELLA *a hidden survivor: A photographic essay by Carlota Duarte,*[1] speak of the call and response of a collaborative documentary project in which the object of the photographs, underprivileged and marginalized, asks to be seen, and the photographer provides "insight" into a life, a privileged viewing of the otherwise socially invisible.

Viewed within the context of a social documentary tradition of Concerned Photography, the *Odella* project is replete with the problems of an imbalance of power whereby one person is in a position to "give" visibility to another. This perspective (one that informs many discussions of documentary photography) foregrounds such issues as the commodification of the subject, cultural voyeurism, and what has been loosely termed the colonization of one group of peoples by another.

In addition, the ODELLA book, unlike much contemporary feminist photographic practice, represents a self-conscious attempt on the part of the photographer, a Catholic nun and a declared feminist, to work within the established tradition of the documentary photo-essay. With its black-and-white photographic style and its excerpts from taped interviews, the book is a ready-made cultural model replete with bourgeois, humanistic implications. Carlota Duarte does not attempt to deconstruct or refuse this established mode, as many photographers do in order to protest against a visual style that now has implications of cultural voyeurism. Duarte's photographs are not unusual. Some are straightforward close-ups of Odella's face, but for the most part they are taken from a middle distance, with available light used in a way that is never obviously dramatic. Their black-and-white style is reminiscent of thirties' documentary (Aaron Siskind was an important figure for Carlota, both as a teacher and in specifically encouraging this project). It is a style that has come to signal the anecdotal, the emotional immediacy of a spontaneously observed daily life.

Yet the ODELLA project sets itself apart from the traditional photo-essay. It jostles the traditional categories of victim and documentarian,

[1] ODELLA *a hidden survivor: A photographic essay by Carlota Duarte* (Boston: Published by the author, 1990). I thank Sherry Buckberrough, Candace Clements, and Carlota Duarte for their helpful comments at various stages in the writing of this essay. I also thank Odella, whose presence in her book and on tapes invited many reflections.

madwoman and healer, model and artist, as well as those of colonized and colonizer so frequently applied to social documentary projects. In understanding how such shifting of categories may occur, a post-colonial perspective can be illuminating. Admittedly, expansion of the terms "colonialism" (and its sequel, post-colonialism) to include any and all discourse on marginality and oppression threatens to make those terms so free-floating as to be useless. However, a perspective that considers the colonized Other to have a right (equal to the colonizer's) to signify on her own terms can be usefully applied to a project such as ODELLA.

Gayatri Chakravorty Spivak, for example, speaks of her strategy as one of exploring "the differences and similarities between texts coming from the two sides which are engaged with the same problem at the same time."[2] Although positing a "same problem" may be construed as harking back to an apolitical humanism[3] (certainly not Spivak's intention), it can also function to displace the emphasis from a generalized perspective of power relations and inward toward the temporality of the photographic act itself as the site of an encounter between two sides. Such a shift gives more importance to the rules of both sides in playing out the (im)balance of power and its consequences rather than emphasizing the helplessness of one.

Carlota's decision to work within the representational structures she has inherited can also be seen according to Spivak's post-colonial view. In one sense it parallels Spivak's critical approach to literatures which is deliberately dependent on Western models. To ignore such models would be, Spivak maintains, to ignore centuries of historical involvement: "I would rather use what history has been written for me."[4]

Odella has also made use of the bits and scraps that history has thrown her way. She clearly prepared for her photographic sessions with Carlota, assembling an array of stereotypical costumes, wigs, props, and poses. She plays to the camera: a blond vamp; a sultry brunette; a man, cigarette in mouth, cocky face beneath the brim of a flat wool cap; a small child waiting for her mother, her face within the parenthesis of two ponytails. Sometimes she seems beautifully self-composed; no makeup, short hair smoothed back, eyes staring directly out of the frame. Other times she seems in disarray, as when she wears a bouffant, blond wig that sits low on her head, which is tilted in open-mouthed allure, a seeming parody of the objectified, subjacent woman within a capitalist, patriarchal order. In such instances, some viewers cringe at her vulnerability on photographic display.[5] Yet a reading of vulnerability is to ignore the book's written text and to ignore the tension generated by the ready-mades of these two women as they are joined together.

[2] Gayatri Chakravorty Spivak, "The Post-Colonial Critic," in The Post-Colonial Critic: Interviews, Strategies, Dialogues, ed. Sarah Harasym (New York: Routledge, 1990), 73. My borrowing of Spivak as a simplified working model of a post-colonialist position is taken from this highly lisible book and does not take into account the subtleties and possible contradictions present in her other writings.
[3] Edward Steichen's The Family of Man (New York: Museum of Modern Art, 1955), a widely traveled exhibition and accompanying book of 503 pictures from 68 countries, is still a model for many photographers and viewers. Conceived, according to Steichen's introduction, "as a mirror of the essential oneness of mankind throughout the world," it disregards the often extreme differences in sociopolitical contexts and the radically diverse subject positions implicated by such differences.
[4] Spivak, "The Post-Colonial Critic," 69.
[5] Viewers were provided with response sheets at all exhibits of the ODELLA photographs. These were a series of general questions and an invitation to write down any thoughts concerning the work. A forthcoming exhibit will also include a section for remarks that are specifically addressed to Odella and will be mailed to her in New Mexico.

When they first met in 1974, Carlota Duarte, a member of the Society of the Sacred Heart since 1968, had recently moved to the low-income, often dangerous area of Boston's South End and was using the camera as a way of meeting her neighbors. Odella, one of the neighbors, was a visitor to the house where Carlota lived with other nuns. Odella was thirty-nine (nine years older than Carlota) and, for five years, had been living on her own for the first time. An abused and neglected child, she had previously been the ward of mental and other state institutions from the time she was nine years old. She had borne seven children, all of whom had been taken from her shortly after birth.

To ask the questions suggested by Spivak's formulation may seem far-fetched. In what ways can these two sides possibly be considered to be "engaged with the same problem at the same time"? In what ways can Odella's "text" ("text" in its broadest sense of indicating a range of messages that can be construed as being put forth by Odella) be thought of as similar to Carlota's "text"? Clearly, any attempt to define a commonality of problems between Odella and Carlota cannot suppose a similarity of dialogue and certainly not a neutral dialogue. Either supposition would deny the separate positions of the two women, although they share some similarities: of major importance to both is their ethnic mixture. Both women are Anglo-Saxon on their mothers' side. Carlota's father is Yucatecan Mexican, Odella's was Native American. Odella takes pride in being part Indian, and Carlota was beginning to examine her little-known Mexican heritage at the time she began the ODELLA project.

The two spend considerable time together aside from photographing: Odella often stops by the nuns' house and shares their holiday meals, they go on errands, there are telephone calls back and forth. It is a friendship, however, developed for the most part across their differences. At times Carlota and Odella exchange places in front of the camera, but never do they exchange poses and costumes. Carlota is seen in simple clothes, with a slight hippie accent of beads or an embroidered blouse in the 1970s pictures, clothes typical of her daily appearance. Carlota also photographs them together talking and clowning. No such pictures of Carlota taken by and with Odella appear in the book. Carlota is represented visually only by a small snapshot of herself as author at the end.

Yet that authorship is contested, even within the book. According to Carlota's introduction, it was Odella who first wanted to be photographed. Odella watched Carlota taking pictures for four or five months, and eventually requested that hers also be taken. She invited Carlota to photograph in her home. From the start, she wanted a book of pictures of herself published. One precedent in her mind was Norman Mailer's *Marilyn*, which she holds to her breast in one photograph. She asked to be commodified. She prefers to be known as just "Odella," perhaps for its value as a brand name like "Madonna," perhaps also for its contrary intimacy. Such a demand for the camera as audience and mirror does not exist in all social documentary photography, but it occurs more often that one might think, or even wish to admit, since to recognize it is to recognize a power and an agency on the part of the "helpless," and subsequently to relinquish a conception of the photographer as the sole authority and author of the work.[6]

The distribution and display of the photographs also suggest a co-authorship. The work was self-published with the aid of grants, and all profits are shared equally by model and photographer. Related exhibits before and after the book's publication have sought a variety of audiences in community centers, libraries, universities, and art galleries.[7] Videotapes of Odella and Carlota, Odella's paintings, and the presence of both Odella and Carlota in the exhibition spaces have also formed the project.

The photographs themselves resist categorization of their documentary style. The hypertheatricality with which Odella plays to the camera opposes classifications of the anecdotal and mundane, replacing the exoticism of impoverishment with a demonstration of a will to be other than impoverished. While surrounded by signs of an indigent and "tasteless" daily life—vials of medicines, canned and packaged junk food, male pinups and pseudo-Barbie dolls and cigarette butts—the deliberate artifice of Odella's self-presentations goes against the grain of the naturalizing realism that could be implied by Carlota's photography. Odella will not be made anecdotal, and Carlota does not impose the anecdotal on her. Both model and photographer avoid turning to lived experience as a mode of radical subjectivity, a mode that so easily rehearses the objectification of its subject. The one exception is the last photograph, which shows Odella looking *at* her photographs rather than composing herself *as* a photograph. It was the one photograph Odella was reluctant to include. Carlota persuaded her otherwise, and its inclusion does draw notice to Odella as a person separate from her other creations and thus highlights her authorial role.

Never does Odella play the *Migrant Mother* to a Dorothea Lange, a role whereby poverty and suffering are rendered as an unproblematic icon of nobility. Neither do Odella and Carlota succumb to a Diane Arbus model of freakishness. Arbus: "You see someone on the street and essentially what you notice about them is the flaw . . . the gap between intention and effect . . . what you intend never comes out like you intend it."[8] Carlota, unlike Arbus, has not sought out the flaw. Her intention was to show the dignity of a being who was already perceived—diagnosed, in fact—as

6. For example, in photographing the shelters built by the homeless in Tompkins Square Park, New York City, during the 1989 summer riots, Margaret Morton encountered hostility at first, but when the park's residents knew the police bulldozers were about to arrive they invited Morton to photograph and, in their words, "to document their homes." Kim Sichel, "Pictures of the Edge: Photographic Representation and the Margins of Society," *exposure* 27, no. 4 (Fall 1990): 52.

7. Major venues have been The Artists Foundation, the Space Gallery, and the South End Library, all in Boston. The pictures were also shown at the Episcopal Divinity School and at Radcliffe's Schlesinger Library, both in Cambridge. At Tufts University the exhibit circulated through nine departments: sociology, psychology, community health, women's center, health services, theater, romance languages, art history, chaplaincy. Some of the photographs were also shown at the Institute of Design in Chicago, at San Francisco State University, and at the University of California–Los Angeles.

8. Diane Arbus, *Diane Arbus* (Millerton, New York: Aperture, 1972).

Photographs by **Carlota Duarte**.
Text by **Odella**.

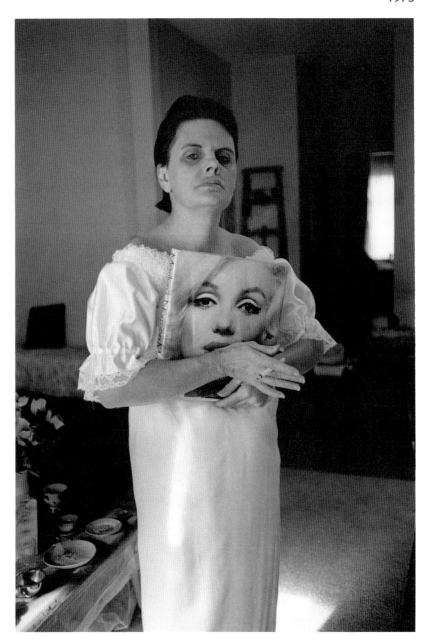

I look like Valley of the Dolls. I look
like an angel in that one, didn't I?
Yeah, I did. Didn't look like I was
married or nothin'. Look like I was a
little saint. I think I was more happy
in the South End, wasn't I? Yeah.
Boy I look like, what do you think I
look like, Valley of the Dolls? (1988)

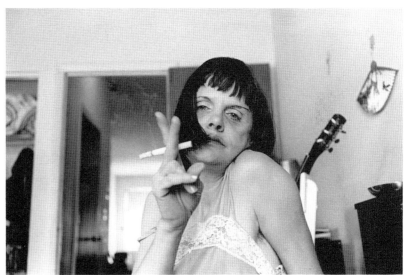

Oh, my God, I look like Bette Davis in this one. What happened to ah, what was the name of that picture? Look at it. Doesn't that look like Bette Davis a little bit? Wow, was I sexy. Can't believe it. I had pretty eyebrows, too, didn't I? My God is that my really hair? (1988)

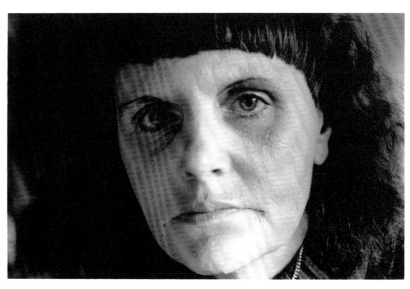

Hauntin' eyes Odella. That's me. And I am goin' to haunt people when I die. I'm comin' back baby. Beware. (1989)

152   Photographs by **Carlota Duarte**.
Text by **Odella**.

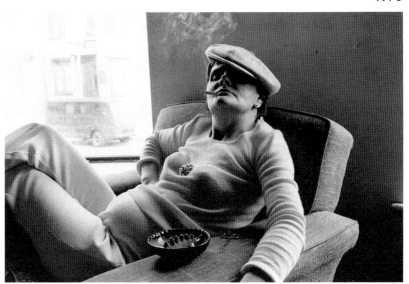

Oh, no! I looked tough didn't I? In every picture I look different. I was tough in this one. I had a good build then. Oh, got the cars showin' an' everythin' out the window, huh? West End kid. Don't mess with me baby. If you do, you know you're gonna get killed. (1988)

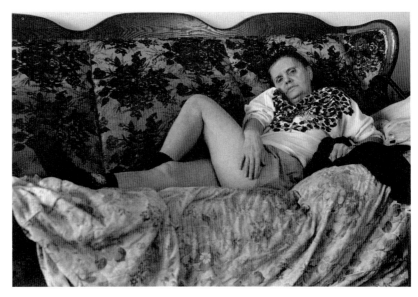

Pin-up Odella. Where'd I get the socks from? Well, my face is old but my body's still sexy. I don't think I'm goin' to lose the body. I might lose my looks, but I'm not going to lose my body, aren't I? I'm not too old lookin'. I hope I don't get wrinkled. (1989)

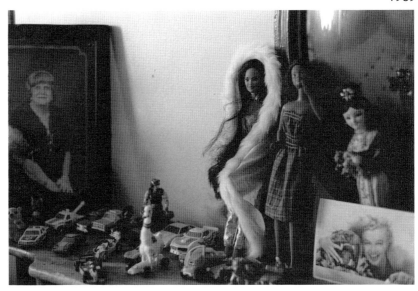

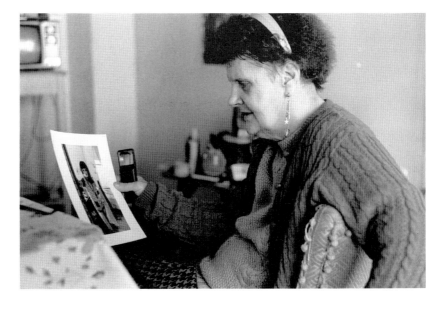

flawed. There are no harsh lights or camera angles, and some pictures that might have seemed awkward were not published. Most important is the flair and vitality with which Odella produces herself throughout the book, undeterred by those gaps between intention and effect, of which she is well aware. Odella's theatricality also serves to camouflage her face as a clearly readable text, a place of anecdotal reference, of categorization.

Carlota, on her part, also resists being visually readable through a maneuver opposite that of Odella's: the sublimation of her artistry and visibility. The two interior still lifes in the book, for example (one of Odella's collection of dolls and toy cars next to a portrait of her mother, and another of her wall phone with a few numbers and a Hershey wrapper taped up nearby), are not like those of Walker Evans's in which an array of humble objects is made elegant as much (or more) by the photographer's eye as by the qualities of the display itself. Here, as elsewhere, Carlota's presence is muted, manifesting itself through the act of presentation rather than through an overt display of her own abilities.

Aside from her "authorial" photograph, Carlota is primarily represented by the caring, humanist, Christian voice of her disembodied words. The implications of nonvisibility and interiority throughout that text—Carlota's aim is "to provide insight into a life"—introduce Odella's construction of a self in terms that are flamboyantly postmodern in their emphasis on exteriority and cultural appropriation: "I want people come *to see* me" (emphasis added). Carlota subscribes to the idea of discovering the interior value of Odella and, by visual as well as verbal implication, of herself. Odella demonstrates the seemingly opposite idea: that what one is is created externally on the spot and for the moment rather than discovered; that the making of a self is primarily a dramatic project, a matter of finding a role and acting it out.

It is also a matter of finding an audience. Odella's need for human interaction of some sort, a longing for others that marks many visual and verbal passages of the book, is a major factor that sets her role playing apart from that of Cindy Sherman, with whom she has been compared by several reviewers.[9] As Sherman has been critically constructed by the art world (a construction far more determining than that resulting from the collaboration of Odella and Carlota) she stages a decentered, disunified selfhood as a social norm outside of which she positions herself by means of her solitary exercise of authority. Odella does not position herself outside of her stereotypes; rather, she participates fully in them, with Carlota and her camera as audience. As one critic noted, Odella's poses, costumes, and fantasies, both visual and verbal, are an affirmation of self instead of a denial or a splintering of self.[10] The various models of power and allure that Odella mimics

[9] For example, Kim Sichel (see note 6); David Joselit in *Art in America* (Sept. 1990): 201; and Nancy Princenthal, in *The Print Collector's Newsletter* (May–June 1990): 66.

[10] Sichel, "Pictures of the Edge," 54.

are constructions of her "real" potential selves, blurred only by circum-   **155**
stance. She has often told Carlota, "I could have been anybody." The
models she chooses are not always those typical of consumer display. In one
video she compares herself to a picture of a wild beast tacked on her wall. "I
look just like him in the eyes. . . . Maybe I was meant to be a lion. But I came
out female, a woman, instead. Oh well. . . ."[11] Odella's creations of a self as
someone other function as a form of resistance to deprivation, and it is
ultimately this resistance that is on display. She resists being cast as victim as
she has resisted other confinements, through exaggeration and at, at times,
violence. She is not figured as are the Famous Men "praised" by Walker
Evans and James Agee in 1939, of which the latter wrote: "It seems to me
curious, not to say obscene and terrifying, that it could occur to an association of human beings . . . to pry intimately into the lives of an undefended
and appallingly damaged group of human beings, an ignorant and helpless
rural family, for the purpose of parading the nakedness, disadvantage and
humiliation of these lives before another group of human beings. . . ."[12]

Agee describes a condition of voyeurism, of "prying," while the ODELLA
project, despite (and/or because of) its emphasis on sexuality and its occasional nude photograph, configures the viewer as spectator, not voyeur.
The privacy characteristic of voyeuristic looking is not only absent but by
definition excluded because spectatorship is part of the meaning of the
display.[13] Like many artists and performers, Odella begins her constructions
of display in privacy. She wanted Carlota to photograph her at home, away
from other eyes, but from the start she intended the photographs to be
made public and was performing for a larger audience, at first primarily
male.

Odella's running commentary throughout the book is a vital element in
the construction of her "spectacle." Her remarks are excerpted from ten
hours of taped conversations with Carlota that, for the most part, recorded
her reactions to the photographs, at times more than a decade after they
were taken. The words suggest the kind of conversational monologue with
another viewer typical of people looking at photographs of themselves: "I
look like Elizabeth Taylor here, gettin' ready to lay on that bed. . . ." "Oh,
my God, I look like Bette Davis in this one . . . wow was I sexy. . . ." Much as
Odella's words construct these home-made performances, they also
deconstruct the very spectacles they set up. "I look kinda draggy in that
black wig." "Oh, I'm gettin' bags under my eyes, right there." "I look like I
been drinkin' all night." It is through Odella's words that we know of her
lucid awareness of the effects of her appearance, an awareness common to
most excluded and disadvantaged peoples who creatively adapt and
recode the commercial cultural products that come their way.[14]

[11] Sidney Storey, *A Visit with Odella*
(Somerville, Mass.: Somerville
Community Access Television, 1990).

[12] James Agee and Walter Evans, *Let Us
Now Praise Famous Men* (New York:
Ballantine Books, 1960), 7.

[13] Here I am indebted to Norman Bryson,
*Word and Image: French Painting of the
Ancien Régime* (New York: Cambridge
University Press, 1981), 37.

[14] See, for example, Dick Hebdige,
Subculture: the Meaning of Style
(London: Methuen, 1980).

The book also contains two pages of fragmentary lines by Odella as well as her Foreword and an Afterword (also excerpted from tapes). Carlota had originally wanted to include a small plastic record of Odella's voice but, owing to Odella's indifference and to technical and financial considerations, this idea was abandoned. Selections from the tapes were made primarily by Carlota, who attempted to transcribe Odella's enunciation as accurately as possible, deliberately leaving grammatical and other "mistakes." At the end of the book project, however, Odella assumed a particular authority over her written text. As the book was going to press she spoke what became her epilogue, a text different from her former commentaries, where, as in the epigraph spoken fourteen years earlier, she had hoped people would "see" her and take an interest in her. In contrast, the final comment she wanted to include is not visually self-reflective but verbally directed outward toward an audience of women as well as men: she advises parents to "listen to the book" and to "take care of your children and don't abuse them." And, she continues, "patients, when they get out, should try to talk to someone who can *hear* you" (emphasis added). Here Carlota's listening has become a part of Odella's voice as the roles of image and language as places of struggle and definition are recognized again on both sides.

A videotape shows Odella commenting on some of the pictures after the book is finally in print: "I've been studying this book, I was up late studying this book," she tells Carlota as she again re-produces and re-lays these images of herself. "That's me, the 'high survivor,'" she says, quoting herself.[15] To become a book that she can quote from is an extraordinary achievement for someone whose command of basic English is flawed to the degree that she has often been diagnosed as speech defective. As with so many "colonized" peoples, language, written and oral, is one of the main factors that have positioned Odella outside the mainstream of power relations. Even when the language of the Other is comprehensible, investigations of a documentary, ethnographic, ethnolinguistic, or otherwise "scientific" nature tend to treat the native informant as objective evidence, so that "the theoretical problems only relate to the person who knows. The person who *knows* has all of the problems of selfhood. The person who is *known*, somehow seems not to have a problematic self."[16] Through this project Odella becomes the known *and* the one who knows, the textual evidence of and for her problematic self.

As Odella becomes a text, Carlota's gesture is to efface her own textuality in a literal way. After beginning the ODELLA pictures Carlota had returned to school, receiving an MFA in photography in 1978, but when she thought the project was complete she lost interest in photographing people altogether and soon stopped. Her subsequent series of photographs

[15] Storey, *A Visit with Odella.*
[16] Spivak, "The Post-Colonial Critic," 66.

were of handwriting, her own and that of friends. In these, the writing is **157** made illegible through reversal, tearing, layering—almost unrecognizable for what it is. A series of paintings from the eighties, delicate, maplike abstractions, also contain faint palimpsests of writing. They form a clear contrast to the bright shapes, colors, and bold lettering characteristic of the figures and landscapes Odella began to paint in 1989, which have been exhibited along with the photographs.

In our society, where visibility is so often a sign of value and textual knowledge a form of power, Carlota's partial effacement of herself in the ODELLA book and her symbolic effacement of writing in her photographs and paintings, occupies a particular ideological, as well as psychological, position. She became a nun soon after Vatican II, the "renewal" within Catholicism when Pope John XXIII initiated a questioning of established dogma and ritual. All aspects of the Church—prayers, dress, ceremonies, and its duties—came under scrutiny and revision during this time. One nun has described her experience of this period as "really being called to the center of everything you believed in and trying to make it real, rather than to everything that the *institution* was. . . ."[17]

The house in Boston's South End founded by the Society of the Sacred Heart in 1970 (four years before Carlota arrived) particularly questioned the nature of ecclesiastical imperialism and its tradition of benevolent power. The founding idea of the program was to have no specific agenda, but simply to live within a deprived area and be acted on according to the needs of the community and its individual members. Each nun was to tell herself, "I am here to do whatever I am asked."[18] Carlota, who was not in any way a professional photographer at the time, was asked, among other requests, to photograph Odella.

The construction of a self by means of an encounter with an Other has been recognized as a component of social documentary photography as well as of colonial and ethnographic projects. The difference of another has been seen as a means of reflection on the self and its boundaries, usually involving a reconfiguration of the other in order to be able to come to terms with the limitations of the self. As in anthropology, ethnography, and other kinds of fieldwork involving activities among other peoples, the social documentary photographer has been understood as defined and validated by her or his "discoveries." That there could be a parallel operation on the side of the Other is usually not an issue. That someone like Odella would be quick to seize the opportunities that came her way, and take time in studying and approaching Carlota would not be considered discovery. It is assumed that the words in the book's title, "a hidden survivor," refer only to Odella, and not to Carlota as well.

[17] Joan Chittister, "Sister Says," in *Once a Catholic*, ed. Peter Occhiogrosso (Boston: Houghton Mifflin, 1989), 12.

[18] Carlota Duarte, conversation with the author, May 23, 1993.

As the book begins to undermine such assumptions and Spivak's "texts coming from the two sides" meet with and modify one another, their engagement "with the same problem at the same time" becomes evident through its play of dramatic oppositions. Odella, recently free from institutionalized "diagnoses," and their resulting deprivations, must reconquer this precarious liberty on a daily basis. Carlota, having recently become a member of an institution at a time of radical change, must reinvent herself and her role as a nun. In many ways their photographic project became an activity that served as a means of transition for both. Through the "evidence" of photography, both women resist being readily known, categorized, and "readable": Odella through the increasing visibility of an array of different selves, Carlota through an increasing invisibility. For Odella, a display of sexuality by means of stereotypes reasserts her presence, her new freedom, and its possibilities. Carlota's renunciation of overt visual and, later, textual display reasserts her commitments to the ideas of public service that were being elaborated within her religious order at the time.[19]

A post-colonial paradigm shift also implicates a critical shift; it implies a relaxation of both our cultural baggage of guilt and our presumed critical authority in favor of strengthening the individual work's authority and potential power. We are quick to praise postmodernist gallery artists for supposedly critiquing a consumer society's effects on the representation of women, but we hesitate to recognize intentionality and artistry when people of different social and professional status launch equally self-conscious critiques but for different ends. It is easier to conclude that subjugation and ignorance exist, on one hand, leaving poverty and abuse pure and uncorrupted by knowledge, and to imagine on the other, a powerful hegemony uncomplicated by insight, doubt, or change.

A project such as *ODELLA* does not resolve the imbalances between the disenfranchised and those in (relative) power. It does, however provide an example of a disenfranchised person gaining access to visibility and language in a public sphere. Although Odella has been damaged to the extent that she cannot function in that sphere with the same control and effectiveness as Carlota, she presents a testimony to her own strength, will, and its possibilities. The project also testifies to the willingness of another to listen, and along the way Odella has learned the power of the listener. In the process, she has provided a definition for, and display of, Carlota's less visible presence. In its delicate balance of contraries, the *ODELLA* project provides an impetus to continually restructure the ethical imagination in ways that take into account the power of the "helpless" and the often unanticipated means by which that power may be realized.

It is a collaboration that continues to have a profound effect on its two

[19] Norman Bryson elaborates a related interpretation in writing about the still lifes by the Spanish monk Juan Sánchez Cotán (1561–1627). "To alter any of these [details] would be to allow too much room for personal self-assertion, and the pride of creativity; down to the last details the painting must be presented as the result of discovery, not invention, a picture of the work of God that completely effaces the hand of man (in Cotán visible brushwork would be like blasphemy). *Looking at the Overlooked: Four Essays on Still Life Painting* (Cambridge: Harvard University Press, 1990), 70.

participants. Carlota now spends part of her time in Chiapas, Mexico, instructing Mayan Indians in photography to enable them to use the camera as a social and pedagogical tool on their own. One project involves Mayan actors and writers using the popular format of the *fotonovela*. At one point during her collaboration with Carlota, Odella had also taken up photography and purchased her own camera (a bright yellow Polaroid), but she never used it to record herself. Living in a particularly dangerous building at the time and acting, as always, according to the necessity of the moment, she photographed people she regarded as threatening. Odella's own camera became a form of protection and surveillance, a shield to reflect the faces of others while masking her own. Since then, profits from the book have enabled her to move to a better home near a brother in New Mexico. She continues to exist on a precarious daily basis, and she also continues to paint. For now, she has no need for photography.

Rationalizing and Realizing the Body

162

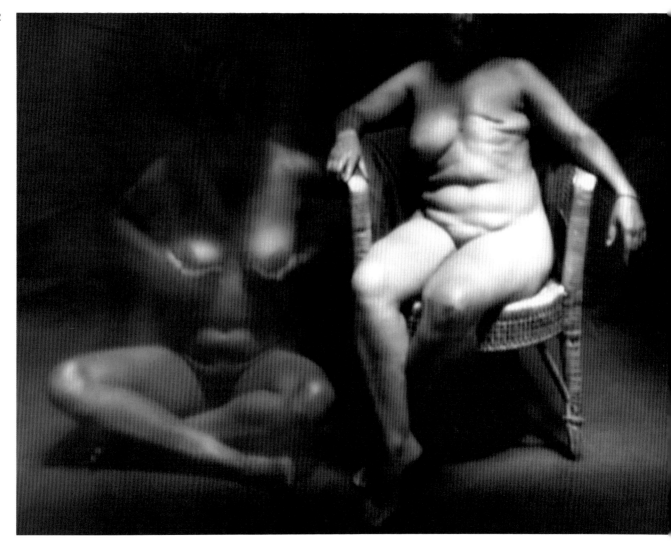

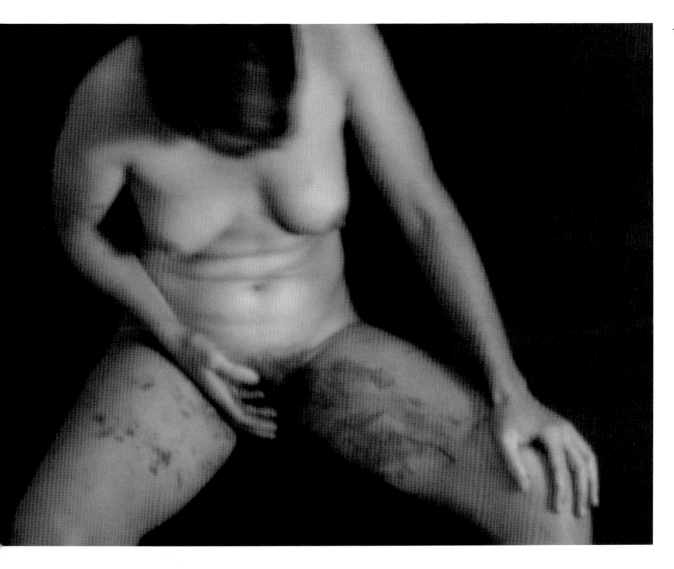

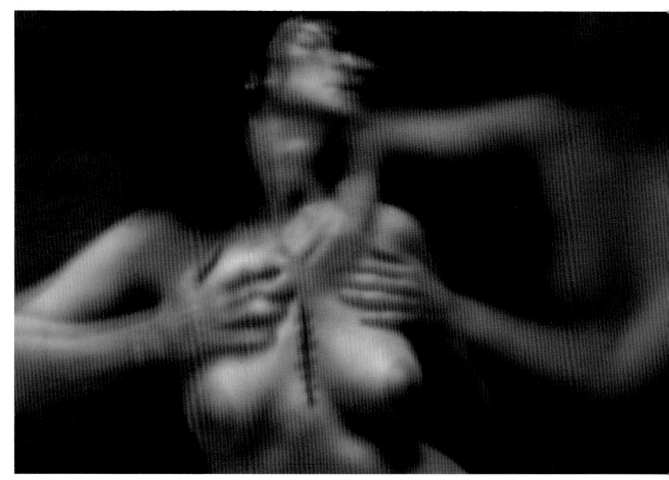

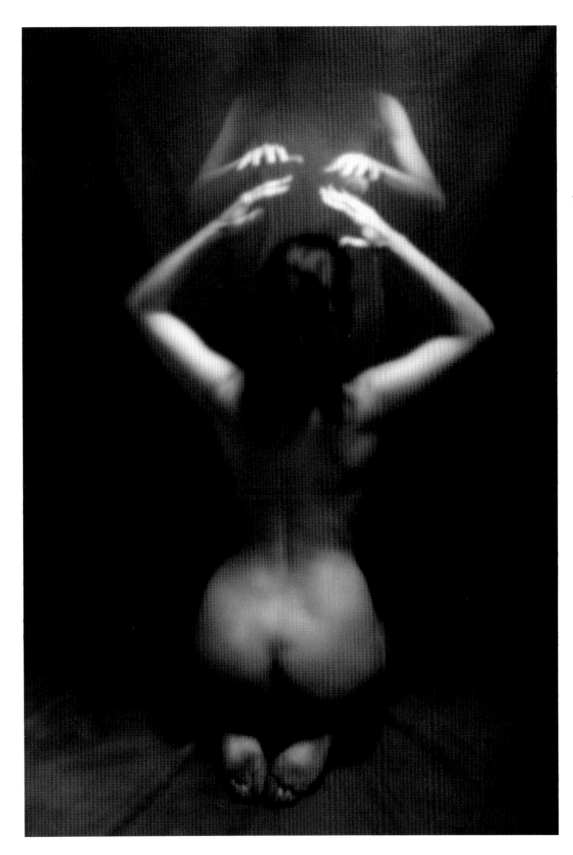

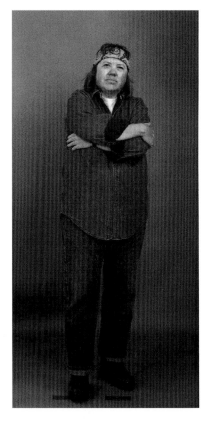
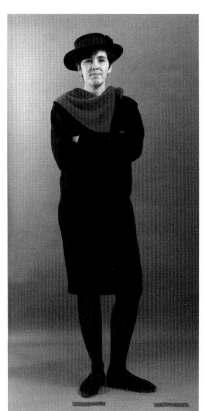
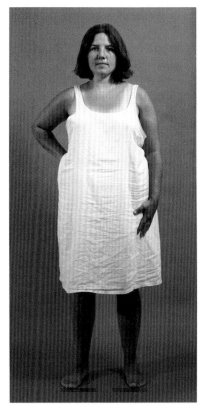
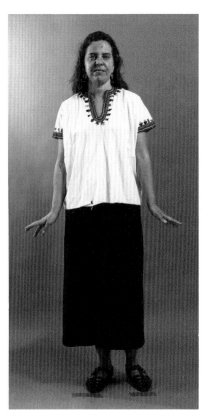

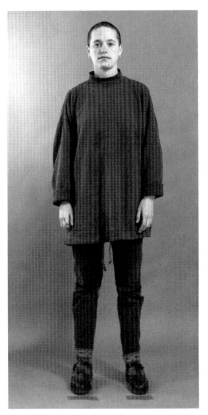

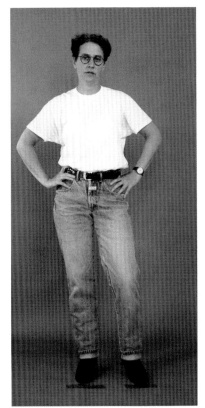

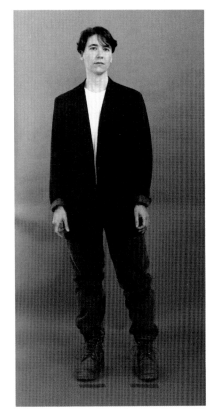

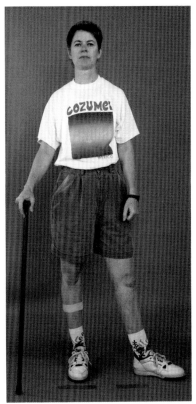

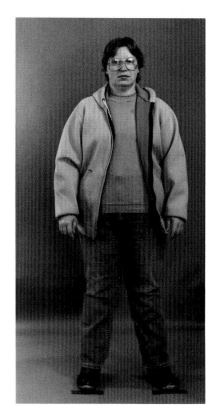
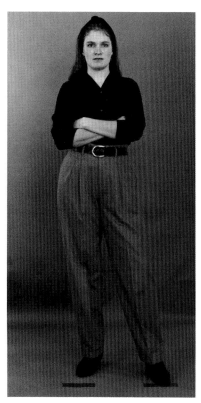
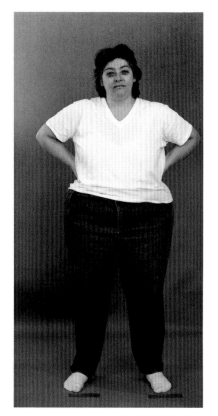
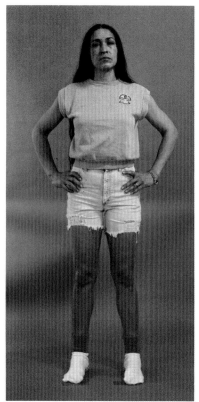

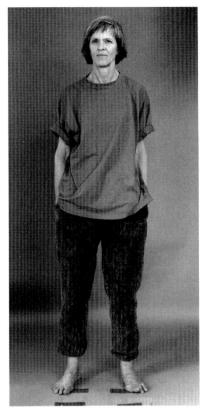

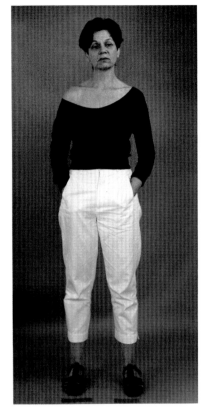

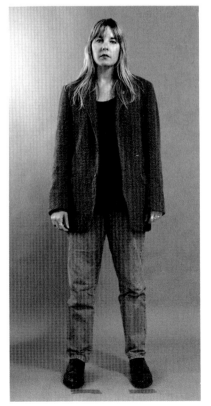

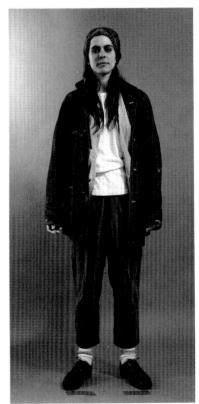

Ann Meredith

from ***The Global Face of AIDS:
Photographs of Women***

Sharon-Confidential
San Francisco General Hospital,
Dr's. office, June 1987
Age: 35
Diagnosis: "AIDS"
Sexual Preference: Lesbian
Transmission: IV drug use

170

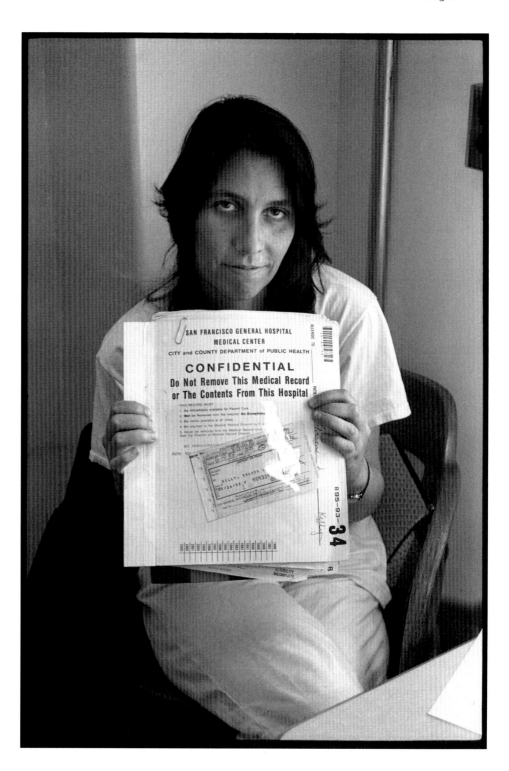

Eleana and Rosa (The little girl has AIDS)
The Elipse/The White House
Washington, D.C. October 1988

Natalie with her daughter, Carolyn and her son, Doug
Sparks, Nevada, August 1991
Age: 46
Diagnosis: "AIDS"
Sexual Preference: "I'd prefer not to be labeled"
Transmission: Heterosexual sex with her husband

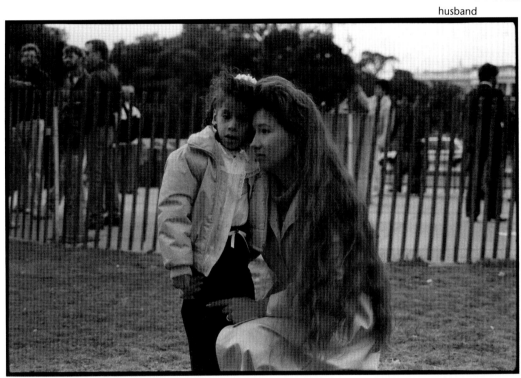

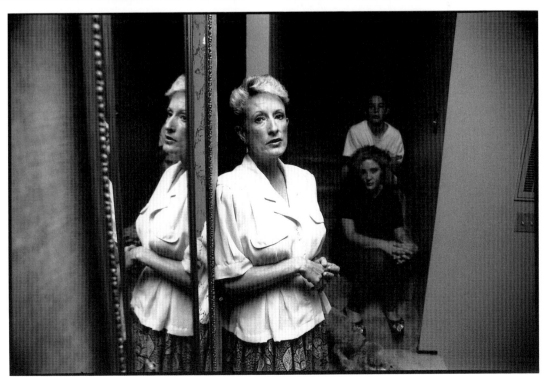

Le onor and Jose
El Paso, Texas, October 1990
Age: 34
Diagnosis: "AIDS patient"
Sexual Preference: Heterosexual
Transmission: "I don't want to put the
blame on anyone or anything"

Rose
Luo-Siaya District Hospital, Siaya, Kenya,
February 13, 1993
East Africa
Age: 26
Diagnosis: "AIDS"
Sexual Preference: Heterosexual
Transmission: Heterosexual sex with her
husband

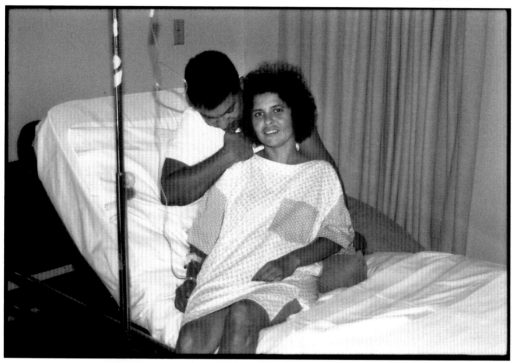

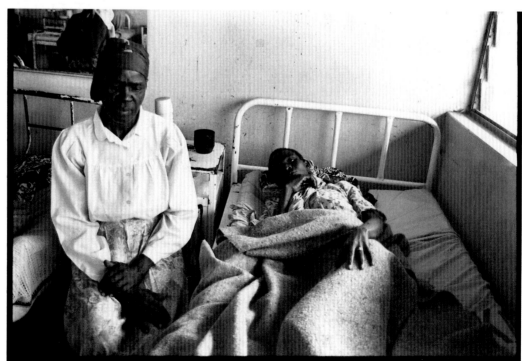

Cheryl and Missy
Washington, D.C. October 1988
Diagnosis: "AIDS"
Sexual Preference: Heterosexual
Transmission: IV drug use

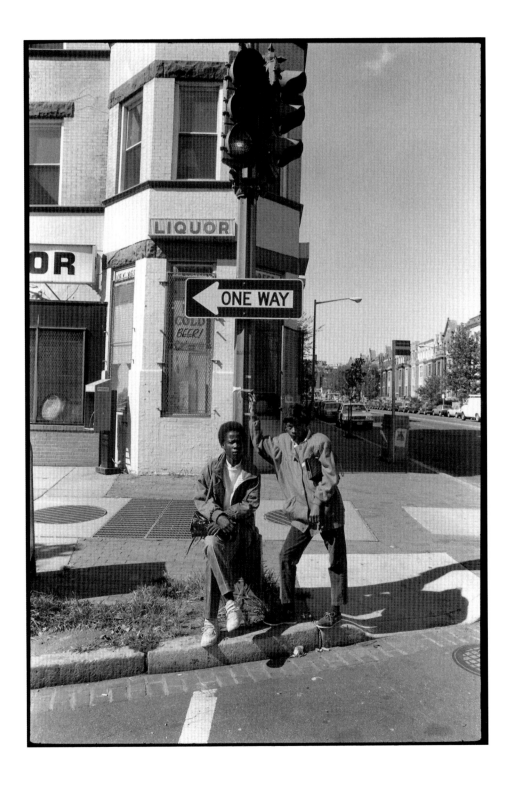

174

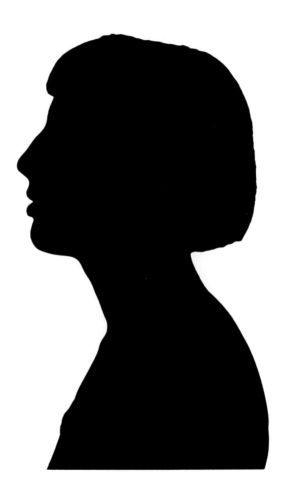

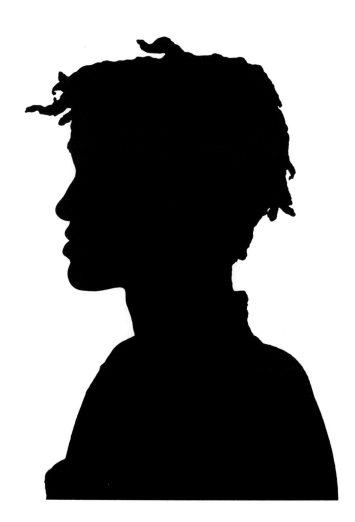

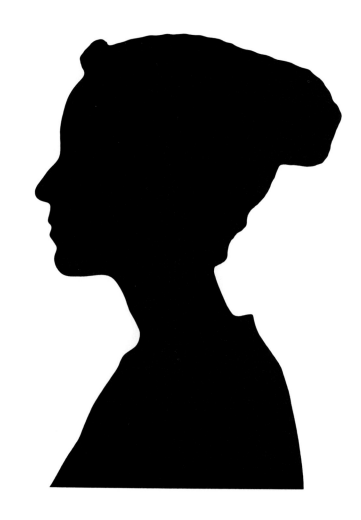

176

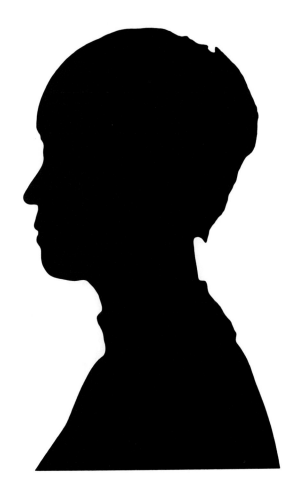

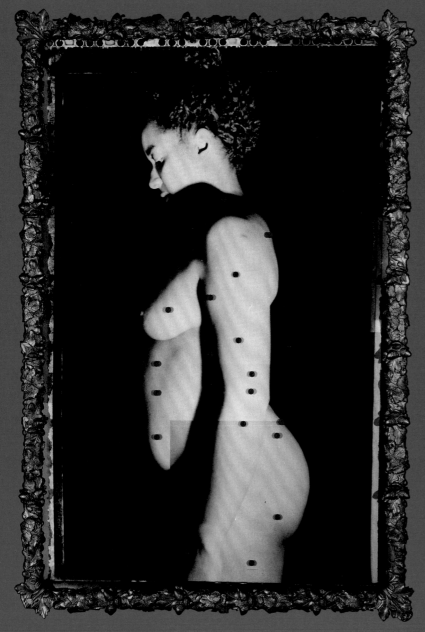

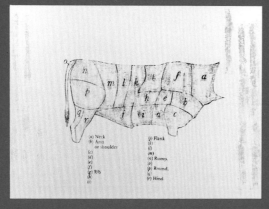

(a) Neck   (g) Flank
(b) Arm   (h)
    or shoulder   (i)
(c)   (m)
(d)   (n) Rump.
(e)   (o)
(f)   (p) Round.
(g) Rib   (q)
(h)   (r) Hind
(i)

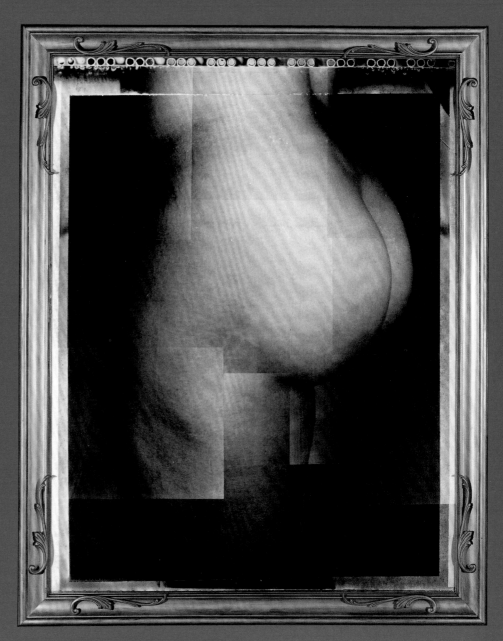

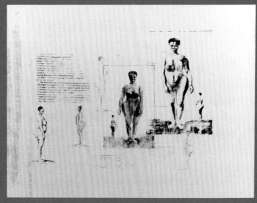

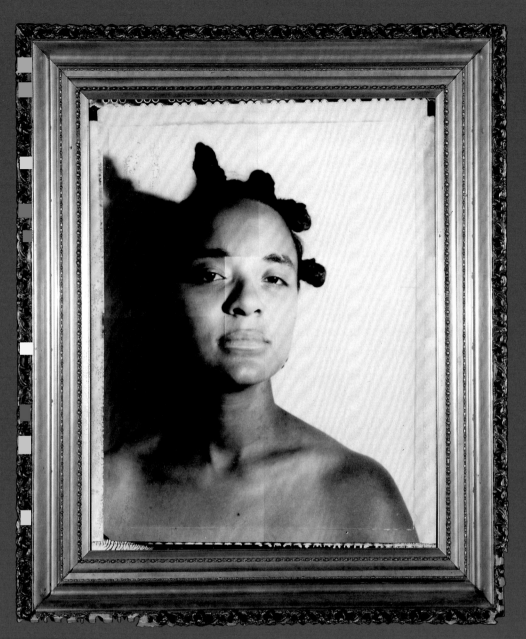

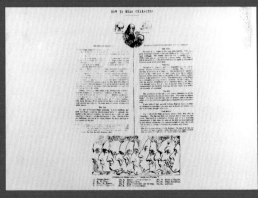

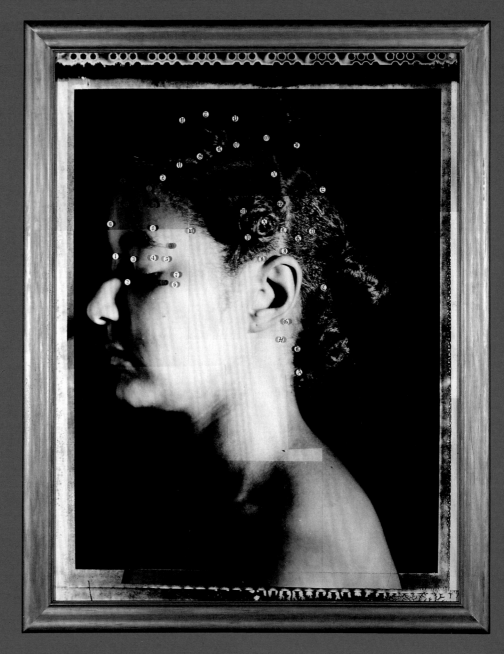

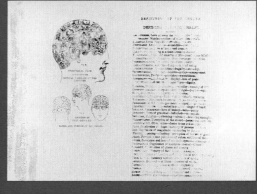

from *X-Rayed* (*Altered*)

182

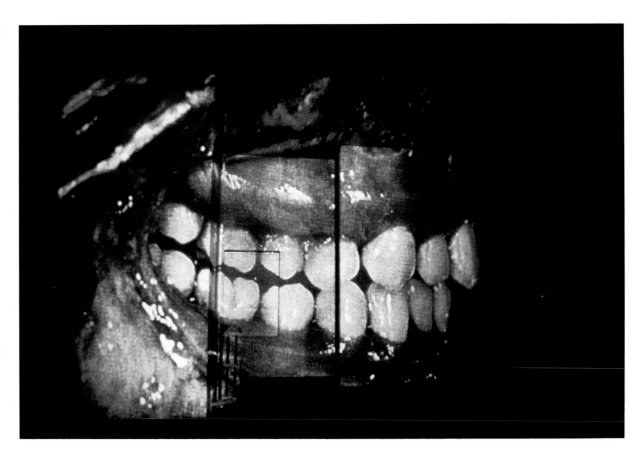

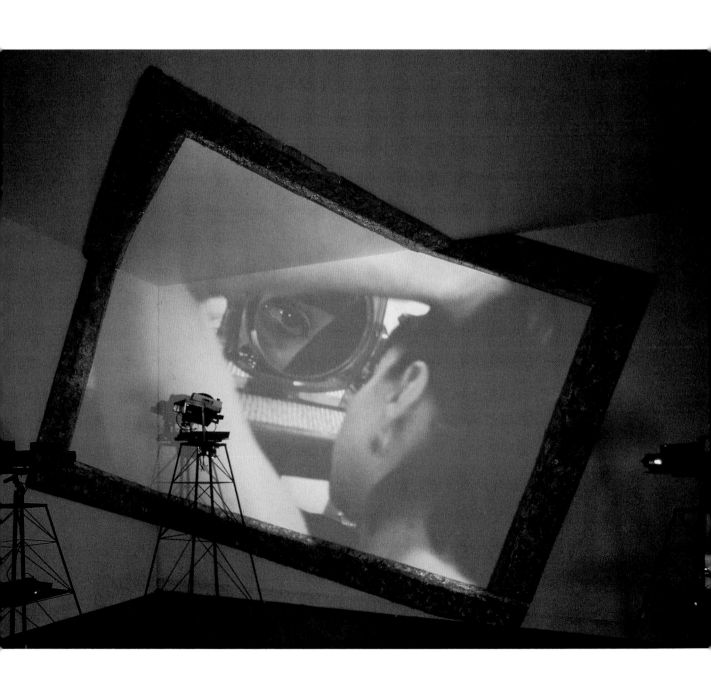

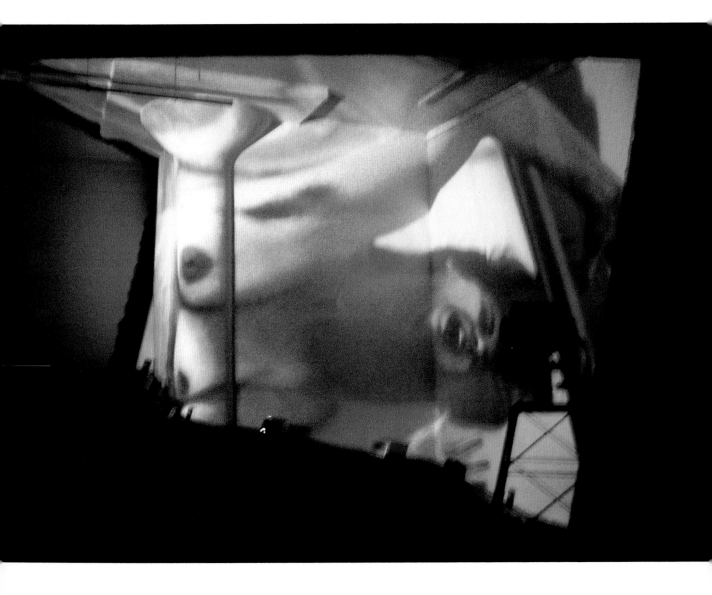

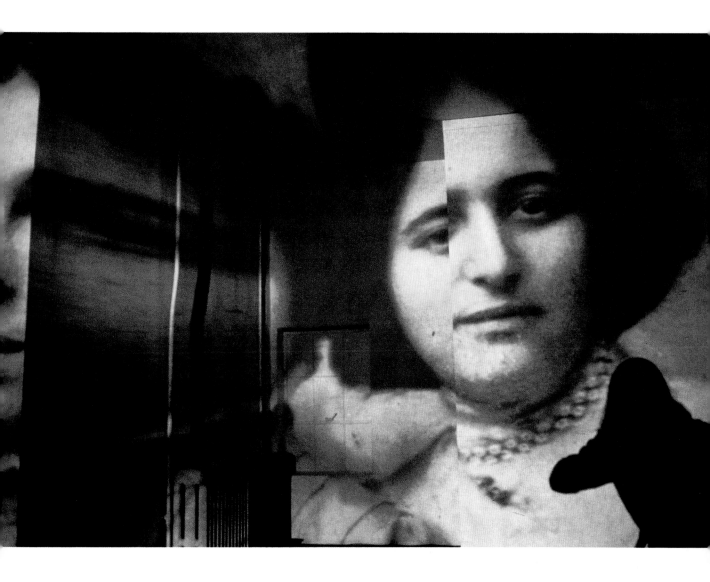

186

May 21, 1993, Berkeley. Restless, I have left my computer and am meandering around the neighborhood. On a sales rack outside a bookstore is displayed *Real Beauty . . . Real Women*, written by "Avon's International Beauty and Fashion Director." Its cover is decorated with a photograph of four women—two young women of color (African American and Asian American) and two Euro-American women (older and younger). Inside the store, I look at publications on women and aging (I have an impending 60th birthday) and also find there a newly created lesbian section in women's studies—this material had been shelved under gay studies till now. I browse through Naomi Wolf's *The Beauty Myth*, and discover Lucy Stone speaking her mind in 1855: "It is very little to me to have the right to vote, to own property, et cetera, if I may not keep my own body and its uses, in my absolute right." Did Lucy Stone possess the sense of certainty of such an "absolute right" that she might know its loss? Did she and her feminist friends talk about how social constructions of women's bodies become internalized, and how hard it is to stay conscious of such influences although one may be resolute about political goals?

How have attitudes of American feminists to their own bodies changed over the last century and a half?

I come home to find a phone message concerning a photograph by Hulleah Tsinhnahjinnie that I had loaned to the Heard Museum. It makes me recall a conversation with her in 1992, when she was considering having both her calves tattooed with a design modeled after that of a nineteenth-century Seminole tattoo for men. I remember, also, a long discussion with Margo Machida, who told me that the assertive ways in which she depicted her body in her autobiographical narrative paintings often offended Asian American men, that assertion went profoundly against the grain of many men's expectations of (and desires for) Asian American women.

How does a woman artist these days represent her own body, and how is that act read by herself and others, in the various cultural traditions of the United States and elsewhere?

As I begin this essay, I feel the resonances in my life of *Sounding the Depths*, a 1992 collaborative installation of sounds, videos, and images by Pauline Cummins and Louise Walsh at the Irish Museum of Modern Art in Dublin. On the museum walls Cummins and Walsh had placed large color photographs of harshly lit, fragmented images of unruly bodies (their own)— bellies and breasts on which were superimposed giant, teeth-bared, wide-open mouths, a reference to Sile Na Gig, the ancient Celtic icon of female sexuality, with its gaping vagina. I had been asked to contribute an essay to their catalogue and, as I grappled with that task at long distance, I began to widen my discussion of representations of the body to include not only the two Irish women's explorations but also those of Sutapa Biswas, of England, and Suzanne Lacy and Yong Soon Min, of the United States. Through a combination of intimate knowledge of their work and lengthy conversations with them over the years, Lacy and Min have come to represent for me in a rather personal way the breadth of the histories and shifts in attitudes among American women artists toward representations of the body.

In my catalogue essay for *Sounding the Depths*, I quoted from the letters that Cummins, Walsh and I had exchanged about the thinking behind their imagery. In the context of Catholic Dublin—a world in which abortion and divorce are illegal—Walsh stated, "[T]he word body is about autonomy, it's the only thing we really have," and Cummins wrote, "I love to use Virginia Woolf's words, 'as a woman I have no country,' but I like to say, 'as a woman my body is my country.' I used this paraphrase during the dreadful anti-abortion campaign in 1984. When we were being told what we could or could not do with our bodies, our country was being invaded."[1]

In my essay on Cummins and Walsh, I wrote of parallels that I sensed between their work and the photographic collage experiments of Sutapa Biswas.[2] For her 1991 Vancouver installation, entitled *Synapse*, Biswas, a London-based artist of Indian heritage, presented life-size black-and-white photographs. This series show the nude Biswas standing, sitting and lying down. Superimposed on her body or cradling it are images of Indian landscapes, people and classical religious cave sculpture (which Biswas had taken while on a visit to India)—these had been projected as slides during a studio "shoot" and the collective image photographed. The particularities of her perspective had allowed Biswas to merge her own body fluidly and easily with those of Indian goddess sculptures. The result was a striking and unabashedly physical self-assurance to her self-representations.

In this *Sounding the Depth* catalogue, together with Biswas' work, I also included work by two American artists, Yong Soon Min and Suzanne Lacy. Lacy's 1976 series, *Falling Apart*, is composed of a roughly torn photograph of herself—a small-breasted, slight figure leaping on raised toes in an undefined space, hair flying, arms outstretched, legs apart—the two halves of her image interrupted by a photograph of raw intestines. Despite the implication of the work's title, the mood is one of ritualistic abandonment. The piece was generated in the context of an intense white feminist community in Southern California and its style shows the exuberance as well as anger of much early American performance art. Lacy is one of the several major Euro-American women performance artists (Carolee Schneemann and Rachel Rosenthal are two others) who have placed the

[1] Moira Roth, "Two Women: The Collaboration of Pauline Cummins and Louise Walsh, or International Conversations Among Women," in *Sounding the Depths* (Dublin: Irish Museum of Modern Art, 1992), 6, 15.

[2] Moira Roth, "Reading between the Lines: The Imprinted Spaces of Sutapa Biswas," in Sutapa Biswas, *Synapse*, a self-printed artist's book, Vancouver, 1991. A more easily accessible catalogue is *Synapse: New Photographic Work by Sutapa Biswas* (London: The Photographers' Gallery; Leeds: Leeds City Art Galleries, 1992).

188   **Suzanne Lacy**
Falling Apart, 1976
photocollage.

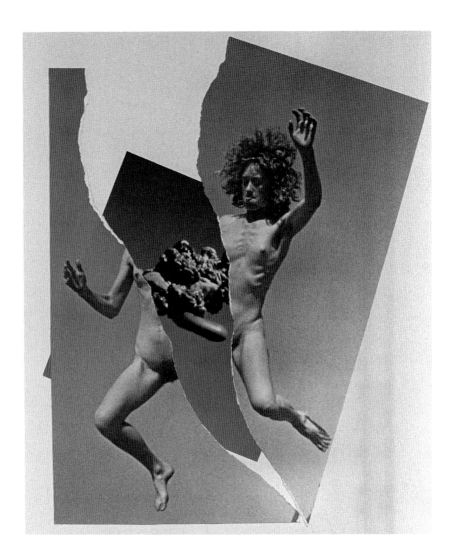

physicality of women's bodies and women's literal voices at the center of their work.

    Images of the works I have seen by Lacy over the years come to mind. Memories of her huge ceremonial gatherings of women—women on the steps of the Los Angeles city hall protesting the Hillside Strangler murders and their media coverage; women of color on pedestals in a Los Angeles sculpture garden; older women of all races dressed in white on a southern

California beach and, in black, in an elegant indoor public space in Minneapolis. Memories, too, of Lacy's more idiosyncratic personal appearances as a young vampire complete with false teeth; her more somber transformation into an older woman; and the series in which she appears nude, ironically pairing herself with the breasts, thighs, and legs of a raw chicken.

I have been equally inspired by Yong Soon Min's highly original blending of contemporary cultural debates with autobiographical experiences. Recently she has been collaborating with Allan deSouza (at first her lover, now her husband). They draw on their personal relationship, on their diverse cultural-racial backgrounds (she is Korean American, he Indian English), and on their theoretical and activist involvements in Anglo-American debates over cultural and sexual differences.

I remember my shock and wry amusement when I first saw a picture of Min inflating a condom into a sausage-shaped balloon and blowing it toward deSouza. On other images of their bodies—sometimes intertwined, sometimes separated—they have written fragmented narratives, a series of words and phrases that revolve around the possibility or not of love and individual relationships in a world rife with racism and colonial history.

Throughout Min's art, autobiographical material has served both as a major inspiration and a source for imagery, but increasingly she is working directly with the body—hers. Why the shift? In my Dublin essay, I quote from a statement of Min's: "It seems . . . that the body in all its contestations cannot be ignored in the constructions of IDENTITY and DIFFERENCE. With the AIDS crisis, there is a great sense of urgency that we formulate new strategies to reclaim our bodies to counter all the misappropriations as well as to point to healthier constructions of sexuality and desire."[3] In my catalogue essay I included Min's 1991 *Demilitarized Desire*, in whic she presented a fragmented, compact image of herself, her arms folded across her breasts, only the lower part of her face showing. Across the body she had stamped "WHERE."

Demilitarized Desire, Falling Apart, Sounding the Depths, Synapse—an intriguing range of titles for women artists to use in representing their own bodies.

I subtitled my Irish essay, "An International Conversation Among Women." I wrote that for the Irish, English, and American artists in the exhibit the body was a site from which they could speak their minds as well as voice their feelings, for all the artists were knowledgeable in contemporary theories of representation. This moment of bringing together thinking and feeling about the body is an interesting time, if—a big proviso—a lively

[3] Roth, *Sounding the Depths*, 17.

190 **Yong Soon Min**
Demilitarized Desire, 1991
video laser print.

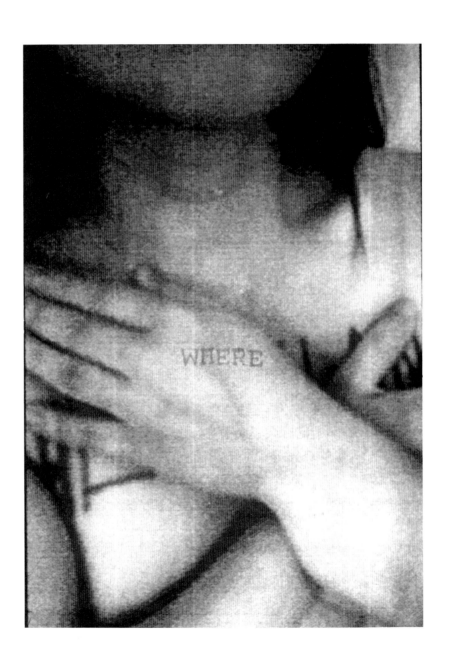

balance can be achieved between the two. All too often, at the moment, there is an acrid polarization between social constructionist theory and essentialist celebrations of the body.

My recent experience with writing on Cummins, Walsh and Biswas, and Lacy and Min, gave me a fresh framework for thinking about American women's representations of the body, particularly in the photographic medium. For Cummins, Walsh, and Biswas, their work was informed by a coupling of ancient cultural associations of women and power and contemporary theoretical discourse about women and their bodies. The older cultural associations seemed to me less directly available for American women. Also, North American feminist history is dissociated from the standard political sphere in a way that the Irish and English feminist histories are not, given the more overt connections between feminism and socialism in those countries. Finally, our twenty-year history of feminist art has demonstrated profoundly ambivalent attitudes toward the female body, producing shifts in attitudes more extreme than anything seen in Europe. American women have been affected by the sexual revolution of the 1960s; by the feminist battles in the 1970s over the issues of abortion, rape, dieting, and notions of beauty; by analyses of media imagery; and by the homage paid in American culture to youth and the concomitant fear of age. Many of us have been deeply affected by the theoretical texts of recent years concerning the problematics of representation around the female body—and lurking behind all this is the entrenched puritanical discomfort with the body and sensuality.

And then there is the matter of history. For the most part, the current burst of critical thinking has not been accompanied by a full-blown knowledge of the women's art movements of the past twenty years. There is still a dearth of publications on this; the first serious survey of the 1970s has only now (1994) been published.[4] There is also an imbalance in research on Euro-Americans' art and that of women of color, and lesbian art history still remains uninvestigated in any depth. We are still waiting for serious international comparative studies. All this comes to mind particularly when one considers contemporary feminist photographers' responses to the body, and their relationship to the yet unwritten history of representations of women's bodies—in performance, painting and sculpture, photography and video—since 1970.

I think about these issues in my teaching as well as in my writing. I am on the faculty of Mills College, where we have only women undergraduates, and thus I am particularly aware of the circumstances in which women art

[4] Norma Broude and Mary D. Garrard, eds. *The Power of Feminist Art: The American Movement of the 1970s, History and Impact* (New York: Harry N. Abrams Inc., 1994).

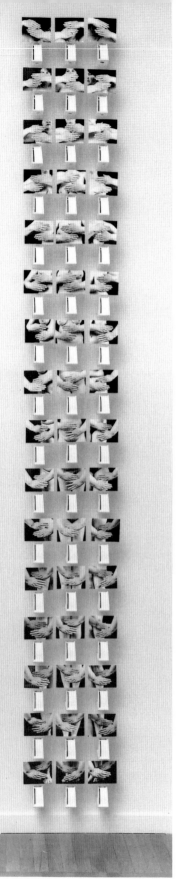

Deborah Lohrke
Untitled (Diet Scale), 1993
ceramic, acrylic, black-and-white photographs, 138" × 17" × 5".

students find themselves these days. At Mills College, the women respond eagerly to art by women of all different ethnic backgrounds, to contemporary theoretical writings on the politics of representation, and to analyses of how gender, race, class, age, and sexual preference are constructed politically, socially, and psychologically. Such discussions are often located within photographic criticism, epitomized by the title of a recent anthology by Richard Bolton, *The Contest of Meaning: Critical Histories of Photography.*[5]

It is interesting and encouraging for me to see work by students in both art history and studio art programs because I sense that their status as students, irrespective of their maturity or age, may allow them a greater freedom in moving around current debates than I experience these days.

This year I watched two graduate students at Mills at work on feminist projects: Pamela Carroll, whose background is a mixture of Canadian Native and German, and Deborah Lohrke, a Euro-American. Reading contemporary criticism in the arenas of feminist and cultural studies, together with studying women's art history, and articulating their own thoughts in conversations and essays, both photographers produced fresh work that took on difficult issues about women's bodies.

Deborah Lohrke, who earlier had assisted Judy Chicago, produced a series of work about her body in which she mixed a wide range of media: photographs, medical sample glass slides, diet scales, silver forks, and sausage casings in water. An untitled work that has come to be called *Diet Scale* is composed of forty-eight miniature diet scales in rows of three to create a strange, narrow, ladderlike column some twelve feet high. On each scale Lohrke balanced a photograph of a small portion of her body, partially covered by her hands (the images range from head to foot). Lohrke's intent was to "create a structure of obsessiveness and repetition much like the process of dieting."[6] In *Pierced Photography*, three forks extend from the wall, each brutally piercing a small photograph of a fragment of Lohrke's body. She commented on the piece: "Body image and consumption of food are constantly tied together in the media, but now the viewer is offered the body image for consumption."[7] Lohrke has stubbornly refused to take sides in the polarization that is rife in critical thought and through her research has constructed a rich and eclectic collection of sources, inspirations, and histories. They range from autobiographical material to current theory, from Wittgenstein on architecture to recent work by Dorit Cypis and other feminists of the 1990s, and from a fascination for mid-1970s investigations of the body by Martha Rosler and Carolee Schneemann to those in *Faith Ringgold's Over 100 Pound Weight Loss Performance Story Quilt*, a recent story quilt by Faith Ringgold about her body, food, and diet.

5 Richard Bolton, ed. *Contest of Meaning: Critical Histories of Photography* (Cambridge: M.I.T. Press, 1992).

6 Deborah Lohrke, "The Measure of Self." Master's thesis, Mills College, Oakland, 1993, 11.

7 Lohrke, "The Measure of Self," 14.

194   Pamela Carroll

When She Stopped Gasping for Breath, 1993
black-and-white photograph,
65" × 40".

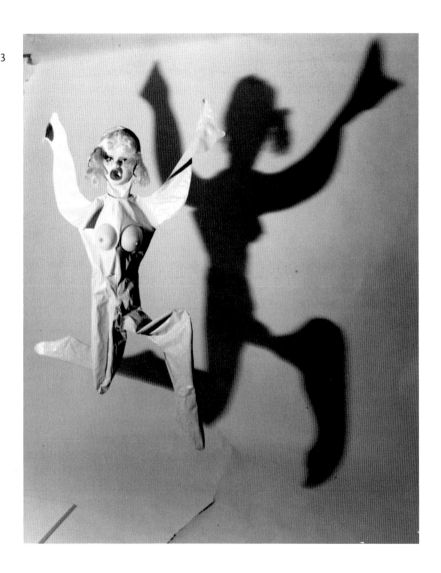

For months, Pamela Carroll grappled with her responses to a white
plastic inflatable sex doll. Over and over she photographed this object,
whose sexual function was all too clear from the gaping holes of its mouth,
vagina, and anus. But how to transform it? For a long time nothing seemed
to work. Visitors to her studio would see Carroll's experiments with different
images and media, but we were always more aware of the powerful,
grotesque presence of the original doll than of any successful attempts to

deconstruct its message visually. Suddenly things started moving. Carroll photographed the doll confronting her reflection in a mirror (at one point the artist's own nude body also appeared there with the doll), and she experimented with dramatic lighting so that the figure became accompanied by her lively shadow. These shadow images were finally to constitute the concluding photographs in *When she stopped gasping for breath*, an impressive narrative sequence that began with close-ups of the doll pinned to a blank wall. During the year, Carroll oscillated between the doll and the subject of her Native grandmother. She is now expanding this second large project to include her German grandmother, and the whole tricky question of how to represent visually the subject of "mixed blood"—a fascinating and little explored subject in art. As she worked in her studio Carroll also read voraciously, and was especially inspired by the texts of two anthologies: *Black Feminist Thought*, edited by Patricia Hill Collins, and *Partial Recall*, edited by Lucy R. Lippard; in the latter, Native writers respond to representations of Native people. Carroll also looked at the work of Lorna Simpson, Carm Little Turtle, Hulleah Tsinhnahjinnie, and other new photographers while she mulled over autobiographical experiences and what family photographic material she could gather together.

Is it possible that a new generation of women artists may increasingly use the camera to address the question of women's bodies in ways that will help disentangle false oppositions of theory and experience, of construction and deconstruction?

I have written so far of women creating images of their own or other women's bodies. Another rich arena for women artists to explore is that of narratives around the male body, and constructions of masculinity that would extend beyond the obvious sexist critiques to address the complexities of race and class, among other factors. One artist who has tackled this issue repeatedly is Pat Ward Williams.

It is easy, when discussing Williams's work, to focus on her sense of history, interest in memory, and techniques that use autobiography, text, and experimental photographic processes. But what struck me most when I first saw the works was their physicality. Certainly, there is the recurring physicality of the wooden constructions that Williams often uses to frame her pieces; most of all, however, there is the physicality of the bodies of black women, men, and children. If you want to look at her art, you have to look at the bodies of the people she portrays—there's no escaping them.[8] Black women's hair is the subject of *Oh, She Got a Head Fulla Hair*, and the large clothed bodies of women from Williams's childhood take over much of the space of *Ghosts That Smell Like Cornbread*. Men appear in Williams's work in an equally extraordinary range of settings and moods. In the witty

[8] For this image and other work by Pat Ward Williams, see *Pat Ward Williams: Probably Cause*, ed. Elsa Longhauser (Philadelphia: Goldie Paley Gallery, Moore College of Art and Design, 1992).

196 **Hulleah Tsinhnahjinnie**
Census Makes a Native Artist
from the series ***Creative Native***,   1992
black-and-white photograph,
40″ × 30″.

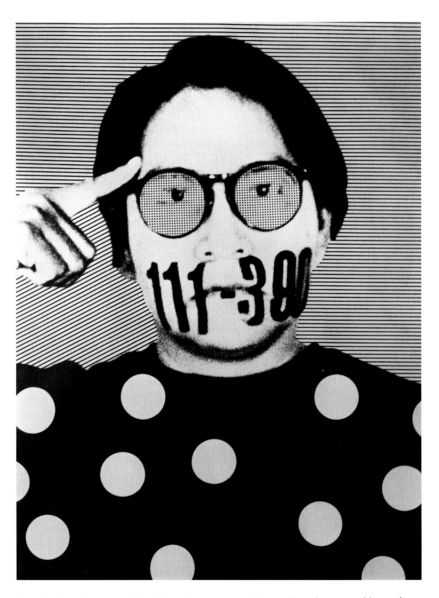

installation, *Beware of the Dog*, viewers can pick up the phone and hear the angry last message of an old lover of the artist; on the wall is an image of the head and nude torso of a man flexing his muscles. But there are other situations of black men which Williams explores with passion rather than wit. In *32 Hours in a Box . . . Still Counting*, for example, we walk around an installa-

tion that contains a large three-dimensional box made up of a series of
photographs of a crouching figure, Henry "Box" Brown, a nineteenth-
century runaway slave, who had himself shipped north in a box to escape
slavery. Finally, there is the uncompromising presence, unmediated by
autobiography or history, of five young African American men who sit
staring directly out at the viewer in WHAT YOU LOOKN AT. This image is enormous (96″ × 192″), and Williams had it placed in the gallery window of the
Moore College of Art and Design. No one walking that street in Philadelphia during Williams's retrospective 1992 exhibition could avoid the
black men's eyes. Neither, while they looked at the men, could viewers
avoid asking themselves that discomforting question (which was stamped
across the width of the image): "WHAT YOU LOOKN AT". We were looking at
men looking at us. But who is the "you" who is looking? Of what gender
and sexual orientation? Of what race? Of what class? Of what age? Such
differences would of course profoundly affect viewers' reactions to the
men's gaze.

In 1993, when I began conceptualizing this essay, I went to Boulder, Colorado, to lecture, but wondered whether I should be there at all, given the
passage in Colorado of Amendment 2 (which would deprive lesbians, gay
men, and bisexuals of any legal remedy against discrimination) and the
resulting call for a state boycott by various groups. During this period I first
saw Caroline Hinkley's *Open Season in the Weimar Colorado*, a work whose
imagery and circumstances moved me tremendously.

    In the left panel of this photographic triptych two nude women run
toward us, one behind the other, heads thrown back, arms raised. The large
central panel depicts a desolate scene of men in a winter, snowbound forest
landscape with faint buildings outlined behind: the foreground figure, his
back turned away from us, has his gun raised; to his right we see the profile
of the body of an escaping hare. The third panel is composed of five fore-
boding images, photographs stacked one upon the other. At the top a nude
woman runs through a barren industrial cityscape. Below are three fragments: the interior of an oven, a figure on a couch (behind it a fragment of
an attendant in a white uniform appears), and a close-up of buttocks. At the
bottom a clothed figure clutches a hare. We see the animal's eyes and body,
but not the face of the man who holds it.

    I first saw this work in Hinkley's home, outside Boulder. The images had
for me the immediate associations of an urgent pursuit conducted in an
eerily silent world, as if I were watching figures speaking in a silent movie.
The sense of agitation came from the recurring images of women running,
echoed in the actions of the hare—bounding in the central frame, but

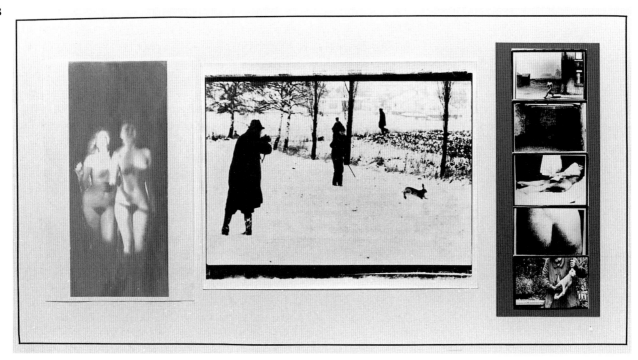

Caroline Hinkley
Open Season in the Weimar Colorado, 199?
mixed media, including black-and-white
photographs and color photographs.

caught in the final image on the bottom right. In that image the man, who grabs the hare by its legs and ears, acts as the finale to the four stacked images above it, as if—again the metaphor of film comes to mind—the viewers had been watching a movie played in painfully slow motion, and this were the final frame.

Hinkley, a white lesbian, had begun this work in November 1992, immediately after Amendment 2 was passed. She said, "It felt like open season when I went driving into town. I was literally afraid of physical violence as well as verbal abuse."[9] She named the work, *Open Season in the Weimar Colorado* to indicate parallels she sensed between the present in Colorado and the Weimar Republic, that glamorous, unstable, and ominous period in Germany between 1919 and 1933 when Hitler came to power. (During the Nazi regime, gays were placed in concentration camps.) For years, Hinkley has been drawn uneasily to the politics and history of Germany, and in *Open Season in the Weimar Colorado* the appropriated images—which she photocopied, then reshot and often manipulated further—are all photographs taken from *Der Spiegel* (the largest current-

[9] In a conversation between Caroline Hinkley and the author, Boulder, February 21, 1993.

affairs weekly publication in Germany), except for the image of the two women, which she found in a book of stills from early Russian films. (Her love of Russian Constructivist colors is reflected in the cadmium red in the left panel, a color echoed in the frame of the right panel.)

Bodies hunted, bodies brutalized, bodies celebrated, bodies weighed, bodies imprinted, bodies of different racial and cultural backgrounds—the bodies of men and children and women are the subjects of these artists' investigations. The artists address the intelligence and the heart of their viewers, and they address, too, the need to seek out change, to act in the real world. In different ways they pose Pat Ward Williams's question, "What you lookn at?"

But as historians, critics, and curators it is urgent that we do much more looking ourselves—not to examine theoretically (yet again) the subject of the male gaze but to seek out new work. This will surely profoundly alter both our theoretical approaches and our sense of the range in feminist photography of representations of women's experiences of bodies, their own and others.

May 26, 1993. There is a synchronicity to the writing of this essay that pleases me. Today, Theresa Harlan—critic, curator, and an old friend—visits bringing original photographs by Tsinhnahjinnie, together with presents: a gardenia and a garland of dried fruits, herbs, and garlic from New Mexico. We talk at length: about the writings of Trinh T. Minh-ha, and a lecture by Pat Ward Williams that she had recently attended. Harlan wants to write on the recent experiments in self-portraiture among Native women photographers. She tells me about Shelly Niro's *I Enjoy Being a Mohawk Girl*, in which the artist and her sisters assume exuberant poses and are extravagantly dressed and made up, and of another series by Niro, *This Land Is Mime Land*. We discuss the wit, imagination, and intelligence among Native women photographers, who are increasingly intrigued with self-representation. We talk about who should speak for whom, and of the pressing need to listen to Native theorists as well as look at Native art, and specifically to seek out the ideas and images of Native women.

Now I sit in my living room with two poster-size photographs from the *Creative Native Series* by Tsinhnahjinnie. I am confronted by her unsmiling, resolute, bespectacled face, her mouth stamped with her tribal enrollment number, and her finger pointed at her head. (A mocking salute? An indication of what's going on inside her head? A suicide gesture where her hand is a substitute for a gun?) One photograph has a subtitle, *Census Makes a Native Artist*, alluding to the recent controversial law according to which only artists who are tribally registered may call themselves "Native" artists if they show or sell in federally funded Indian spaces. Here Tsinhnahjinnie presents a decided twist to the sometimes rather abstract discussions about representation. She asks us, Who decides on whose identity? Does the artist have a right to her self-naming? And surely the underlying question is, Whose body is it, anyway?

If Tsinhnahjinnie and Lucy Stone, whose words I quoted at the beginning, were to meet in some futuristic space, despite their differences in historical time, race, and class they might well come to some basic agreement over the need for the "absolute right" not only to one's body but to one's self-identity as women.

Sex and Anxiety

THE DESUBLIMATION OF ROMANCE
THE SUBLIME   THE ROMANTIC

SUBLIMATE: v. To refine and exalt, to heighten, to elevate to a place of dignity or honor, to make noble, grand or holy (Psychoanalysis). To direct the energy of an impulse away from its primitive aim to one that is higher in the cultural scale, as to sublimate sexual curiosity into artistic or scientific production.

ROMANCE: v. To write or tell of the picturesque, to indulge in extravagant stories pertaining to chivalry or heroic adventure, often alluding to fictitious wish fulfillment.

DE: Freely used as a living prefix to form words with these meanings:
1. Down, as in depose, put down, deride, laugh down.
2. Separation, off, away, as in desist, to stand off, to send away.
3. Intensification.
4. Reversing or undoing by action, as in deform, decapitate, dematerialize, decentralize, declassify, deflesh, etc.

These selected excerpts from partial definitions are edited for emphasis as the accompanying images were edited from a contact sheet (or originally from "real life"). *Fictions "borrowed" from fact, pictures "stolen" by speed and sleight of hand. A depiction of gender dilemma, an obsession with subject/object identification? Oh, that absent OTHER, the camera position that you as viewer must take from me, the PHOTOGRAPHER, evokes the ambivalence **of a woman** as distanced voyeur and **of a woman** as unwilling but present participant, connected to the subject by mutual oppression, as well as, mutual desire to please.* You as viewer stand in my place, imaginary camera as inadequate shield. Depth of field set from here to infinity, next to fastest shutter, zone focused. Frame. Expose.

I want you to see that ***IT IS A PRETTY PICTURE.***
Yet, I know that ***IT IS*** **NOT** ***A PRETTY PICTURE.***
CONSIDER THE DIFFERENCE.

Yes, pleasure in looking. Control by looking. Labor? The process, the craft and the product (the photograph). Appropriation, objectification, misrepresentation? Corrective vision. A purview of discontent. Look again. Recognize a complex and emphatic sexual investment in looking and longing for meaning.

To look, to be looked at, to look back again and again.
The critical look back, the defiant look back,
At the work place, the home place, the same place, the other's place.

THE ROMANCE IS OVER.

I followed them for hours, secretly watching them flirt, cuddle, kiss and caress. I took great pleasure in their pretended search for privacy, their play and reproach, their harmless sparring. They never let on that I was watching. Oblivious to the harried traffic, street hawkers and transient purveyors of bad faith, they seemed the perfect picture of a world unto themselves. All at once, I envied and pitied them at the same time.

CONSIDER THE DIFFERENCE

202

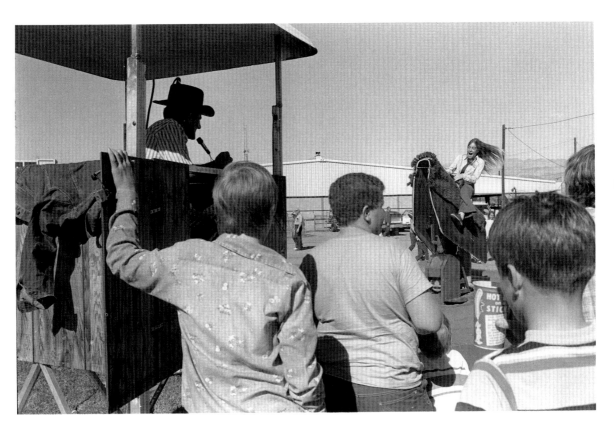

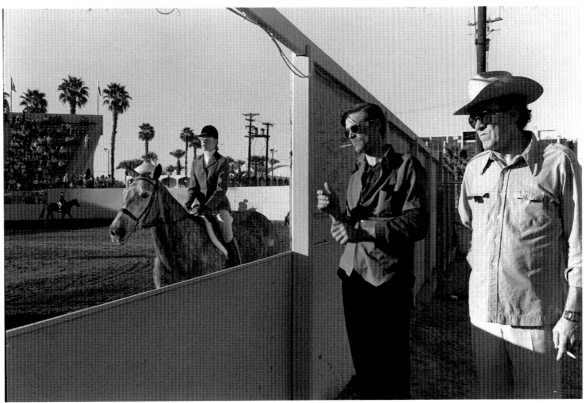

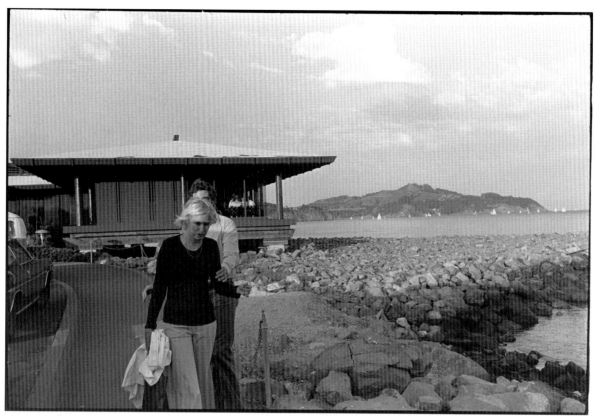

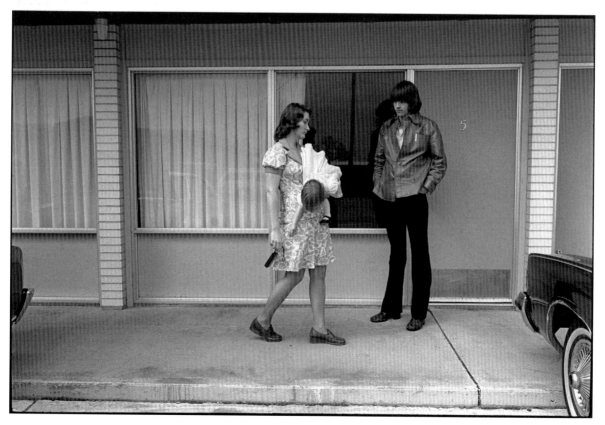

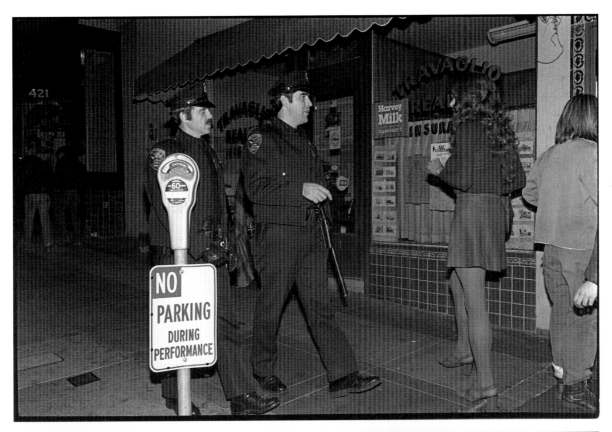

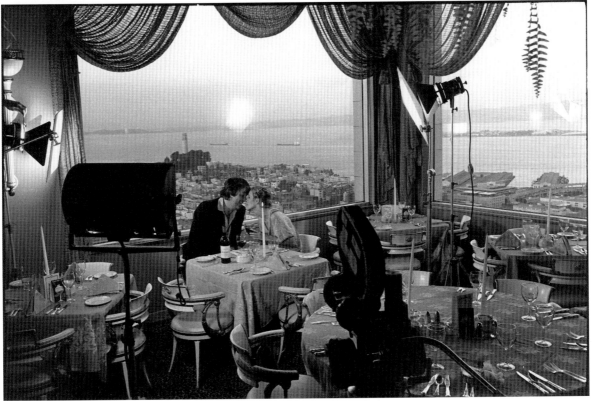

206

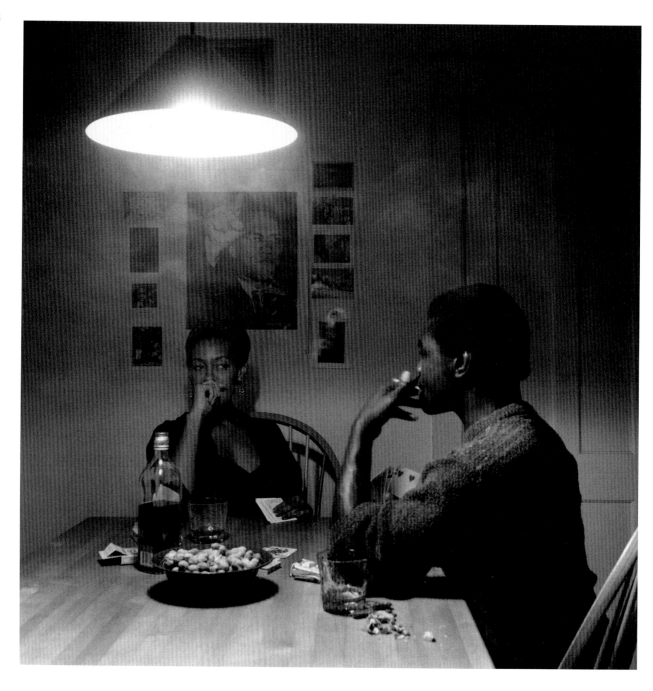

Seeking clarity and purpose, she spoke about the problems with her momma who said, ``There's a difference between men and women. I can't tell ya what to do. But I can tell you that I sided with men so long I forgot women had a side. Truth slapped me so hard up-side my head, I cried for days, got so I couldn't wash my own behind. Shonuff blue. Biggest fool in the world. Turning my back on friends for a piece of man. Oh sure, I've had a man or two—I mean with a capital ``M''—but like a good friend, hard to come by. But look, ya got a good man, man puts up with mo a yo mess than the law allows. If he loves ya, ya best take yo behind home, drop them guns on the floor and work it out. Ya gotta give a little to get a little, that's the story of life.''

He felt her demands for more than he could presently give would cause her to lose a good thing. She felt his lack of compromise around her simple needs would soon have her singing,

I love you Porgy,
don't let him take me,
don't let him handle me
with his hot hands.
If you can keep me, I
wants to stay here
with you forever and
I'll be glad.

She went on a little run with a friend, and when they got back her girlfriend told what she had did. He cried big crocodile tears at the thought of another mule in his stall. So hurt by her infidelity, he felt Frankie and Johnny might have to be played out for real. This was the beginning and the end of things.

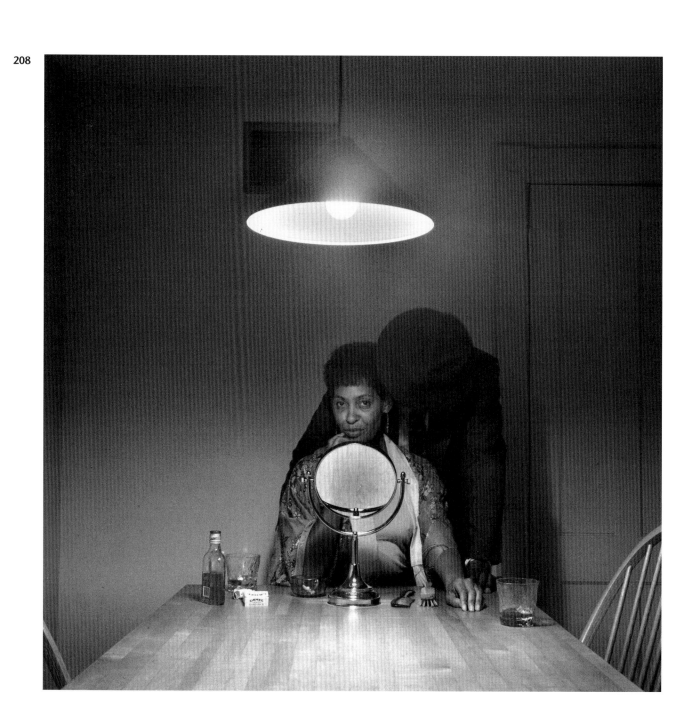

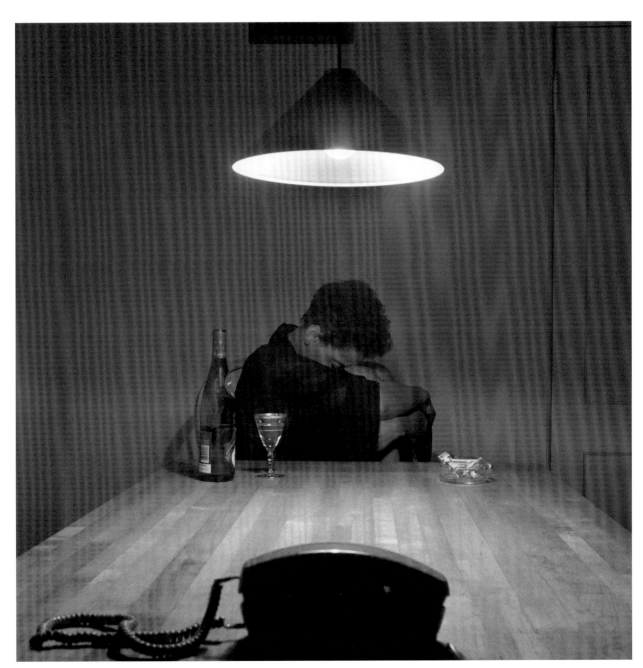

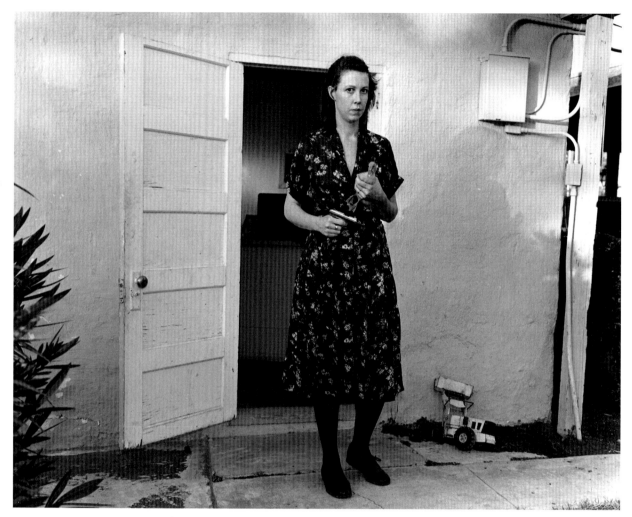

The Vegetarian

For a long time she could not remember what had actually happened. The police said she had shot him twice, once in the chest and once in the head. It was the second shot—the one to the head—which finally stopped him.

In a way, he had asked for it by taunting her ceaselessly, calling her "stupid" and "veggie-brained." On that Sunday he had been drinking heavily and by evening was feeling mean and looking for a fight. The children were at her sister's but were expected back for supper. She boiled water for spaghetti and continued to ignore his attempts to start a quarrel.

In drunken frustration he ran out to the backyard yelling "I'll make you listen to me." He stumbled back with two of the children's baby ducks in his big hands. "How about duck soup? I'll make duck soup for the happy family!" He dangled one of the squawking ducklings over the pot of boiling water. She screamed at him to stop. Having caught her attention, he laughed and let it drop. Scalding water splashed out of the pot. In the midst of the commotion she ran for the hall closet and returned with the little handgun he had bought for her to protect herself.

He was holding the second duckling over the bubbling pot and laughing maniacally. She made her choice.

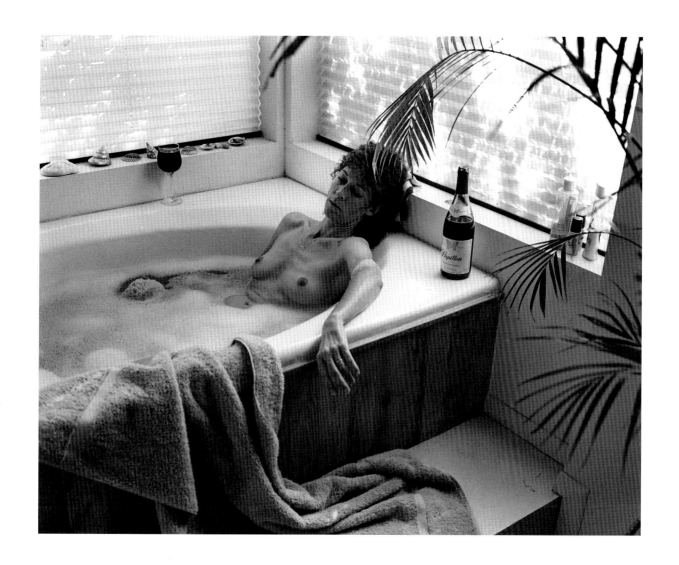

Ex-Wife

It made her angry to think of him with that woman until she realized that eventually his sweet young bride would desire babies. Since he wasn't very good at saying "No" to a pretty face, he would comply.

It pleased her to imagine him, at his age, struggling with diapers and strollers, his lust domesticated by a joint checking account.

Cheerfully, she poured another glass of wine and savored the knowledge that life would dole out its own brand of justice.

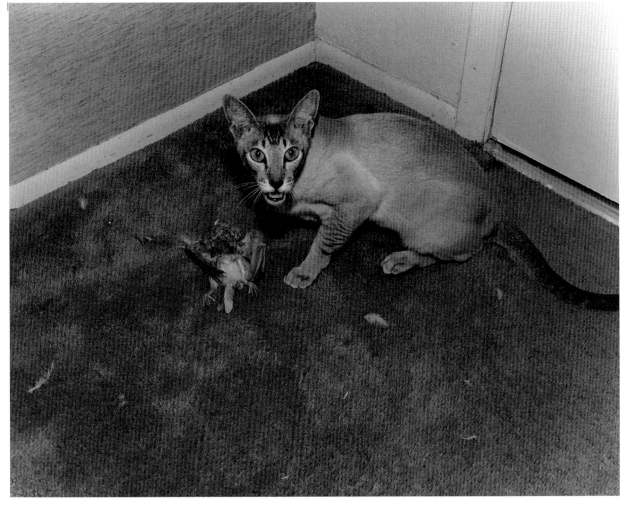

Malice

Although they were no longer on speaking terms, she thought of him more often now than when they were living together.

It infuriated her that he claimed so much of her attention. Despite valiant efforts to have nothing to do with him, she was rarely free of his insidious presence.

In the shower, images of him with his pretty mistress appeared before her tightly shut eyes, making her scream obscenities until she grew hoarse. Not a night passed in which he didn't disturb her fitful dreams with lewd suggestions.

What was it that enabled him to invade her mind any time of the night or day, like an incubus determined to torment his hapless victim, then act as if nothing had happened when he chanced to meet her on the street?

How could she prove she knew he was trying to drive her crazy?

Who would believe a jilted woman?

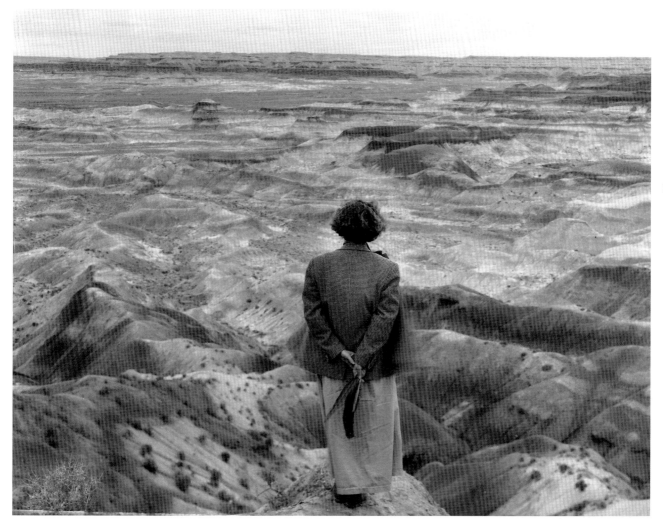

Hawks

She stood on the bluff and stared into the expanse of desert spread out like a relief map before her feet and wished she could fly or, better still, lose herself and become a bird, perhaps a redtailed hawk with a four-foot wing span and eyes that could detect rodents from five hundred feet above the earth. A creature capable of navigating wind currents without the aid of charts or numbers, immersed in life on the primal level, where instinct dictates the rules of the game.

What would it be like to live in the blood, outside of thought, clean and simple, always present, even to death?

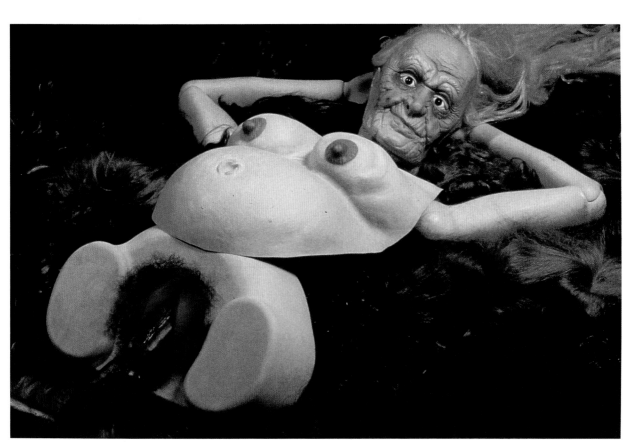

214

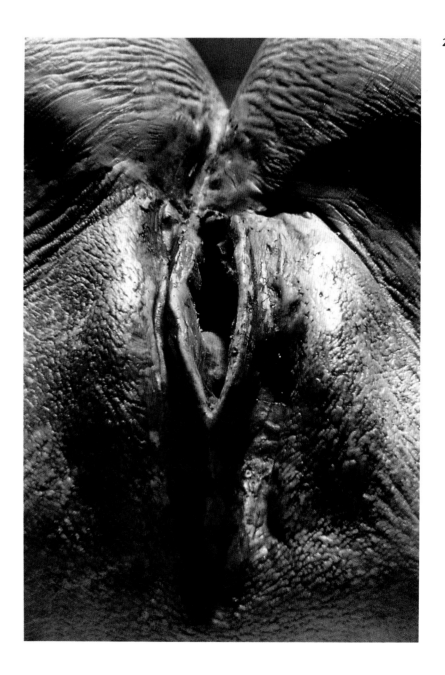

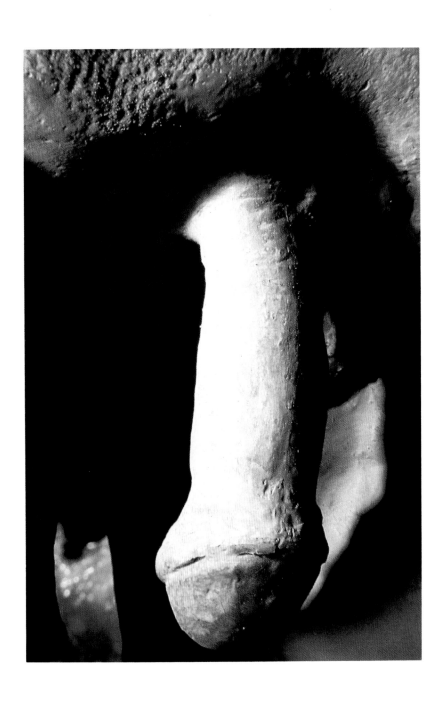

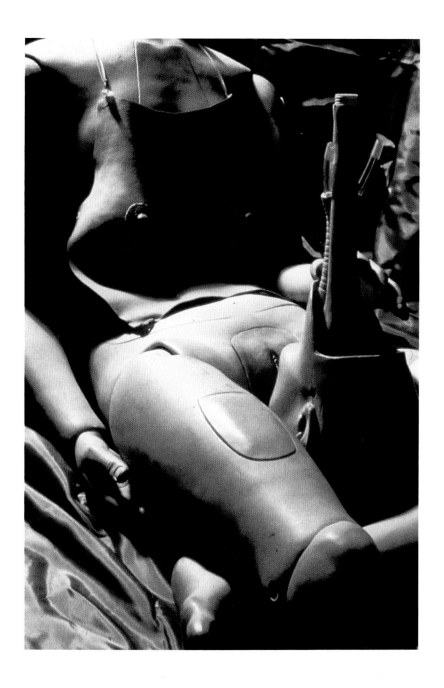

218

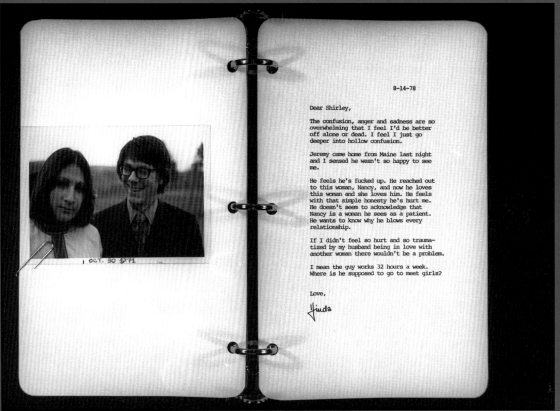

8-14-78

Dear Shirley,

The confusion, anger and sadness are so
overwhelming that I feel I'd be better
off alone or dead. I feel I just go
deeper into hollow confusion.

Jeremy came home from Maine last night
and I sensed he wasn't so happy to see
me.

He feels he's fucked up. He reached out
to this woman, Nancy, and now he loves
this woman and she loves him. He feels
with that simple honesty he's hurt me.
He doesn't seem to acknowledge that
Nancy is a woman he sees as a patient.
He wants to know why he blows every
relationship.

If I didn't feel so hurt and so trauma-
tized by my husband being in love with
another woman there wouldn't be a problem.

I mean the guy works 32 hours a week.
Where is he supposed to go to meet girls?

Love,

Hilda

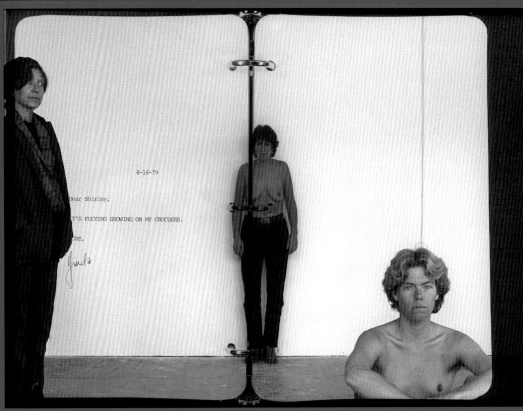

4-16-79

Dear Shirley,

T'S FUCKING SNOWING ON MY CROCUSES.

OVE,

Hilda

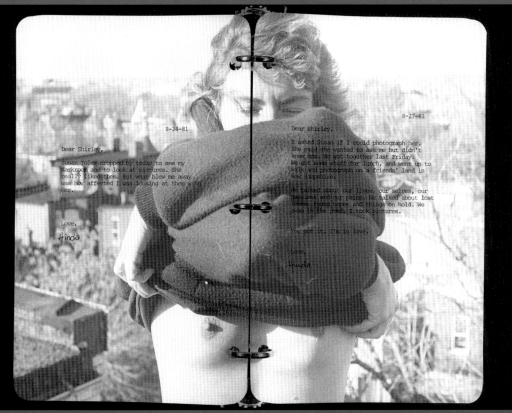

8-24-81

Dear Shirley,

Susan Toler dropped by today to see my
darkroom and to look at pictures. She
really liked them. But what blew me away
was how affected I was looking at them with
her.

Love,

Hinda

8-27-81

Dear Shirley,

I asked Susan if I could photograph her.
She said she wanted to ask me but didn't
know how. We got together last Friday.
We got some stuff for lunch, and went up to
walk and photograph on a friends' land in
New Hampshire.

We talked about our lives, our selves, our
passions and our pains. We talked about lost
loves, found hopes and things on hold. We
swam in the pond. I took pictures.

You got it: I'm in love.

Love,

Hinda

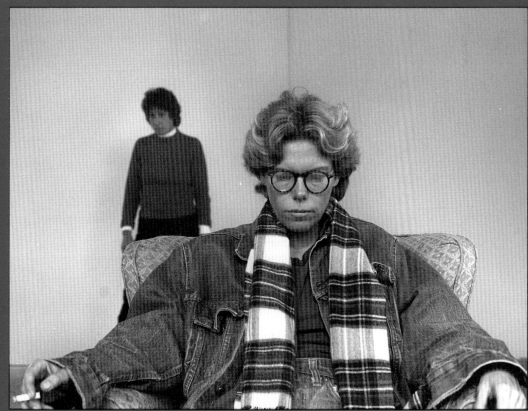

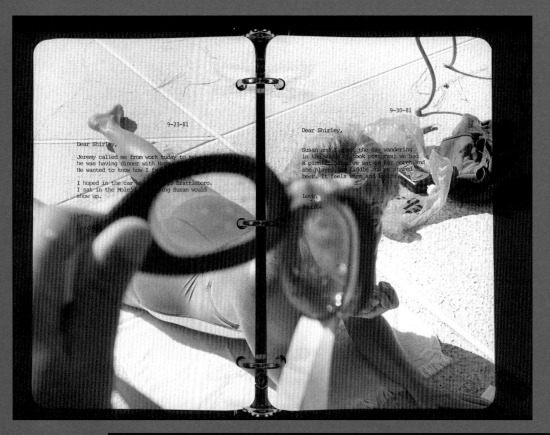

9-23-81

Dear Shirley,

Jeremy called me from work today to [tell me]
he was having dinner with Nan[cy].
He wanted to know how I fe[lt].

I hoped in the car [and drove to] Brattleboro.
I sat in the Mole[y's] [hop]ing Susan would
show up.

Love,

Hinda

9-30-81

Dear Shirley,

Susan and I [spent] the day wandering
in the [woods. I] took pictures; we had
a picnic; [then we] sat on her porch and
she played [the] fiddle [and we] shared a
beer. It feels warm and loving.

Love,

Hinda

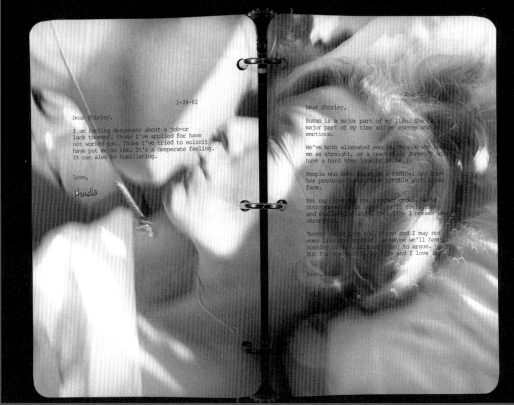

1-24-82

Dear Shirley,

I am feeling desperate about a job-or
lack thereof. Those I've applied for have
not worked out. Those I've tried to solicit
have put me on ice. It's a desperate feeling.
It can also be humiliating.

Love,

Hinda

2-2-82

Dear Shirley,

Susan is a major part of my life. She [is a]
major part of my time and my energy and [my]
emotions.

We've both alienated people. People who [know]
me as straight, or a teacher [or] Jeremy's [mother]
have a hard time looking at me.

People who know Susan as a radical and know
her previous lover, have trouble with a new
face.

Yet our love for one another grows. We've
both [grown] in new ways. It feels risky
and challenging and I feel like I possess new
strength.

Twenty years from now, Susan and I may not
even like [each] other, or maybe we'll have
nothing to [say, or everything] to argue.
But for now [this is] my life and I love it.

Love,

Hinda

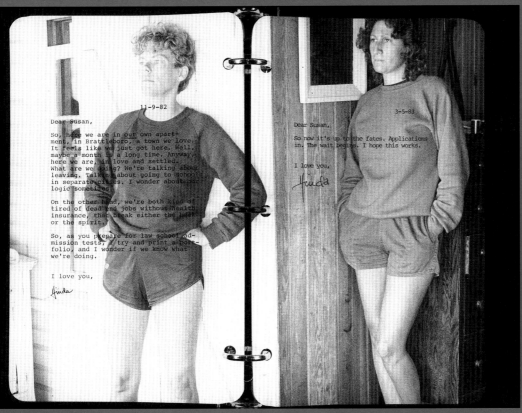

11-9-82

Dear Susan,

So, here we are in our own apartment, in Brattleboro, a town we love.
It feels like we just got here. Well,
maybe a month is a long time. Anyway,
here we are, in love and settled.
What are we doing? We're talking about
leaving. Talking about going to school
in separate cities. I wonder about my
logic sometimes.

On the other hand, we're both kind of
tired of dead-end jobs without health
insurance, that break either the back
or the spirit.

So, as you prepare for law school admission tests, I try and print a portfolio, and I wonder if we know what
we're doing.

I love you,

Hinda

3-5-83

Dear Susan,

So now it's up to the fates. Applications
in. The wait begins. I hope this works.

I love you,

Hinda

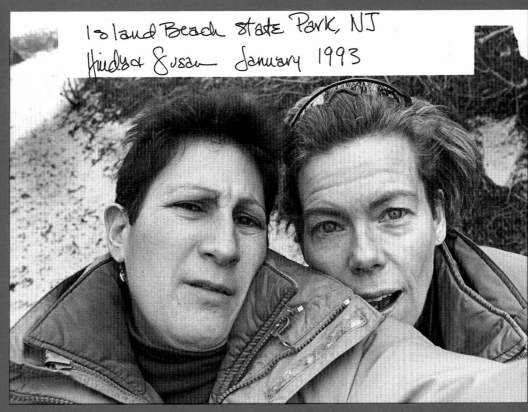

Island Beach State Park, NJ
Hinda & Susan   January 1993

from *The Ballad of Sexual Dependency*
Cibachrome color photographs,
ongoing since 1978

Mark and Mark, Boston 1978

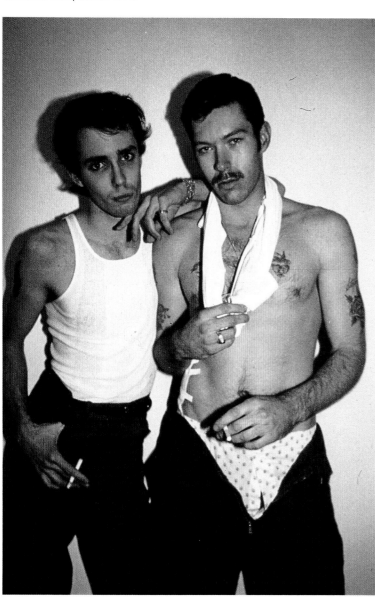

Philippe M. and Risé on their wedding
day, New York City 1978

(*bottom*) Greer and Robert on the bed,
New York City 1982

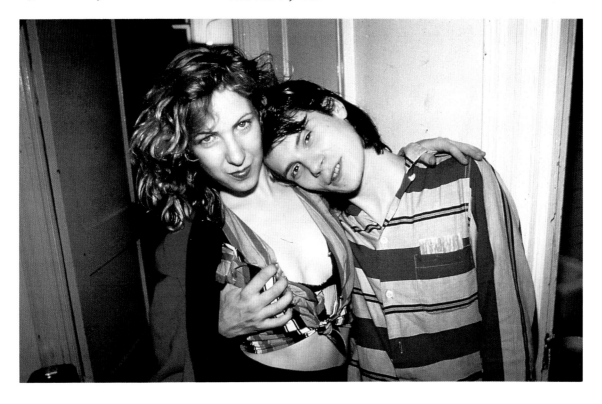

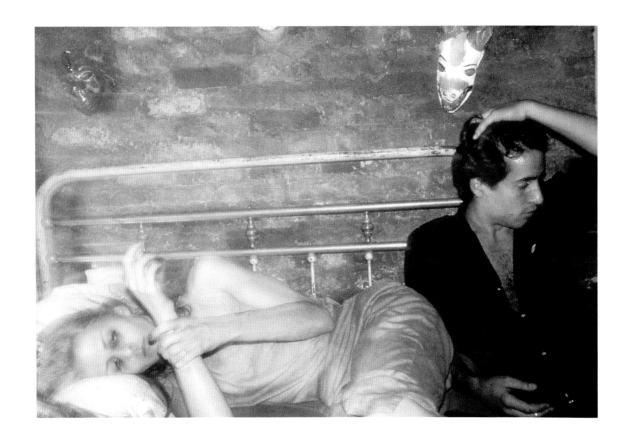

Philippe H. and Suzanne kissing at
Euthanasia, New York City 1981

(*bottom*) Joey and Andres in bed, Berlin
1992

224

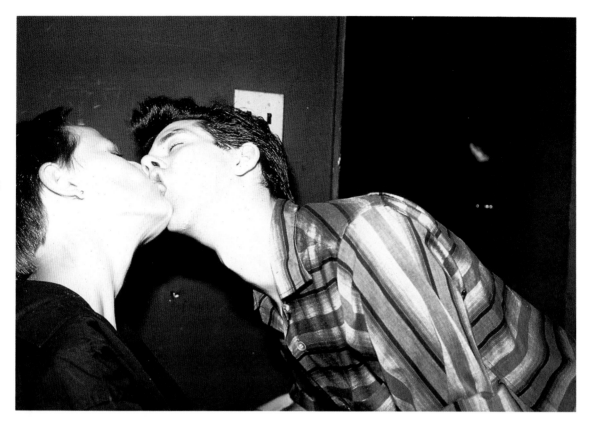

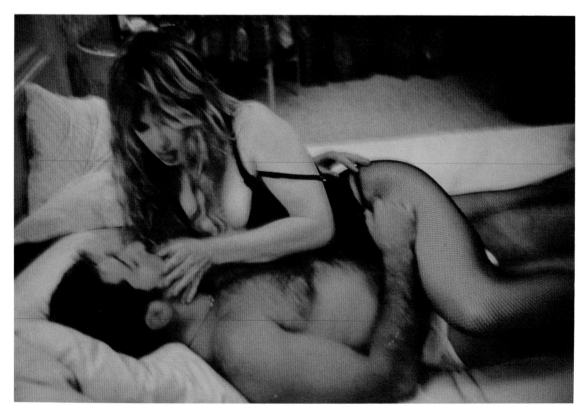

The Hug, New York City 1980

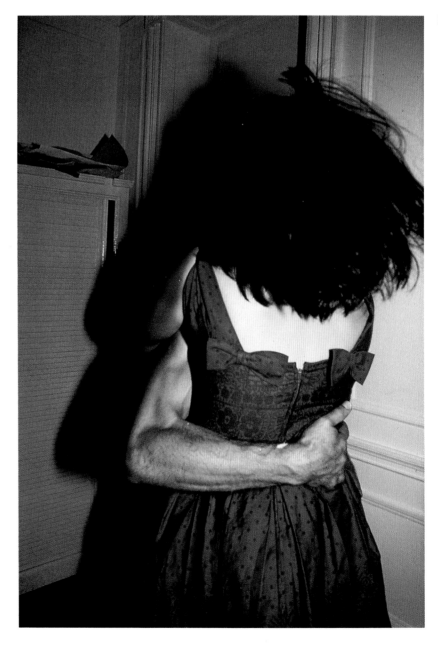

Catherine Lord

226

Face it, it's what you have to do to be an artist these days. You have to mimic the academics. So it's grad school, crits, and the whopper of them all, the nightmare from which you will never wake, the Review of the Thesis Show, that moment of separation, abuse, denial, and confrontation, transference and countertransference, boredom and panic, an apologia for excellence produced by an apparatus all of us profess to critique but that we profit from as much as it profits by us. We assume our positions as furniture in the white box: The Work, The Student, The Faculty. The work does not speak for itself, and it is our job, on the faculty, to ensure that words are pronounced about what we hope we cannot entirely reduce to words. In the art biz, just as Foucault wrote about sex, what is said to be unspeakable, unknowable, and indescribable is surrounded by all sorts of sneaky devices to incite us to speak about it, compulsively and constantly.

So we sit on the floor of the white box, you and I, the faculty, and prepare to discuss the work. You are the artist, a woman of color. Your name is out there. Your work, powerful and uncompromising, much sought after by a mainstream hot to capitalize on changing population demographics (a k a multiculturalism), rests on the irrefutable grit of injustice. You use what you need—drawings, texts, photos, objects—to represent those you claim as your people to themselves. You know that what goes unseen, or unheard, can neither sustain the memories that constitute a culture nor structure an imaginary that might transform the present, much less enable another future. You know that unless you work to produce and control your representation, you do not, did not, and will not exist. You execute the work of material culture, controlling scale, perspective, installation, and context. You have made a career of speaking out about injustice. History you like. Theory you don't. Your work comes from your life, you say, not from theories that prescribe what you should make, that speak about you after the fact, that measure you against standards that are not yours, that cripple you when you walk into your studio. You have no use for feminism—notoriously white and middle class—for it has given you nothing. You distribute the signifiers of a (heterosexual) femininity throughout your work and your speech. You believe there are other ways of knowing than the intellectual, and that those other ways, which you call the spiritual, are in your possession. You represent yourself as the barometer, the arbiter, the muse, and the prophet of your people's needs. I have listened to you speak, eloquently and for hours, in this vein.

The work has been made by a young woman who has for some time been in the process of coming out as a lesbian. In several senses her debut, the exhibition is beautiful, both compelling and tentative. She has arranged various objects so as to suggest that gays and lesbians have existed throughout history, at once embedded in systems of kinship and expelled from them by the rhetoric of hate. In one part of the work, silhouettes of black footsteps on the floor point toward a row of mirrors. Each pair of footsteps is labeled with a term of kinship: daughter, father, son, sister-in-law, cousin, etc. The point is to pick one's shoes, stand in them, look in the mirror, and realize that one—anyone at all—can be seen as homosexual.

We, the faculty, speak vaguely and favorably of various small formal choices, by way of warmup, and then begin to focus on the footsteps and the mirrors, talking to each other through the student, whose voice we quickly drown. This work speaks to everyone, you say, because it speaks through family and everyone has a family. Everyone has somewhere to stand here. You like the work because its makes its point about homosexuality with subtlety. You feel included. It's important not to exclude the viewer, you say , but to draw him in. And, you say, as if relieved at the epiphany, the work shows us that homosexuals are complicated, that they have all sorts of different ways of looking and dressing. Not every lesbian has short hair and piercings and tattoos, you observe.

My name is also out there, as a dyke, a writer, and a feminist. I am white, which is to claim nothing more than that I have been raised to believe I am white. A child of the sixties, I have done my share of speaking out about injustices, and overhauled my share of reactionary art institutions. I have some notoriety as a tough administrative type with decent politics about gender and race. I have been out of the closet so long that I have lost the door, and I am well aware that the glass ceiling in my tenured radical office is just above my head. I have ensured that you too will become a tenured radical, in your own office, with your own ceiling.

You have never read a word I have written. Nonetheless, you maintain that I write incomprehensibly erudite French theory, derivative and out of date, which I force on impressionable young artists to destroy their creativity. I represent logos, not eros, and so I make them afraid, you say. You have told me, many times, that my problem is that I have no spiritual practice.

This is part of our histories.

Now, believing that politics and therefore political change happens in all sorts of unlikely locations, including backwaters like schools and cultural institutions, I cannot let your remarks pass. Or perhaps by now I have a mind like a tattered bumper sticker: THINK GLOBALLY ACT LOCALLY and HOMOPHOBIA IS A SOCIAL DISEASE. Too, there is plenty of time to kill, and besides that, I want coming out to be a glorious thing for this young woman. I know how much she will need this memory, and I want it to exist on her turf, on the most expansive of queer terms, terms that contain the possibility of camouflage, a militance deep and fierce, camp, as well as surprising alliances, sexual and political.[1] I suppose I have another bumper sticker in mind: ASSIMILATION IS NOT LIBERATION.

There is no place I can stand in this work, I say. None of these footsteps fit. As a queer, I'm outside these structures. They are the institution of heterosexuality, not some sort of natural, universal, ahistorical phenomenon. I'm not a mother, or a daughter, or a husband, or a wife. This statement is preposterous to you, and so we argue. You say that every woman is someone's daughter, every mother a mother forever, no matter what. No, I say, I've been disowned by my family, and my child was taken away by the courts when I came out as a lesbian. My family is my queer friends, and the woman with whom I've lived for years, and cannot marry. If I die before her, I know that my family will fight to take from her what we have earned together, and what I would give to her. (This is fiction. In my anger I have sunk to soppy docudrama, claiming as my own the terrible histories of lovers and lesbian legends. The documentary of my life would star loving kin who, knowing they will be penalized for speaking of my lesbian life-style in their heterosexual universes, generally opt for silence about my very existence. As my mother said when I came out to her, "I'll respect your choice, dear, but it will make cocktail parties more difficult for you.") This place where we both work, I go on, would not accord my partner the benefits it would routinely bestow on the survivor of one week's heterosexual married coupledom. The terms which you assume to be universal are the system of your privilege, from which I am entirely excluded. In your system, I am unnamed, and being outside your language, I do not exist and cannot be conceived. (This bit of lowbrow philosophizing I have lifted from the filmmaker Derek Jarman's queered, and brilliant, *Wittgenstein*). I go on to speak about those that the institution of the family supposedly protects, about the suicide rate among gay and lesbian youth, about the thousands of gay and lesbian children forced to become refugees from families that declare them immoral, perverted, unsafe, and delinquent, families that literally wish them dead. I talk about hate crimes and gay bashing. I restrain myself from belaboring the point I believe I am making so eloquently by bringing up the subject of AIDS: it would be just too obvious.

I notice the student listening, wide-eyed. She reminds me that this is not about her work, or about her family, which supports her choices, whatever they might be, and which accepts her for who she is. You remind me that your people can't afford to lose any of their children and have, against terrible odds, tracked the ties of blood. Stubborn, I retreat to talk about recuperating the history of deviance. If this sounds like theory, it is also my native language, the only language that allows me to think myself in the

[1] I hope the word "queer" can mean for a few years more what it means to me now, despite its trendiness, writing in the summer of 1993: a militant *nonessentialism* with the distinct possibility of alliances in unlikely places. See, for example, Teresa de Lauretis's "Queer Theory: Lesbian and Gay Sexualities, An Introduction," *differences* 3, no. 2 (1991), and Alexander Doty's chapter, "There's Something Queer Here," in his *Making Things Perfectly Queer* (Minneapolis: University of Minnesota Press, 1993), 1–16. By the way, I've visited and worked in diverse locations, which means that the incidents and characters included in this essay, myself included, represent no single individual or institution. I thank Diane Neumaier, Connie Samaras, Millie Wilson, and Connie Wolf for their close readings of this essay. Any suggestions that I've ignored are in this case my problem alone.

territory to which you have exiled me. "It's just like the motherfucking tree falling in the motherfucking forest," I think inelegantly to myself. "If no one's there to see family, it doesn't fucking well exist."

It has not been a glorious moment in pedagogy. We both know that we are supposed to be making alliances at the end of some rainbow or another. As we wander out of the white box, making collegial small talk, you speak to me of your son and say to me, with a laugh, "You're always so logical. Do you nurture *anything*?" The utterly predictable late twentieth-century pain of my life flashes up: the lover and friends with cancer, unimportant and underresearched breast cancer, friends dead and dying of AIDS. I make privacy for myself by playing your caricature of me. (Perhaps you recognize the strategy?) "No kids," I say. "Cats. I have two cats. And a garden."

Unfortunately, this exchange is neither private nor personal. Our words demolish certain possibilities as they shape others. We are positioned in and by institutions. Having spoken, our thoughts will have consequences for ourselves and for others.

Unfortunately, too, what has transpired has been an unremarkable interchange. You are merely one more homophobe, operating by willful ignorance and systematic erasure. Smug in the privilege you derive from heterosexuality, it is invisible to you as an institution, and therefore, tolerance is the highest state to which you aspire. In this regard, you are no better and no worse, no more enlightened and no less vicious, than any of your heterosexual peers. Let me multiply this you, then, shatter the monolith before the foundations are completed, and invite the whole epic heterosexual cast into my fairy tale. You are, all of you, under no lived incitement to questioning, curiosity, accuracy, information, respect, knowledge, diffidence, analysis, or interest in regard to the way that the particular sexual practices I prefer have constructed me as a member of a culture in binary and forcibly public opposition to what you assume to be merely your private sexual pleasures. You have made it clear that you'd much prefer it if I consented to treat sexuality as some sort of voluntary difference. You have made it clear, in many subtle ways, that it would be appreciated if I didn't raise the issue of sexuality at inappropriate or inconvenient moments, if I agreed to let the matter drop as silently as a stone off the end of the PC mantra: race–gender–class–parentheses–sexuality–end–parentheses.

Those of you who are heterosexual white feminists have chanted yourselves to sleep with the mantra. To many of us, you have difficulty with everything *but* gender, which is the source of both your oppression and your blindness to other experiences of oppression. That is, your obsession with gender and what you call sexual difference is exactly bounded by your investment in heterosexuality and in whiteness. In the language you speak, "race and gender are treated as if they are mutually exclusive categories of experience."[2] This has produced, among other things, a racism that is legendary *except* in the stories you tell yourselves. You feed the maw of culture that constructs visibility and awards cultural credibility— conferences, books, jobs, shows, grants—long lists of yourselves, and your men, with only an occasional colored, queer, or queer-colored tidbit. You profess an endless curiosity, inviting those you minoritize to instruct you in the errors of your ways, then forgetting what they told you. You don't learn enough about other cultures to figure out that gender isn't a universal script.[3] Your read on our queer gender play is a projection of your own obsessions: you patronize our drag queens because you think they want to imitate you, and you patronize our butches because you think they want to imitate your men. When confronted with these "problems," your solution is a display of masochistic (not the kind involving the articulated pleasure of bottoming out) guilt feelings, which are neither legitimate nor useful. "Guilt is *not* a feeling," writes Barbara Smith. "It is an intellectual mask to a feeling. Fear is a feeling—fear of losing one's power, fear of being accused, fear of a loss of status, control, knowledge."[4]

Some of you heterosexuals, male and female, suspect that I make an issue, as you phrase it, of my sexuality, only to get a better seat on the marginality train. Others insist I merely want to absolve my guilt as a privileged white woman. When you convey in the diverse ways you believe are reasonable that you would prefer me to keep my sexuality private, all of you mean, among other things, that it would be better if I didn't do with other women what you can choose to do with the objects of your various desires in your "public" spaces. As Eve Sedgwick has written, "public names the space where cross-sex couples *may*, whenever they feel like it, display affection freely."[5]

Unlike queer theorists, however, you, my colleague, recognize that "public" is hardly a racially neutral concept, having a venerable history of meaning reserved for whites only. You recognize that "public" space is a space of control and surveillance that functions to discipline, to preclude, to foreclose, to hamper, the freedom of those who cannot pass the privilege spot check of the moment. (Remember the poetic justice of John Single-ton's exposing the refusal to screen his *Poetic Justice* in neighborhoods afraid to show anything that might actually interest a "less affluent element." Consider the penalties for diverse interracial looks.) Unlike white heterosexuals, you understand that since capital fattens itself on the bodies of labor, both reproduction and the very act of sex become instrumental. You understand that when sex itself is used to enforce hierarchies of power, privacy will never be a universal privilege. As Jackie Goldsby has written

[2] Valerie Smith, "Split Affinities: The Case of Interracial Rape," in *Conflicts in Feminism*, ed. Marianne Hirsch and Evelyn Fox Keller (New York: Routledge, 1990), 272.

[3] See, for example, King-Kok Cheung, "The Woman Warrior versus The Chinaman Pacific: Must a Chinese American Critic Choose between Feminism and Heroism?" in Hirsch and Keller, *Conflicts in Feminism*, 234–51.

[4] Barbara Smith, introduction to "And When You Leave, Take Your Pictures With You: Racism in the Women's Movement," in *This Bridge Called My Back: Writings by Radical Women of Color*, ed. Cherrie Moraga and Gloria Anzaldua (New York: Kitchen Table, 1981), 62.

[5] Eve Kosofsky Sedgwick, "Queer and Now," in *Wild Orchids and Trotsky: Messages from American Universities* (New York: Penguin, 1993), 249.

about African American culture in relation to nineteenth-century ideologies of race: "If (hetero)sex constituted a form of freedom, so did the right to keep it private. As long as black sexuality was a market commodity, white voyeurism was an always-present threat, as black sex was subject to public inspection ('interventions' made in the name of rape and lynching). Silence, then, affords a measure of control. . . ."[6]

Nonetheless, all of you heterosexuals tell me that you hope I can be realistic enough to understand that the wrong kind of look or touch or word in a public place will only attract the wrong kind of attention, and perhaps even violent assault. ("You're too happy," screamed the man who tried to run me and one of my lovers down with his car.) The implication is that if I'm not realistic in abiding by your terms for tolerating me in the public space that you control, I deserve exactly what I get. Yet any homosexual touch, even any homosexual thought, in what you insist is a sacred private place—the bedroom—merely places me in yet another unprotected area of your heterosexual architecture. You are already waiting for me, with all the force of the state, in the closet to which you banish me for what you say is my own good.

This means, among other things, that one or another of you will attempt in sundry furtive ways to have removed from casual view those pictures on your colleagues' office walls that you say will offend young or innocent or unsuspecting students, those pictures that you say will call unwanted attention to all artists dealing with risky material of wider political importance. It is our job, you would have us believe, to protect college students from the irreparable damage they might suffer in surprise encounters with representations of leather dykes or naked faggots with hard-ons. You remove the material by which we teach each other, and you, exactly how to fuck without dying. You have assumed, as teachers and parents, the privilege of protecting the young from what you yourself do not wish to see. Knowing that articulating a domain for ignorance adds up to the successful exercise of power, you collaborate in consigning the details of my culture to oblivion.

So there we are, just the two of us again, you in the castle of your skin, me in the temple of my desire. Neither of us is entirely to blame for this mess. Neither of us represents, or can be reduced to, our "culture" or our "people." We are, counterproductively and predictably, two pawns bickering on the margins. Inasmuch as power accrues to the center, and neither of us two middle-aged women will ever, ever, ever in our lives get there, we jockey for proximity, two more bitches in a catfight. Yet we know, having watched, how the margins are used by, and use, the mainstream. It's not always as egregious as the rhetorical impedimenta of Cultural Diversity

6 Jackie Goldsby, "Queen for 307 Days: Looking B(l)ack at Vanessa Williams and the Sex Wars," in Sisters, Sexperts, Queers: Beyond the Lesbian Nation, ed. Arlene Stein (New York: Penguin, 1993), 126.

Week (or month, or day). It's also the forced competition outside the Anglo center (preferably but not necessarily male, or straight): one minoritized culture fights against another, queers of color have to choose which minoritizing term is more *them* ("Did you invite me here to talk abut my orgasms or my people?" asks performance artist Camelita Tropicana), dykes have to fight gay men of any race for visibility (as Adriene Rich observed some time ago, lesbians are caught between two patriarchal cultures, homosexual and heterosexual), gays and lesbians of color battle the nauseating racism of their white counterparts, and so forth. Perhaps essentialism is attractive mainly because it is the most endurable position for the long haul: hybrid, compromised, paradoxical, doubled, punning, or passing identities take endless work and unrelenting self-consciousness, always with the threat of appropriation, never the relaxation of "authenticity."

Still, I insist on understanding your heterosexuality, an institution about which I claim the privilege of outrageous generalization. Not only are some of my best friends heterosexual, but I am hardly slumming: your heterosexuality is the world I have inhabited all my life. I want to talk about your homophobia, but even as I write the work again my pain dims to your abstraction. One pretentious clinical label gives no immunity against the stupid, brute fact of hatred. What is it that bothers you heterosexuals about us queers?—not the redneck neo-Nazi fundamentalist lunatic fringe, trotted out on every talk show to "balance" the compulsory spectacle of homosexuality, but you, the liberal, tolerant, educated, progressive, middle-class intelligentsia. You excuse, distance, and use those possessed by the more extreme forms of your own feelings, while using them for camouflage. Even though some of your best friends are gay or lesbian, why is it that you change the subject when I raise a queer topic, or when I ask you to speculate about the origins of homophobia? What is it exactly that you're not saying when you keep describing my people as "androgynous"? Why is it that you cannot look me straight in the eye when I use the word lesbian? Why do I know it would be better for our friendship if I didn't tell you that when your daughter becomes a dyke she will leave behind her a trail of deliciously broken hearts?

You cannot get your lips shaped around the word "queer," or else you mumble when you try to pronounce this one syllable, as if, I speculate, ambivalence has numbed your vocal cords. Or perhaps when you get your mouth around the word, the very muscles that give you speech produce the echo of other phrases, casually used: "queering the deal," "queer as a three-dollar bill," "smelling something queer," etc. You often worry about how effective I can be, because of my image, as a spokeswoman for our progressive, feminist causes. You suggest to me when students complain about my ideological slant, my bias toward an alternative life-style, my presentation of sexually explicit material, that, having pushed it, having made an issue of it, I ought not to be surprised at the repercussions. Your speech, which you confuse with our knowledge, can never be more than the sum total of the silences you decree.

"I don't see how heterosexuals stand to talk to each other for all those hours and hours," a passing friend and occasional drag queen once said to me. "They're *soooo* boring." Indeed, chronic erotophobia takes its toll on the art of conversation. From my side of the queer fence that it is impossible to straddle, you have designed a world in the image of your terror. For me to "make an issue" of my sexuality—to remind you firmly of the contrary when you assume that I am just like you except for what I do in private, that I am not at all like you except for what I imitate in private, that I either do (or do not) see all women as potential sexual objects, that I do (or do not) want children, that I do (or do not) really wish to be a man, that I do (or do not) hate men, that I do (or do not) get off on aspects of your fantasy life— in short, for me to insist on the specific pleasures of my sexual difference is to suggest to you that it is possible and necessary to speak, even enjoy speaking, of what you bury within the silence of your family or your pornography. For me to speak of sex, of what it is I like to do with or for or to other women, much less other "women," for me to insist that not to speak of it would be *your* problem, for me to fuck with your sacrosanct notions of gender (how can a queer lesbian speak otherwise?) is to suggest that your desires, like mine, could play sweet havoc, with the body politic. The closest you get these days is talking about "performing gender," but I have a hunch you haven't heard the applause yet.

You don't understand that heterosexuality is not what you do in bed, and that homosexuality isn't what I do in bed, either—or in bars, or baths, or basements. For me to attempt to subvert your thoughts is necessarily to pro- duce myself in your image of the unnatural, the spectacularly monstrous woman. For me to speak of sex is to make a spectacle of myself. To insist that queer sex can not only be spoken of, but more, that it is liberatory to speak of it in crass and kinky detail, will likely send you into a homosexual panic. Being a member of the intelligentsia you will not, of course, bludgeon me to death, or as close to it as you can manage, knowing that you can evade responsibil- ity for your own violence by taking uncontrollable revulsion as a legal defense. "Personally, I don't mind what it is you do in bed," all of you have said to me, in one way or another, displaying what you believe to be toler- ance while disinfecting the borders of your pluralism, "but it is not culture."

Since this is, sadly, not a fairy tale, you, my colleague, will go on to make alliances with the most reactionary of the old guard in order to run an anonymous smear campaign about a lesbian takeover. You will make lists of queer faculty and students to demonstrate bias. You will take queer students aside to explain to them that they are occupying more than their quota of space. After all, you like history, not theory. You conduct a witch hunt, in secret, while remaining a revolutionary in public, speaking eloquently and at length about justice and freedom.

Perhaps this would be an opportune moment to introduce all of you to Elephant Lesbian. Dressed in her very best finery, she would crowd you into her humble abode. She would explain through her thick British accent, while slurping loudly on her tea, that despite her appearance (and from this side of the fence, her appearance is awfully seductive), she is a human being, just like you. I think this character in *War on Lesbians* is video-maker Jane Cottis's brilliant invention, a strategic incursion on the mainstream that ought to vanquish with giggles all crusades to find more freaks to tolerate. But I suspect you wouldn't think it was funny, which is to say that you would call it didactic, or specialized, or obvious.

While I'm making introductions, those of you who are academically inclined may as well meet, if you haven't already encountered him in your closet, Elephant's friend Mr. Marlon Riggs, Miss Loud Snap-Happy Signifying Butch Girl, the latest hit in your world of "theory divas and culture queens." Mr. Riggs, whom you have appointed Race and Sexuality Resident Expert, suffers in equal proportions from the afflictions of being an artist, being black, and being queer. She wonders how, or whether, or why, or when to speak at all. She tells you what she knows you're thinking: "[D]oes she comprehend discursive intertextual analysis, can she engage in postfeminist, neo-Marxist, postmodern deconstructionist critique? Does she understand the difference between text, subtext, and metatext? Does she know she's part of a subaltern universe? Can she, in a word, *really* read?" She has your number: "My mouth moves, but you hear your own words."[7]

It's enough to drive anyone back to bed, but let's have a little more realness about that particular piece of furniture. For a middle-aged lesbian to speak of her sexual pleasures is also to make a spectacle of herself among her supposed allies in queerness, that is to say, young dykes and faggots. (Since their discovery of Queer Nation, homesteaders have stamped the new territory—artists, academics, and the manufacturers of commodified fantasy anxious to capture another market percentage. Everywhere one turns these days, there's another Q, from glossy magazines to academic journals to *Star Trek* to cars.) The Q word functions on an edge of explicit

[7] Marlon T. Riggs, "Unleash the Queen," in *Black Popular Culture: A Project by Michele Wallace*, ed. Gina Dent (Seattle: Bay Press, 1992), 99–105.

sex, and there, just as in the straight culture we queers don't want to share, **235** youth has the edge on visibility, and with it the edge on agency in sexual representation. Teresa de Lauretis and Sue Ellen Case and Eve Sedgwick and Judith Butler (though she's rated a fanzine called *Judy*[8]) simply do not have the same instant cultural zing as (*not!*) Madonna's fabulous tattooed pierced skinhead lesbian freaks, who, by the way, have names, Allistair Fate and Judie Tolentino. Even one of the latest lesbian attempts at making a conference which included talk about sex, and sex, rather than a lot of longwinded sublimation of desire—that is to say the L(esbians) U(ndoing) S(exual) T(aboos) conference held in New York in the fall of 1992— managed to incorporate the fortysomething crowd only in a panel about bed death. Pun intended, hardly anybody came.

And rare indeed is the young faggot (or old faggot, or faggot of any color) who works to overcome both his ambivalence about the bodies of women as well as hyperoblivious delirious fuckbuddy misogynist guy bonding in order to register the sexual agency of a middle-aged dyke. Caught between the maternal and the ridiculous, we partake fully and inexorably in the spectacle of the aging female body, which is to say that our sexuality is pushed to the margins, and we are relegated to the representational territory of unrequited loneliness, or, yawn, romantic love and flabby couplehood.

So there we are again, you and I, artist and writer, in our middle-aged female bodies, driven apart by this thing called family. My people, middle class and white, have built what they piously call family on the forced labor of a succession of underclasses, including your people. My people have broken all sorts of families in order to build our nasty little empires, foreign and domestic. What has historically been my "natural" privilege is precisely what you have fought to trace, to name, and to preserve. We both know these histories. Predictably, you insist on the transcendence of a privilege threatened, I resent the denial of a privilege once assumed. This does not mean that your culture is any more homophobic than mine. Inasmuch as sexuality is a racialized category, however, your middle-aged femaleness has been informed, though not determined, by a cultural nationalism that figures the family differently than mine. In defense against the empires of whiteness, race becomes, forcibly, a category of political identity invested with profound desires for authenticity, "disproportionately defined," in Paul Gilroy's words, "by ideas about nurturance, about family, about fixed gender roles, and generational responsibilities."[9]

Having blurred disparate, distinct national and ethnic identities into one great fiction called "color," having colored my own vision, where then am I positioned, as a middle-aged white (queer) lesbian, in relation to ideas

8 Not that Butler accepts the zine as an honor. The preface to *Bodies That Matter* takes exasperated issue with the use of "Judy," pointing to "a certain patronizing quality" and the effort to recall her to "an apparently evacuated femininity." See Judith Butler, *Bodies That Matter: On the Discursive Limits of "Sex"* (New York and London: Routledge, 1993), ix–x.

9 Paul Gilroy, "It's a Family Affair," in *Black Popular Culture: A Project by Michele Wallace*, ed. Gina Dent (Seattle: Bay Press, 1992), 307.

of whiteness? (By white, I mean an undertheorized signifier that does not refer to skin color but to the *trope* of race. One translation from theory into English: Clarence Thomas.) Writing inside this edifice, whiteness is a privilege I naturalize to invisibility, expediently and unconsciously, inasmuch as the successful performance of class, skin lightness, religion, education, etc., affords me access to privilege. Whiteness both organizes my knowledge and conceals itself as an object of my analysis: this whiteness, in Richard Dyer's words, "seems not to be there at all . . . secures its dominance by seeming not to be anything in particular."[10] The whiteness affords me, among other things, the right to look,[11] the right to speak, the expectation of being heard. This whiteness constructs me as a social being. This whiteness has been thoroughly sexualized. As Richard Fung points out, white culture, gay and straight, views "Asians" as undersexualized and "blacks" as hypersexualized. "Since whites fall squarely in the middle," he writes, "the position of perfect balance, there is no need for analysis, and they remain free of scrutiny."[12] This whiteness resists the most reasonable suggestion that, given the history of miscegenation, it is a complete fiction.[13] This whiteness makes me, historically and potentially, as much your oppressor, as a woman of "color," as any "white" man.

Writing inside this whiteness, I'm aware of a fear that my knowledge and my acknowledgment will align precisely with an institution and an insult called racism. I'm aware of a fear that speaking these issues will raise attack by those determined, for various complex reasons, to essentialize a fiction of social difference called race. "Whiteness" informs, however, but does not entirely describe or determine my subjectivity. After all, I'm stubborn, and I'm queer: I won't accept the condition of my skin as a terminal illness. I'm interested in shifting my place, speaking from both within and without these categories, from those queer locations where the codes don't quite read.

Yet at the same time, for you and me, something else functions between us, as women. As a white woman, I am in relation to white man the second and dependent term, the currency of exchange, the psychic dumping ground that shores up the boundaries of his identity. I function for you, perhaps, as a convenient displacement, less able to fight back, and less useful as an ally. I suspect that as a lesbian—that is, not a woman at all in a heterosexual (white) economy—I am an even easier target. Since you do not have to identify with me as woman, I can be doubly constructed as a white. As a member of the class of lesbian women, I am doubly removed from the white center.

This, of course, leaves your (and my) queer sisters and brothers in the middle of a minefield, not a mantra, declining their (non)choices while

[10] Richard Dyer, "White," *Screen* 29, no. 4 (Autumn 1988): 44.

[11] The phrase belongs to Jane Gaines, in her thorough critique of white feminist film theory, "White Privilege and Looking Relations: Race and Gender in Feminist Film Theory," *Screen* 29, no. 4 (Winter 1988): 24.

[12] Richard Fung, "Looking for My Penis: The Eroticized Asian in Gay VideoPorn," in *How Do I Look?*, ed. Bad Object-Choices (Seattle: Bay Press, 1991), 145–46.

[13] See, for example, Adrian Piper, "Passing for White, Passing for Black," *Transition* 58 (1992): 4–32.

picking their way through the undetonated bombs of whiteness, family, nation, culture. In this territory, camp takes on a multitude of other meanings, some of which are a drag and some of which suggest an enormous potential for transformation.

How to put an end to what is not a fairy tale? We won't live happily ever after, but here's a shopping list for the road.

1. Since we queers are notorious workaholics, we make changes in the very fabric of what there is to be learned. Instead of waiting until it's too late, we start in kindergarten, and we get copious federal funding to help us figure out how to teach complex pleasures to the young. We'll demolish the edifice that has enforced the institution of heterosexuality by the hysterical, panicked repression of talk about bodies, about sexuality, about pleasure, a repression increasingly evident in the classroom, where the institutional machinery deployed to contain sexual harassment is increasingly marshaled against the representation, verbal or visual, of any material about sexuality. When our children hit college, they will encounter, if they haven't already, the work of a very queer list. Besides the characters in the footnotes to this essay, among them will be Richard Fung, Cheryl Dunye, Cecilia Dougherty and Leslie Singer, Cherrie Moraga, Shu Lea Cheang, Thomas Harris, Lyle Harris, Fred Wilson, Millie Wilson, Kobena Mercer, Isaac Julien, Essex Hemphill, Michelle Parkerson, Pratibha Parma, Marga Gomez, Glenn Ligon, Sapphire, Gloria Anzaldua, Sadie Benning, Ray Navarro, Laura Aguilar, David Cabrera, Len Miller, Meena Nanji, Octavia Butler, Samuel Delaney, Kate Bornstein, Dorothy Allison, zines like *Pocho*, *Judy*, *I ♥ Amy Carter*, and *Hothead Paisan*, the Five Lesbian Brothers, Pomo Afro Homos, Hunter Reynolds, the Sisters of Perpetual Indulgence, Deb Kass, Guillermo Gomez-Pena and Coco Fusco, Doug Ischar, Bob Flanagan, Eileen Myles, Jewel Gomez, Douglas Crimp, Dionne Brand, Jamaica Kincaid, Hilton Als, David Wojnarowicz, Nan Goldin, Catherine Opie, George Lamming, Claude McKay, Minnie Bruce Pratt, Joanna Russ, Yvonne Rainer, Greg Bordowitz, Leslie Feinberg, Gayle Rubin, Annie Sprinkle, bell hooks, Joan Nestle, James Baldwin. . . .

2. That partial, even whimsical, list would be the beginning of our core curriculum. We'd call it "Bending the Canon." We would, for example, make up a course called "Chopping the Phobia off Homophobia: Home Economics Remodeled." We would start with the erotic, specifically the essays of Audre Lorde. Writing in 1978, without ever once using the L word, her insistence on erotic truth is, in retrospect, fiercely queer. "[T]hat deep and irreplaceable knowledge of my capacity for joy," she writes, "comes to demand of all my life that it be lived within the knowledge that such a satisfaction is possible." It's part of our home economics course because Lorde

makes her statement penetrate with an extraordinary domestic memory, resonant in its lubricious reversals of private and public, whiteness and color:

> During World War II, we bought sealed plastic packets of white, uncolored margarine, with a tiny, intense pellet of yellow coloring perched like a topaz just inside the clear skin of the bag. We would leave the margarine out for a while to soften, and then we would pinch the little pellet to break it inside the bag, releasing the rich yellowness into the soft pale mass of margarine. Then taking it carefully between our fingers, we would knead it gently back and forth, over and over, until the color had spread through the whole pound bag of margarine, thoroughly coloring it.[14]

Since it's home ec time, this would be followed by a rereading of Virginia Woolf, a white lesbian whose critique of the workings of privilege has been vastly underestimated, on making bread.

3. We queers get to stop playing your idea of the political, which can only be separated from the spiritual by erasing the political's roots in community, and enjoy the formal, aesthetic, decorative, and obsessive pleasures of our queer obsessions. What fascinates us is never trivial. As Eve Sedgwick writes of literature: "We [queers] needed for there to be [cultural] sites where meanings didn't tidily line up with one another, and we learned to invest those sites with fascination and love. . . . For me, a kind of formalism . . . was one way of trying to appropriate what seemed the numinous and resistant power of the chosen objects."[15]

4. Working at those points and intersections where racism (or homophobia, or sexism) does *not* entirely describe us to ourselves, we queer not just the idea of nation but of family, of culture, of race, of state. We take care to make the strategically pleasurable alliances for which we are notorious.

5. We take, and make, the language we need to speak and hear, the representations by which we see and are seen. We think about Samuel Delaney's map of straight talk and street talk, the one marking learning while concealing the violence of privilege, the other marking a banal and repetitious ignorance that conceals fact, wisdom, and poetry.[16] We believe Delaney when he says that these are issues of life and death, so we intuit that the moral to the story involves, at the least, some healthy skepticism about all our many voices. We give our greatest intelligence to refusing expediently constructed borders between the languages of theory and history, between theoretician and artist, between academic and creator, between intellectual and anti-intellectual. Most of all, we take to heart the words of Mikhail Bakhtin, quietly queering his assumptions about gender:

14 Audre Lorde, "The Uses of the Erotic: The Erotic as Power" (Paper delivered at the Berkshire Conference in 1978), in *The Lesbian and Gay Studies Reader*, ed. Henry Abelove, Michele Aina Barale, and David M. Halperin (New York: Routledge, 1993), 339–43. The title of this class is, of course, a play on Jewelle L. Gomez and Barbara Smith, "Taking the Home out of Homophobia: Black Lesbian Health," in *Piece of My Heart: A Lesbian of Colour Anthology* (Toronto: Sister Vision, 1991). See also Gloria Anzaldua's "Fear of Going Home: Homophobia," in *Borderlands/La Frontera: The New Mestiza* (San Francisco: Spinsters, 1987), 20.
15 Sedgwick, "Queer and Now," 242.
16 Samuel Delaney, "Street Talk/Straight Talk," *differences* 5, no. 2 (Summer 1991): 21–38.

Language, for the individual consciousness, lies on the borderline between oneself and the other. The word in language is half someone else's. It becomes "one's own" only when the speaker populates it with her own intention, her own accent, when she appropriates the word, adapting it to her own semantic and expressive intention. Prior to this moment of appropriation, the word does not exist in a neutral and impersonal language . . . but rather it exists in other people's mouths, in other people's contexts, serving other people's intentions: it is from there that one must take the word, and make it one's own.[17]

[17] Mikhail Bakhtin, quoted in Henry Louis Gates, Jr., editor's introduction, "Writing 'Race' and the Difference It Makes," in *"Race," Writing, and Difference*, ed. Henry Louis Gates, Jr. (Chicago: University of Chicago Press, 1986), 1.

Crossing Over: Reimagining and Reimaging

242

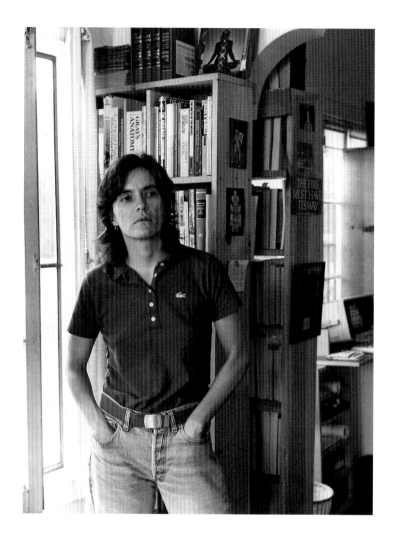

My latina side infuses my lesbian side with chispa
& pasión. I am a lifelong lesbian and I think that
women hold powerful promise for changing conditions
on the planet. You think I look hostile? Maybe
it has to do with a passion for and an impatience
with a vision. Maybe it comes from comparing
what could be with what is. ¡! Y qué?!

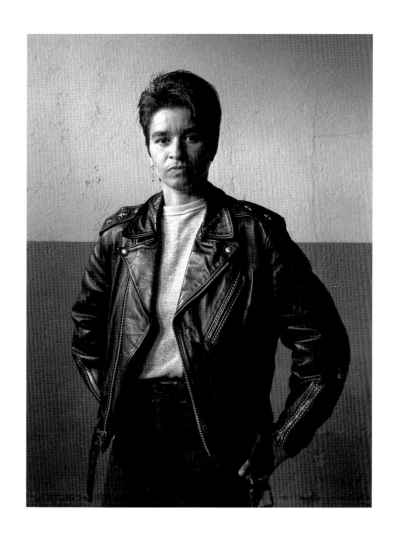

My mother encouraged me to be a
court reporter...
I became a lawyer

Carla Barboza Esq.

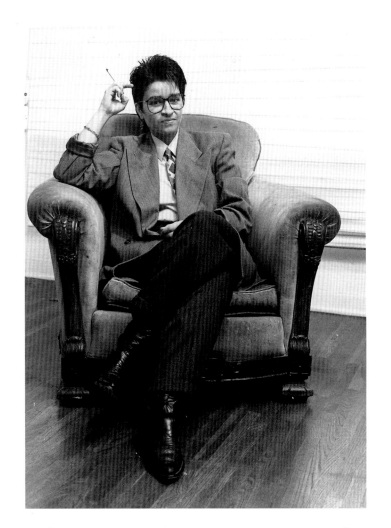

I used to worry about
being different.
Now I realize my differences
are my strengths.

Carla

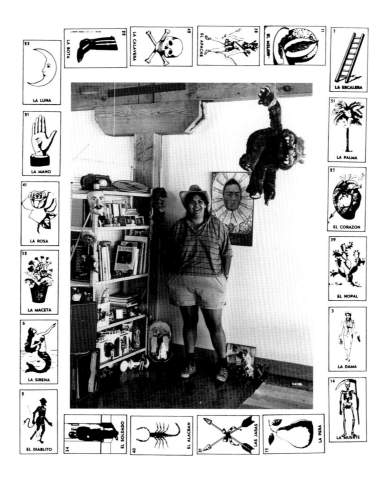

I'm not comfortable with the word Lesbian but as each day go's by I'm more and more comfortable with the word LAURA. I know some people see me as very child like, naive. Maybe so. I am. But I will be damned if I let this part of me die!

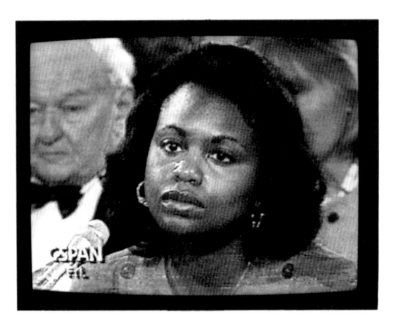

Hero

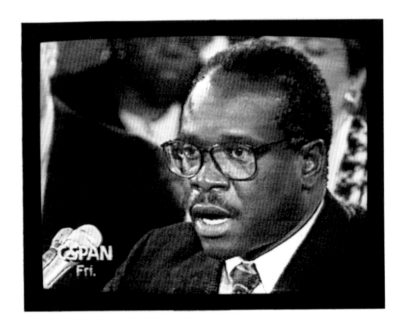

Lech

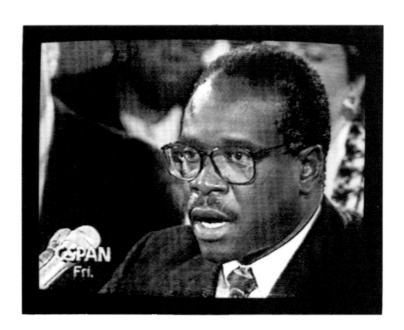

Victim

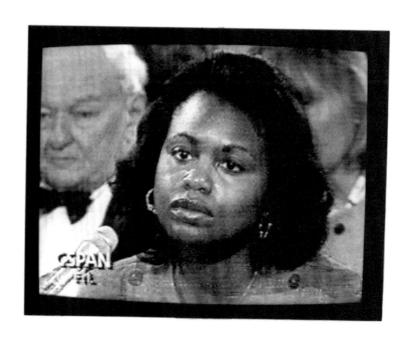

Pawn

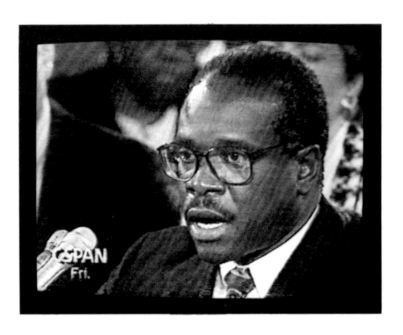

Uncle Tom

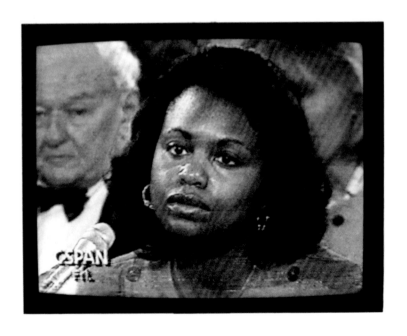

Lesbian

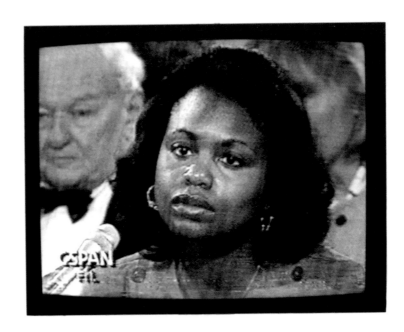

Uppity

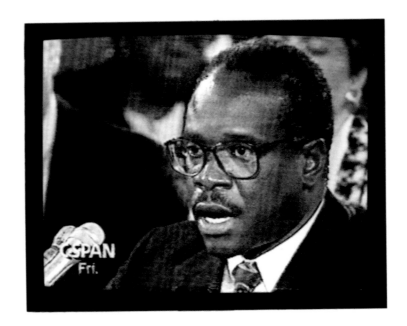

Stud

Carm Little Turtle   from *Earthman Series*

Earthman Playing Chihuahua Love Songs He
Thought He Heard in Taos

250

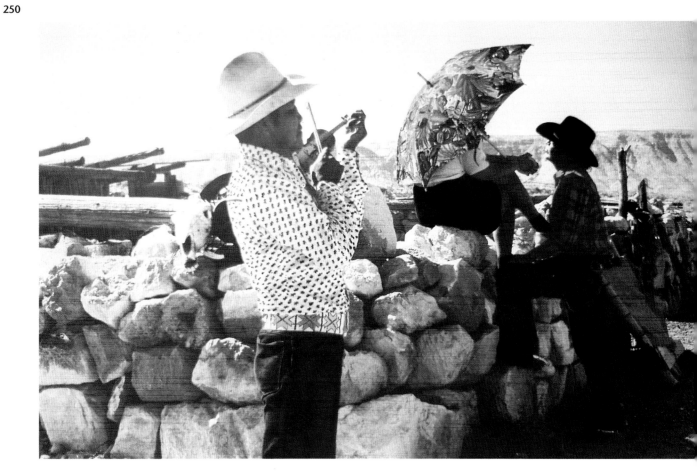

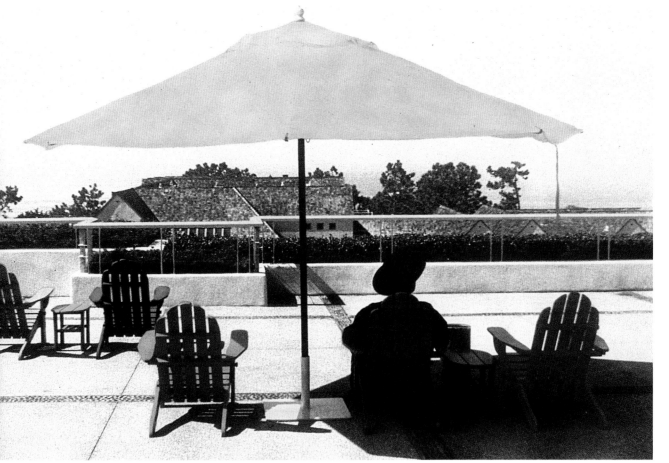

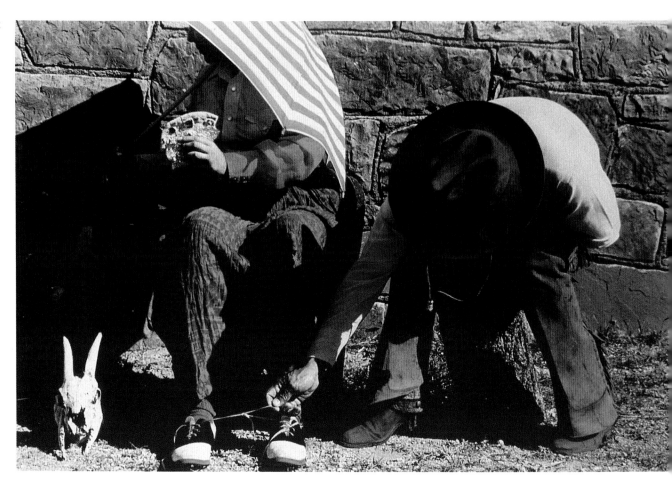

Earthman Thinking About Dancing with
Woman from Another Tribe

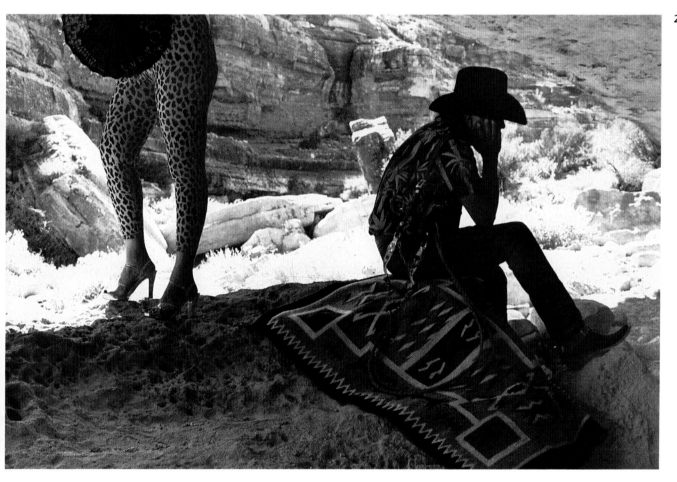

Chief

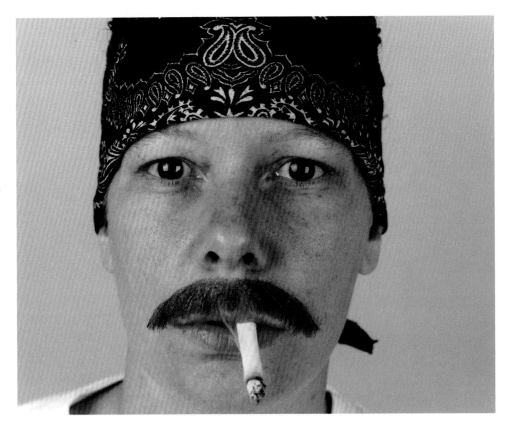

254

Whitey

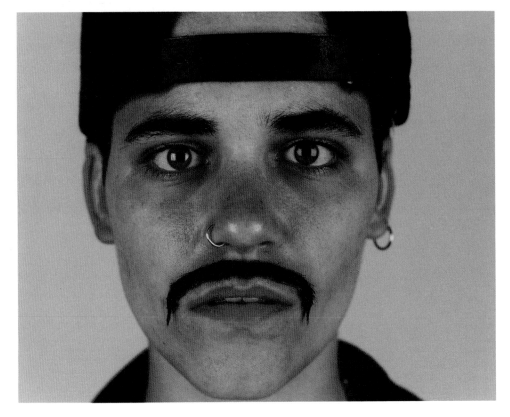

Chicken

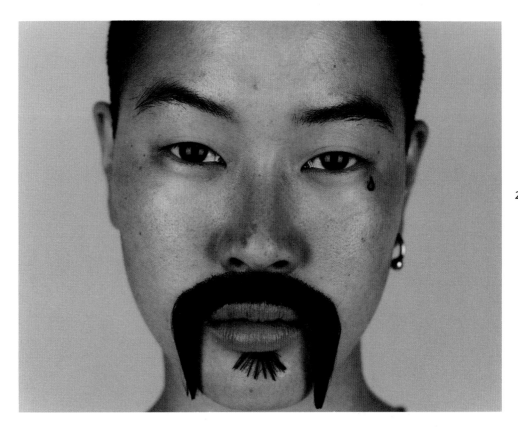

255

Oso Bad

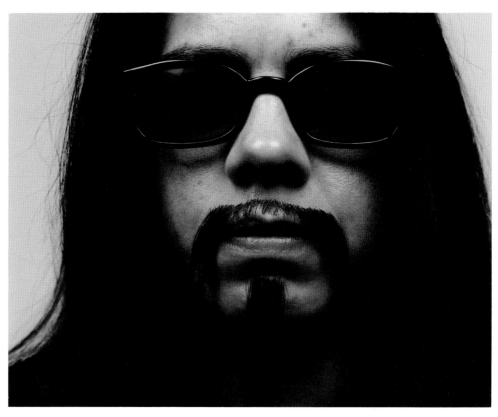

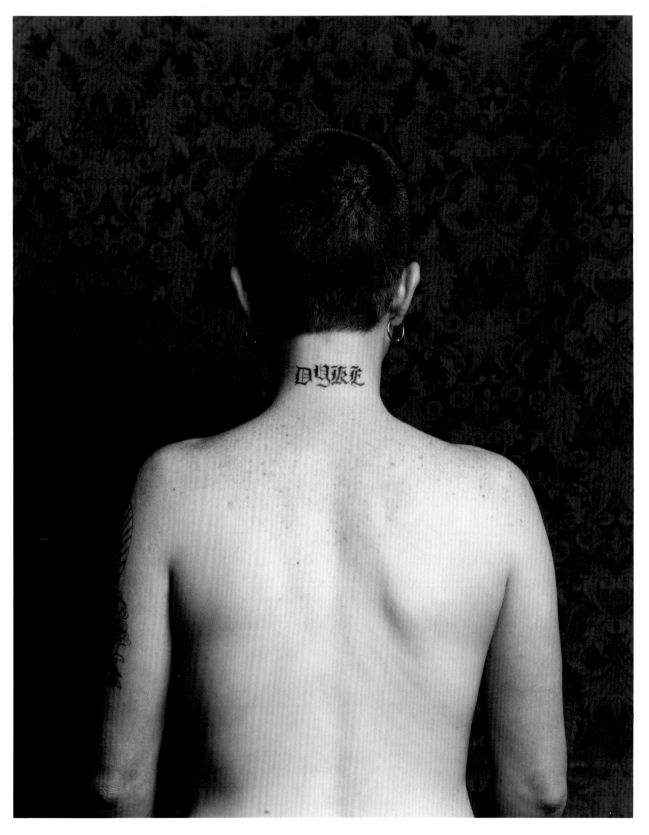

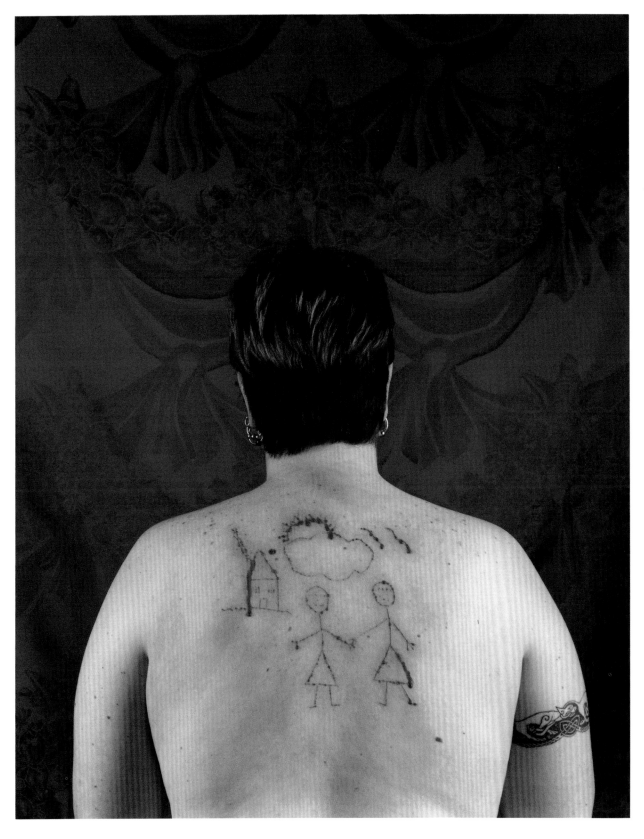

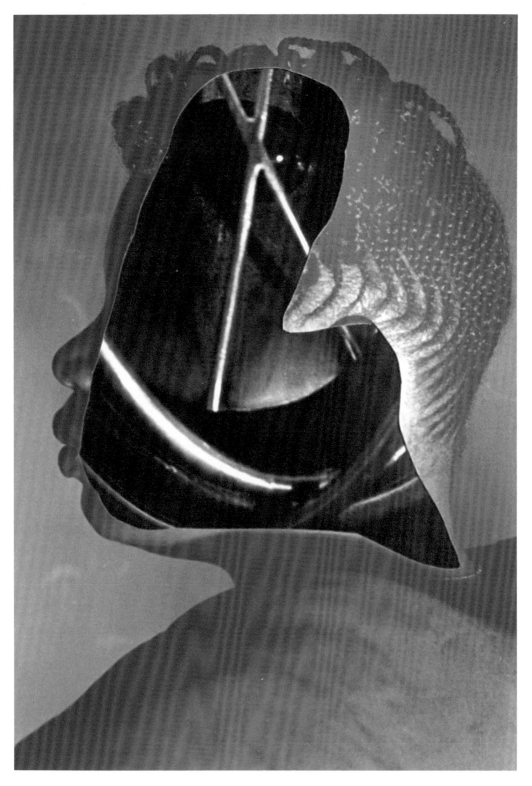

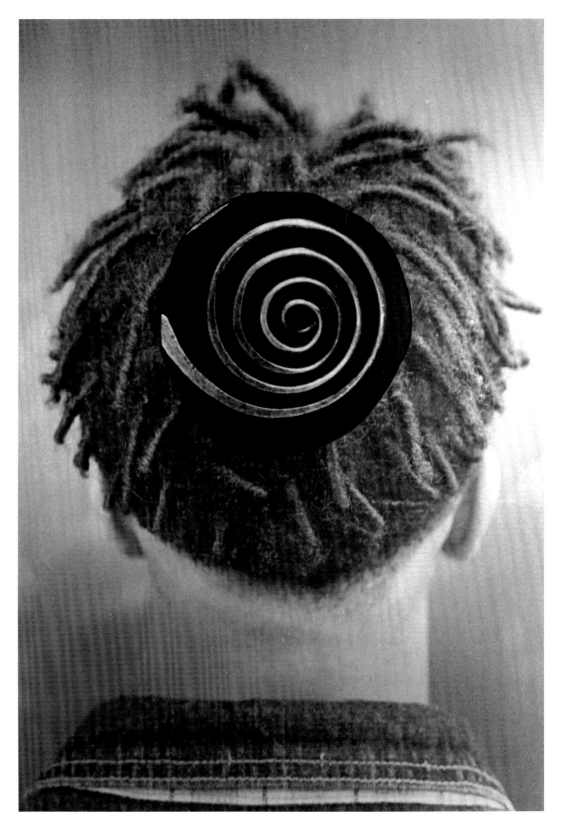

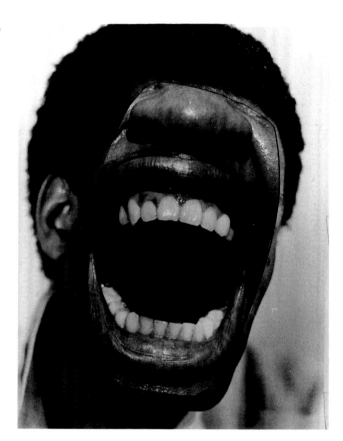

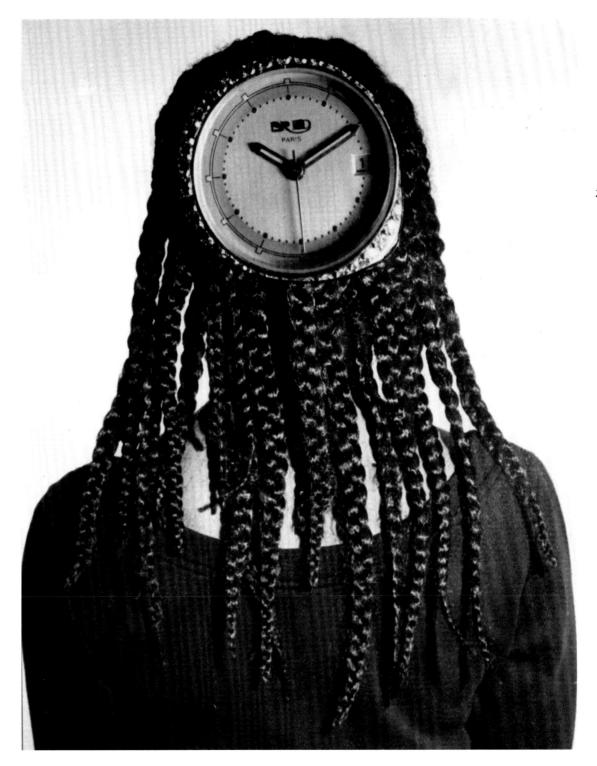

262

"Racism is a visual pathology,"[1] notes African American artist and philosopher Adrian Piper, and Asian Americans have been victims of the visual pathology of racism since coming to this country in the 1800s. The late nineteenth- and early twentieth-century hysteria of Asians taking over the United States was named the "Yellow Peril," for the perceived color of Asian skin, and a famous caricature from World War II, entitled "How to Spot a Jap," gave explicit visual instructions on perceiving the supposedly distinct physical differences between the benevolent Chinese, who were allies of the United States in World War II, and the evil Japanese.

Throughout the twentieth century Asians and Asian Americans have been rigidly stereotyped in popular literature such as Sax Rohmer's *Fu Manchu* series, and in film and television, from the sexless inanities of Charlie Chan and Mr. Moto to the superhuman martial arts achievements of Bruce Lee. Asian women in particular operate under the burden of meeting the double expectations perpetuated by the popular media—to fill the mythical shoes of seductive temptresses such as Anna May Wong and Suzie Wong while simultaneously upholding the legend of the docile and subservient geisha girl.

In the work of the Asian American women artists examined here, photography allows each artist to reclaim her identity and her self-image in the face of aggressive stereotyping. The mechanical medium of photography allows these artists to fight fire with fire, utilizing the language and power of the photographic image to correct imbalances in representations of Asian Americans. The artists often directly confront and dispel false images, exposing the lie of stereotypes and one-dimensional caricatures through manipulation and appropriation of source material. They also create a new visual legacy for Asian Americans by defining themselves on their own terms, in their own visual language, and by countering and contradicting the fallacies of popular culture and the predominant beliefs these fallacies reflect.

Betty Lee

Chinese American photographer Betty Lee, currently living and working in Los Angeles, uses photography, text, images from Chinese and Hollywood films, and archival photographs to redefine images of Asian Americans. Born and raised in Illinois, Lee discovered at an early age the contradictions and complexities of the mediated image. In a letter to the author written in 1993, Lee stated, "I am in love with the power of the photograph because as a child it was the best means I had to the outside world. In a small town in the Midwest we were the only Asian family in our community. I spoke

[1] Adrian Piper, "The Critique of Pure Racism," *Afterimage* 18, no. 3 (Oct. 1990).

Betty Lee
Miss America, 1989
black-and-white photograph,
40″ × 50″.

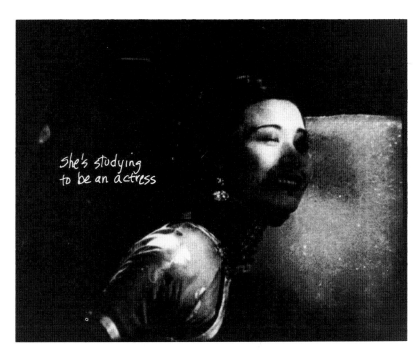

Chinese at home and English was my second language. But the visual language in photography became the ticket to the outer world."[2]

Lee also noted the importance of popular photography in her choice of media, and recounted her ultimate realization of the falsity of those images. "I was profoundly influenced by the work of photojournalists of the 50s and 60s and the visual reportage in *Life* magazine had a tremendous impact on why I chose photography as my preferred medium," she recalled in the letter. "Ironically, I now criticize how these images are used in the media and advertising in my own work, and how it skewers representations of Asians and Asian Americans."

Her early series of large black-and-white photographs, consisting of collages of images from mid-twentieth-century Chinese cinema and hand-written texts, testifies to the nefarious influence of popular culture in distorting identity and self-image.

Why the Wongs Won't Name Their Daughters Susie (1989, gelatin silver print, 40″ × 50″) refers to the indelible stereotype of the Asian good-time girl, the hooker with a heart of gold, as portrayed in the seminal Hollywood film, *The World of Suzie Wong.* In it a Chinese woman mournfully regards the text, "the belief you become what you are called," asserting the Chinese conviction that the spoken word has the power to affect reality. *Miss*

[2] Betty Lee, letter to author, 1993.

America (1989, gelatin silver print, 40″ × 50″), shows a Chinese woman wearing traditional dress, her face obscured by shadow; across the face of the photograph are written the words, ''she's studying to be an actress.'' This piece refers to the beauty queen mythos as a commentary on women's socialization and the futility of Asian women attempting to fit the model of the buxom blue-eyed blonde. *Grace in Rear Window* (1989, gelatin silver print, 40″ × 50″), a simple collage of an Asian woman's head on Grace Kelly's body, languorously reclining before Jimmy Stewart's admiring gaze, is another poignant comment on the impossibility of Asian women achieving the false ideal of the all-American woman.

Lee's later series, *Contemplation of the Journey Home*, uses rephotographed photocollages to question the Eurocentrism of mainstream culture. Of these images she has written, ''As a Chinese-American I have always been compelled by issues dealing with two intertwined but different heritages. [This series] is a search for personal history that is critical because, [viewed] as a Chinese-American, the representation that abounds in our popular culture is not entirely relevant to me. My goal is to address these issues and hopefully project some of the complexities of race and culture that are not always apparent'' (letter to the author).

The Temple of Amah (1990, gelatin silver print, 40″ × 50″) juxtaposes an image of Lee's grandmother (*amah*, in Chinese) with Greek and Roman statuary and urns. Here Lee usurps ''classical'' Western history with personal identity. *The Centurion* (1990, gelatin silver print, 40″ × 50″) portrays a Chinese American soldier standing on top of severed heads from classical statuary, while *Contemplation of the Journey Home* (1990, gelatin silver print, 40″ × 50″) floats several Chinese American elders above the ruins of a Roman temple.

By topping these icons of Western civilization with images from her personal history, Lee makes a statement about the dominance of European culture and her wish to upset that balance of power. In correspondence with the author she noted, ''So much of the visual representation in popular media, education, and the arts reflect what is basically rooted in Western culture. The rest of us are rendered invisible.'' In this series Lee turns the cultural scheme of things upside down, giving us the Chinese American version of the hierarchy and significance of specific cultural icons.

Diane Tani

Born and raised in San Francisco, Diane Tani uses color photography, photosculptures, and public art to address issues of personal identity and political empowerment.

Diane Tani
Duel, 1989
color photograph, 20″ × 16″.

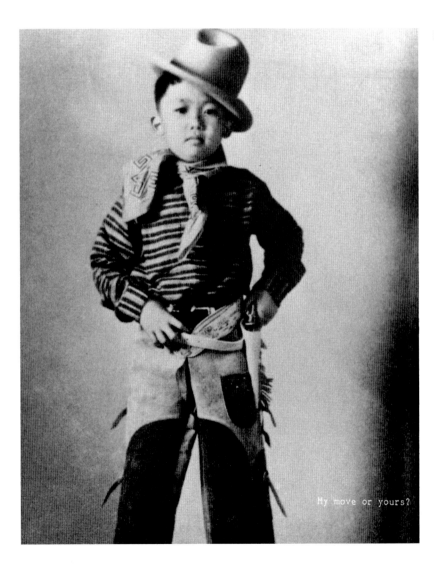

She notes, "My work has developed from the personal and the explan-
atory to the public and provoking. It is no longer sufficient to define myself,
alone and isolated. It is important to recognize the circumstances in which
we all live and interact."[3] This statement reflects Tani's awareness of the
power of the image to influence public thought and opinion, and the interaction of art, politics, and social concerns in her work as an Asian American
photographer.

[3] Diane Tani, artist's statement.

Tani's earlier work dealt directly with countering pervasive stereotypes of Asians in popular culture, which many perceived as harmlessly entertaining caricatures. In her artist's statement she said, "I question the image and identity of Asian Americans, specifically, and the acceptance of these portrayals, generally. I wish to attack stereotypes and the complacent acceptance of them." Tani's series of chromagenic photographs appropriates images from advertising, film, and television, often inverting or altering each photograph's chroma or otherwise manipulating the original image. Laid over these images are statements dealing with racial and identity politics, often in terse, declarative sentences that mask the underlying tensions the sentiments belie. *Communique* (1989, chromagenic photograph, 16" × 20") juxtaposes a rephotographed black-and-white video image of a classic geisha girl and a sword-wielding samurai with the plaintive text, "The only ones I knew were from television." *Stereotype* (1989, chromagenic photograph, 16" × 2-") also uses a rephotographed video image, of a man poised to thrust a knife, seppuku-style, into his belly , with the text, "the term oriental may not seem derogatory but the public had a long time to associate it with a multitude of stereotypes—charlie chan, suzie wong, madame butterfly." The scan lines from the video source tape emphasize the artificiality of the image, which is underscored by Tani's text spelling out the pervasiveness of racist misconceptions.

More subtly stated is *Duel* (1989, chromagenic photograph, 20" × 16"). In this enlarged snapshot an Asian American boy about six years old, duded up cowboy style in chaps, a bandanna, and a five-gallon hat, stands ready to draw his six-shooter from the toy holster slung over his hips. The boy stares challengingly at the camera, his gaze emphasizing the text, which inquires, "My move or yours?" Here Tani uses Western conceits of masculinity to articulate a radical Asian American sensibility, reclaiming the upper hand in the struggle for self-determination and self-articulation.

Tani's most recent work with the Women's Work project in San Francisco also emphasizes the empowerment of a traditionally disenfranchised population, namely, women who have been victims of domestic violence. Commissioned by women's apparel manufacturer Liz Claiborne, Inc., in an interesting collaboration among the corporate clothing manufacturer, social service agencies, and visual artists, including Tani,[4] Women's Work placed artists with various domestic violence organizations to create a body of work that was displayed in bus shelters and on billboards throughout San Francisco.

Working with the Asian Women's Shelter, Tani created a series of photographs that combined images and text, translated into Korean, Chinese, and English, that addressed the cause and effect of domestic

[4] Other participating artists included Barbara Kruger, Carrie Mae Weems, Susan Meisalas, and Margaret Crane/ Jon Winet.

violence. Through this process she gave voice to the women in the shelters while dealing with her own misconceptions about battered women. Of this work she has said, "I confronted my own myths about domestic violence; instead of fractured, broken women I saw empowerment, sustenance, resolution" (artist's statement). One image in the series, a woman's arms folded defensively over her belly with text that states, "Every 15 seconds a woman is beaten by her partner," simply and forcefully recounts the prevalence of abuse, while the tag line in the corner of the billboard listing the phone number of a local domestic violence hotline offers a chance for escape.

Another piece deals with the cycle of violence from parent to child. Placed in bus shelters in predominantly Asian American neighborhoods in San Francisco, the piece includes an image of a wide-eyed Asian child with the statistics, "91% of abused women say that their children have seen their beatings. 63% of all abusers have seen their mothers abused or were abused as children. They Look, Listen, Learn, and Repeat." In her statement, Tani wrote, "We decided that an image with a child was important in licking domestic violence—a controlling tactic between partners—with child abuse and the cyclical nature of learned behavior along with emphasizing the effect family violence has on the entire family." Tani noted the collaborative nature of the decision-making process as well as the extensive consideration of the broader social concerns that led to the creation of the piece. Both process and result in the Women's Work project meshed with Tani's existing concerns for using creative work as a means for social commentary, empowerment, and cooperative image-making.

Yong Soon Min
Korean-born artist Yong Soon Min immigrated to the United States as a child, thus making her a member of the "1.5" generation, the term for Korean Americans born overseas but primarily raised and educated in the United States. This generation feels it is somewhere in between their parents' generation, which grew up in Korea, and those Korean Americans born and raised in the United States.

Addressing her generational hybridization, Min's proactive and politically charged work deals with issues of identity, acculturation, and self-articulation, attempting to present a true and accurate portrayal of concerns of the Asian American community. She states, "In order to ensure that our distinct voices are heard in the groundswell of a multicultural chorus, we must stand our ground and assert the value of our own personal and collective experience."[5] In *Defining Moments* (1992, series of six gelatin silver prints, 20" × 16") Min uses a silhouette of her own head and upper

[5] Yong Soon Min, "Comparing the Contemporary Experiences of Asian American, South Korean and Cuban Artists," in *Asian Americans: Comparative and Global Perspectives*, ed. Shirley Hune, Hyung-chan Kim, Stephen S. Fujita, and Amy Ling (Pullman: Washington State Press, 19XX), 285.

268   **Yong Soon Min**
from ***Defining Moments,*** #4:
Kwang Ju Massacre,   1992
black-and-white photograph,
20″ × 16″.

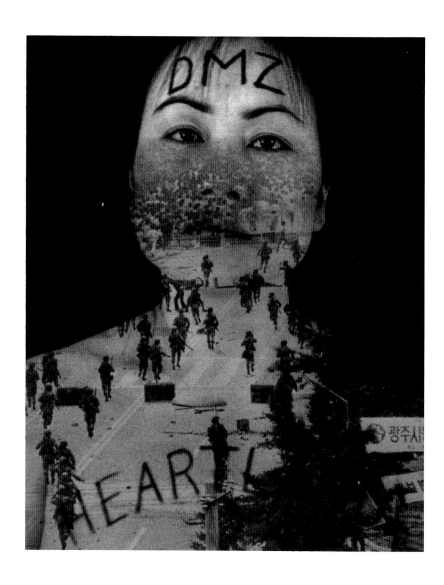

body overlaid with images of significant events in her personal and cultural
history, including the year of her birth, which also marked the end of the
Korean War; the date of the Kwang Ju student uprising in Korea in the
1980s; and the date of 1993's Los Angeles civil unrest, which occurred on
Min's birthday. She notes the connection between her personal history and
a broader Korean experience, stating, "The importance of history in formu-

lating my own identity is undeniable. Once I felt I had a grasp of alternative history, a history of my Korean roots that was denied or suppressed, that there was a role model, it gave me incredible strength. You realize that you have this connection and that you are a part of this continuum."[6] By using her own body in *Defining Moments* as a site for historical events Min literally remaps her identity, finding within her own physical existence the history and memories of her culture's conscience.

The artist's book *Occupied Territories* (1991, accordian-style book, 3" × 5" pages), created in collaboration with Allan de Souza, further uses the body as a place of political and social significance. Throughout the book are photographs of Min's and de Souza's nude torsos, smooth and hairy, printed in positive and negative, which are overlaid with coiled barbed wire and typewritten text. Referring to Min's and de Souza's respective origins as Korean American and South Asian via England, the text on one page reads, "From the far corners of Asia / with our own histories / territories of occupation and division / internally exiled / on either side of the Atlantic." Again in this piece Min and de Souza emphasize the merging of the personal and the political, articulating their perspective as Asians of the diaspora.

Min's large-scale installation work, which uses photography as one element among many, also traces personal history as a means of examining social and political concerns. In *deCOLONIZATION* (1991, mixed media installation), images include a repeated print of a Korean woman and little girl, with the men in the original family picture cropped out, and a photograph of a girl in traditional Korean dress standing in front of a military vehicle. A Mylar overlay spells out the word OCCUPIED in cutout letters, while the text partially reads, "I'm your mama san, miss saigon, mail order bride— I'm yours." Here the litany of stereotypes obscuring the photograph suggests the imposition of Western thought on Asian cultural values. Another overlay relates a letter from mother to daughter recalling the beginnings of a military action near their home that changed their lives, again implying the merging of personal and global history.

Min also uses photography as a metaphor for the socialization of values and mores in *Make Me* (1989, four-part photographic installation, 20" × 16" each), which manipulates photographs of Min's hands and face by splitting, mirroring, and joining the two halves of the image to form a distorted portrait. Cut-out block letters over the rearranged visages spell out the phrases "model minority," "assimilated alien," "objectified other," and "exotic immigrant." These phrases, combined with various hand gestures suggesting silence, submission, and pulled-up "oriental" eyes, indicate the suppressed anger and frustration caused by the words literally carved into Min's image.

[6] Yong Soon Min, "Home Is Not a Birthplace . . . ," *Korean American Community* (July 13, 1991).

Broader Applications

In addition to their individual creative production, Lee, Tani, and Min are also involved with various artists' organizations in their respective home bases. Through these organizations they expand on the progressive concerns evident in their creative work, giving these beliefs broader social and political applications. In California Lee is a board member of the Society for Photographic Education's Western Region and served as an organizer for the 1992 Western Regional Conference. She has spoken widely on issues of identity and the creation of a collective self-image at venues throughout the country, including the Conference on Visual Literacy and the College Art Association's 1993 conference.

In San Francisco Tani is a member of the Asian American Women Artists' Association (AAWAA), an artists' organization that works for the visibility and support of its associates. In collaboration with art historian Moira Roth, Tani is active with *Visibility Press*, a small press that has published limited-edition catalogues of artists Bernice Bing, Betty Kano, Brian Tripp, and Flo Wong. Through these activities Tani merges her aesthetic and social concerns, as a cultural worker promoting the advancement of the Asian American artists community.

In New York City Min is active in *Godzilla*, the Asian American artists' collective that publishes a newsletter, holds monthly meetings, and advocates for Asian American visual artists. Among their activities last year was a successful protest surrounding the absence of Asian American visual artists in the 1992 Whitney Biennial. As a result of their actions, artists exhibiting in the 1993 biennial included Asian Americans Christine Chang, Shu Lea Cheang, and Kip Fulbeck, among others. Min also cites the significance of the Min Joong (people's art) movement in South Korea as a model for artist-activists who combine collective political action with the creation of a progressive cultural aesthetic.

In their creative work and their work in the artistic community these artists have begun to reverse some of the damage wrought by popular culture on the image and identity of Asian Americans. By reappropriating the language and power of the photograph, and by manipulating negative imagery, pop culture icons and stereotypical representations, they have turned the tables on their oppressors. They have taken the means of their degradation and redirected them, turning them around and creating a new lexicon and iconography of an Asian American aesthetic.

For these artists photography becomes a weapon for righting the indignities of the long history of wrongdoing against their community. Their mastery of the master's tools gives them the ability to present a more accurate, eloquent expression of Asian American histories and voices.

Rerepresenting Representation

ARTWORKS

Ann Fessler — *Ancient History/Recent History*
Betty Lee — from *Contemplation of the Journey Home*
Deborah Bright — *The Management of Desire*
Diane Neumaier — from *Metropolitan Tits*
Susan Jahoda — from *Theatres of Madness*
Mary Kelly — from *Corpus*

ESSAY

Abigail Solomon-Godeau — Representing Women: The Politics of Self-Representation

ANCIENT HISTORY
RECENT HISTORY

An Ongoing Examination of
Art History Survey Texts
by

Ann Fessler

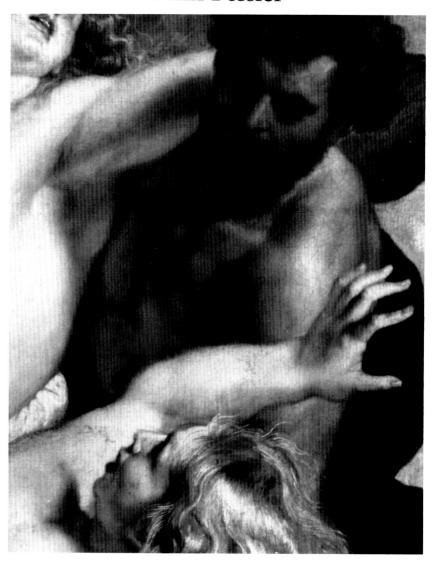

"His *Rape of the Daughters of Leucippus* . . . recalls forcibly Titian's *Rape of Europa*. . . . The act of love by which Castor and Pollux, sons of Jupiter, uplift the moral maidens from the ground draws the spectator upward in a mood of rapture. . . ."

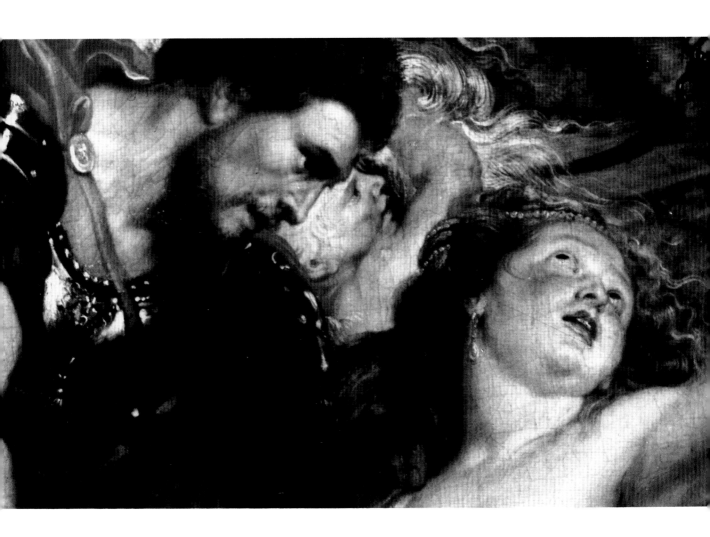

The female types . . . are traversed by a steady stream of energy. .

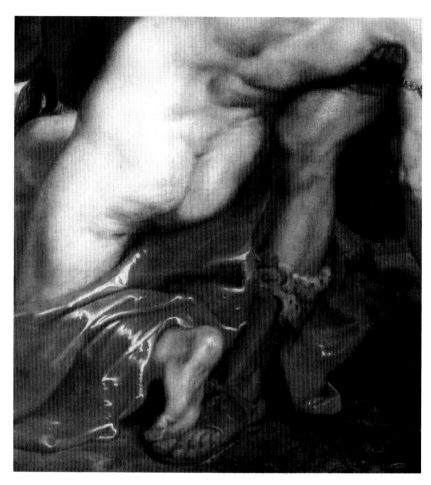

The low horizon increases the effect of a heavenly ascension, natural enough since this picture . . . constitutes a triumph of divine love;

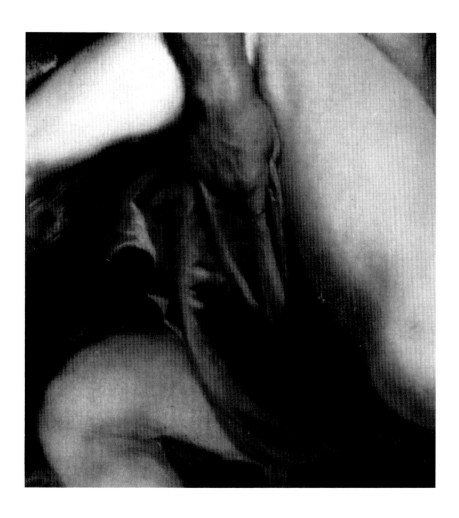

the very landscape heaves and flows in response to the excitement of the event."

Frederick Hartt, *Art: A History of Painting, Drawing, and Architecture*, 3rd ed. (New York: Harry N. Abrams, 1989).

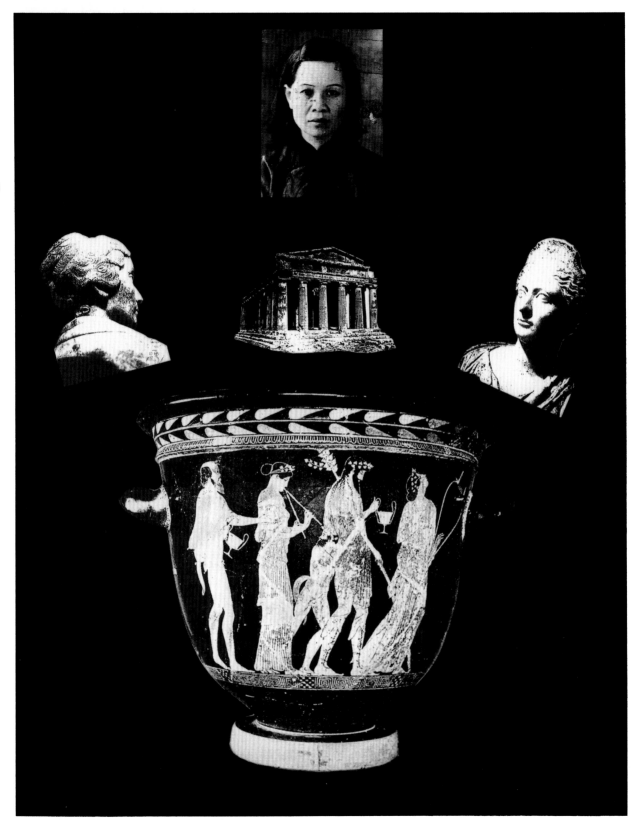

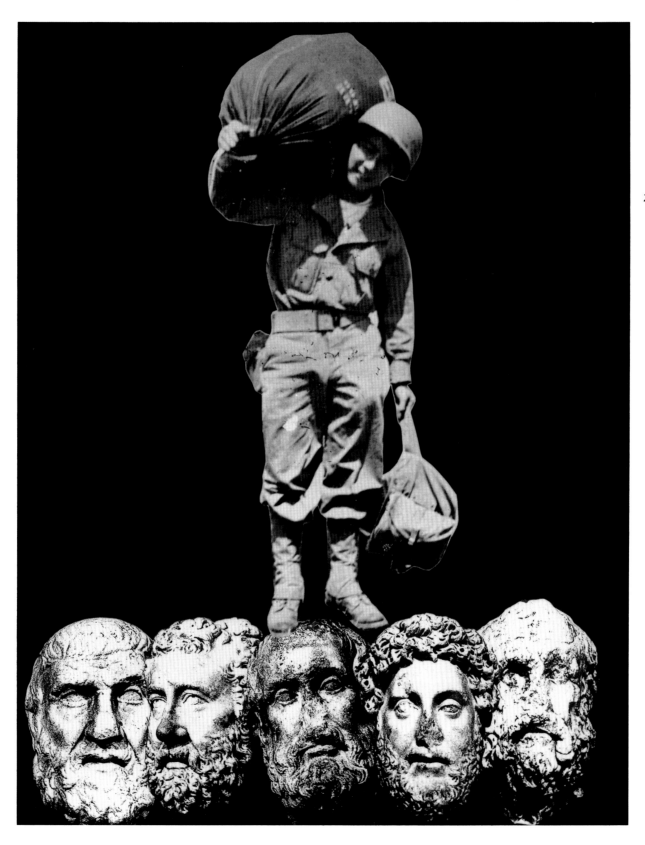

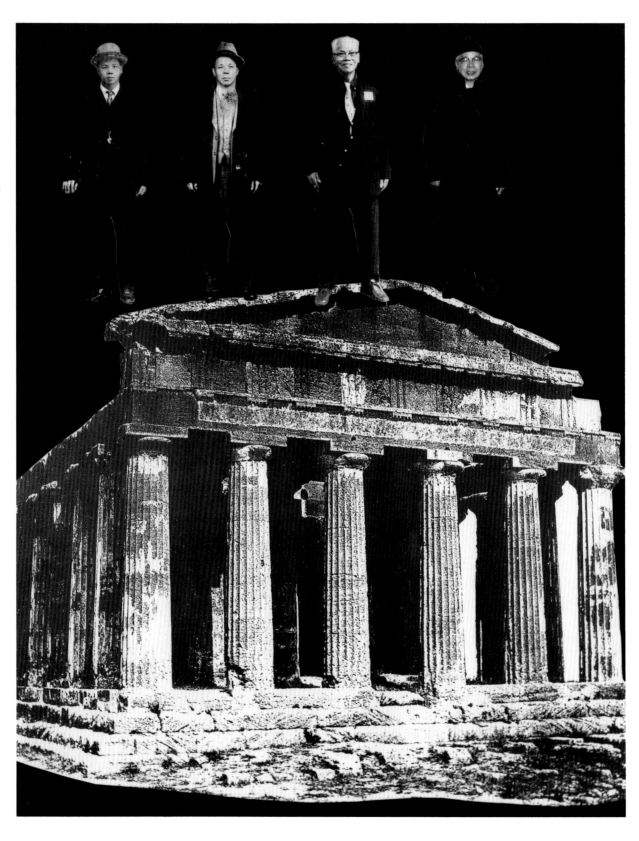

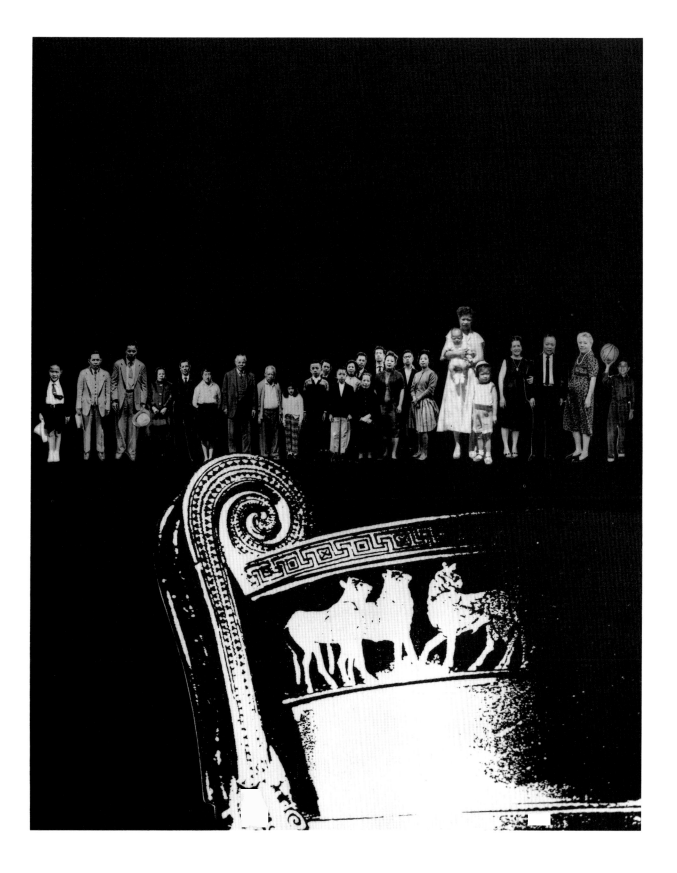

Deborah Bright

The Management of Desire
(an unmodified radical response)

280

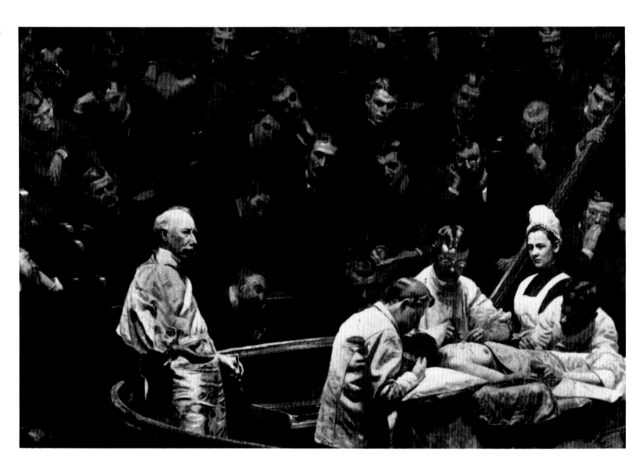

Thomas Eakins, *The Agnew Clinic,* 1889

She did not see herself as a victim. Many thought her desires

My attention gravitates to the figure of Nurse Clymer in Eakins' painting.

unnatural. Between her and her lover they still had three—one

Save for the unconscious patient hovered over by the assisting physicians,

more than most couples, she said. Scientists were searching

she is the only woman present in the operating amphitheater. She stands

for the gene that would identify her condition. Some asked why

stiffly at the surgeon's elbow—impassive, stoic, solid as a pillar—

281

she didn't have reconstruction. The doctors thought they had

seemingly unmoved (or is she transfixed?) by the mastectomy before her.

managed her disease. (They're losing the war against it!) She

In contrast to the immobility of the two women, the male doctors and

was no longer a believer. Her body reminded them of their own

medical students present a bustle of activity, animated by the master

mortality. She was put in a high-risk category. Her mother had

who directs and explicates the scene. The surgeons and anaesthetist busy

warned her on several occasions. 130,000 would be diagnosed

themselves with their required tasks, dividing the patient's body into

that year. Some said it was her Type C nature. Others said it

distinct zones of labor. Leaning, stretching, craning their necks to watch,

it was her Type L nature. Perhaps it was her sinful nature.

the students are, by turns, fidgety, bored, and anxious, but confident of the

There was no family history. Her body reminded them of chaos.

script. The painter included himself in the canvas as the spectator being

Her father was a doctor. He asked her about her symptoms. He asked

briefed at the extreme right. His portrait was painted by his wife who,

her if she was saving any money. She has a preexisting condition.

it's been said, was a very talented artist.

Each recurrence is more resistant to cure.

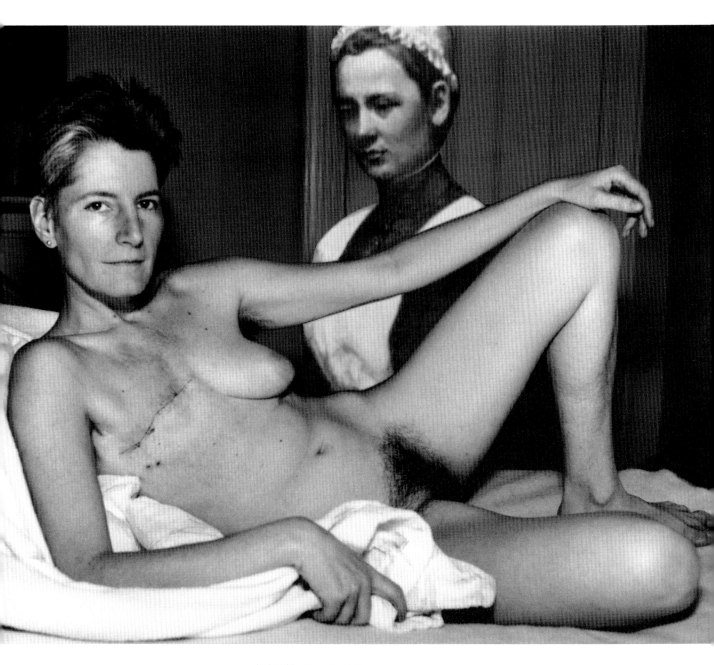

Assisted by Mary Ann Nilsson

284

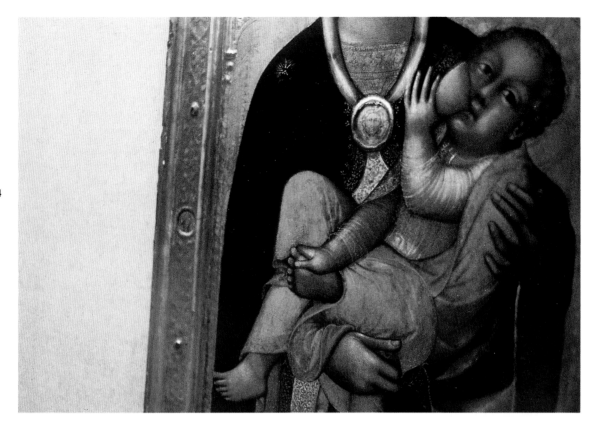

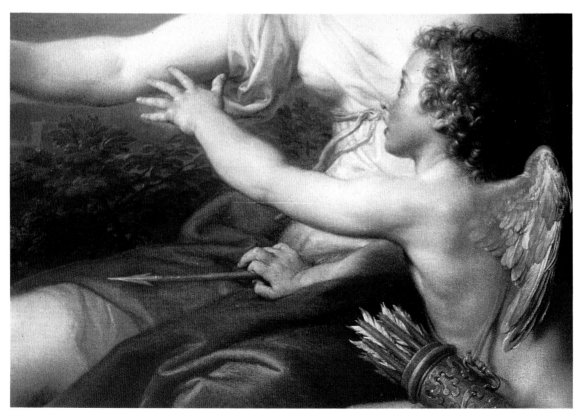

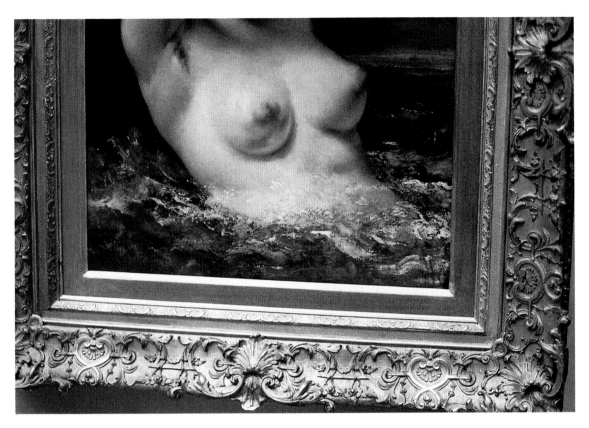

285

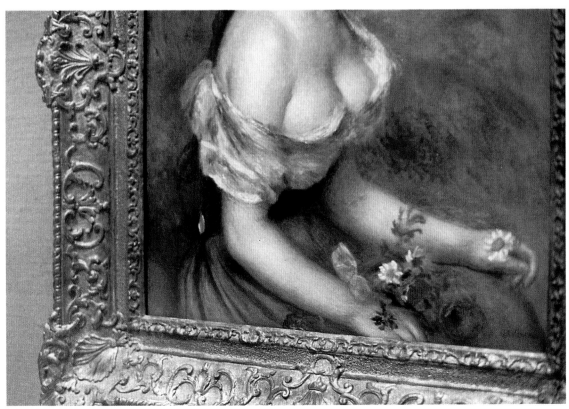

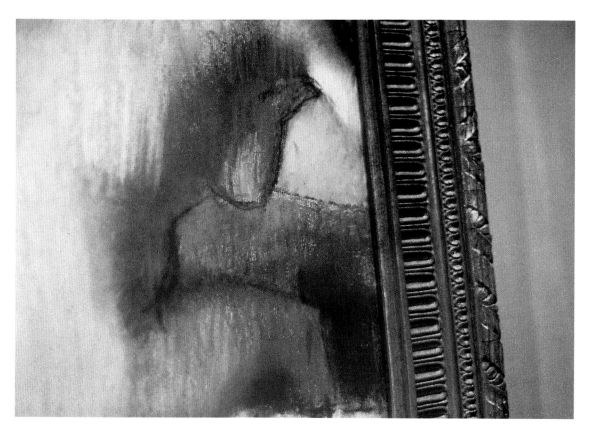

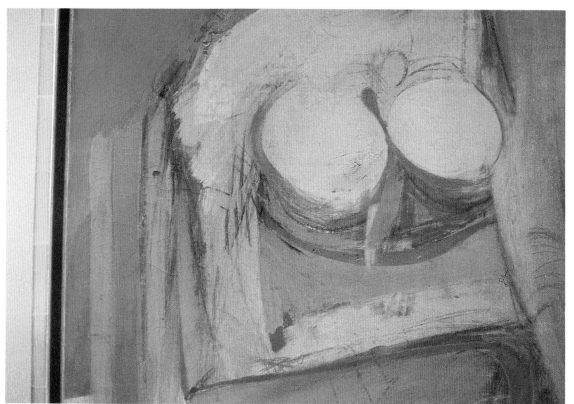

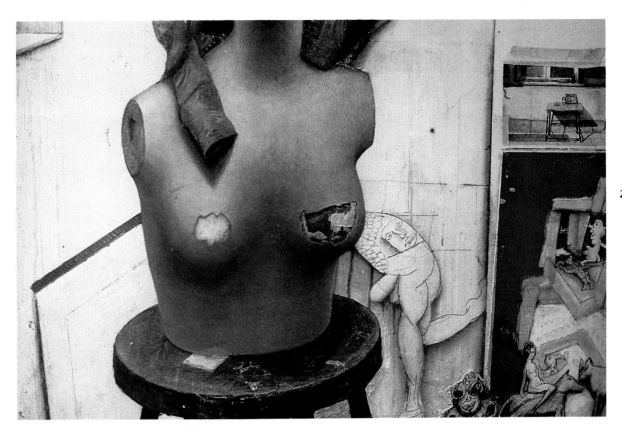

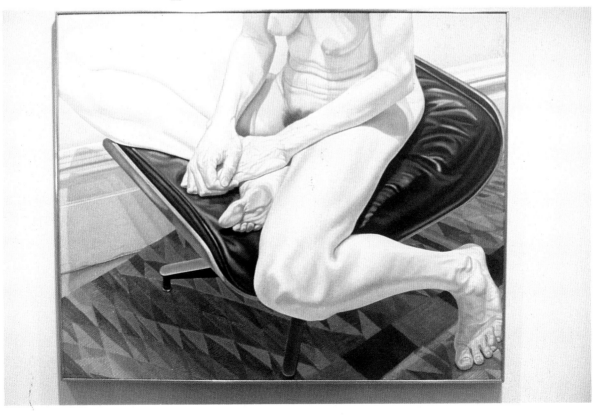

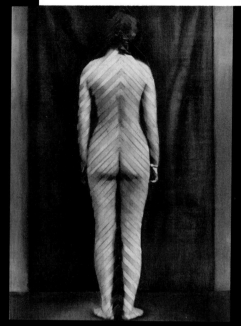

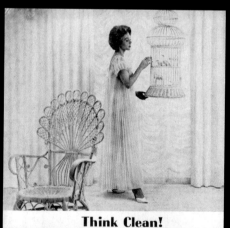

Think Clean!

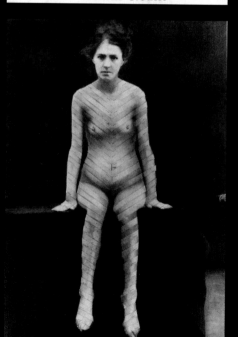

Whilst researching at the New York Psychiatric Institute I was confronted by a series of nineteenth century photographs and case histories of women diagnosed as hysterical and insane. Twisted bodies and faces, simultaneously gazing inward and outward, appeared frozen: stilled at the instant of misrecognition. Sitting and standing before the camera, coerced by the mechanical power of their own reflected images, they submitted: they were, finally, what they had become. Hysterical.

Accumulations of evidence jolt the fragile strata of memory, demanding exposure. Words and images form to name the raw, uncovered surfaces of sadness and anger. I had found what was inextricably bound and connected to my own past and present. In re-writing their stories I was re-writing my own.

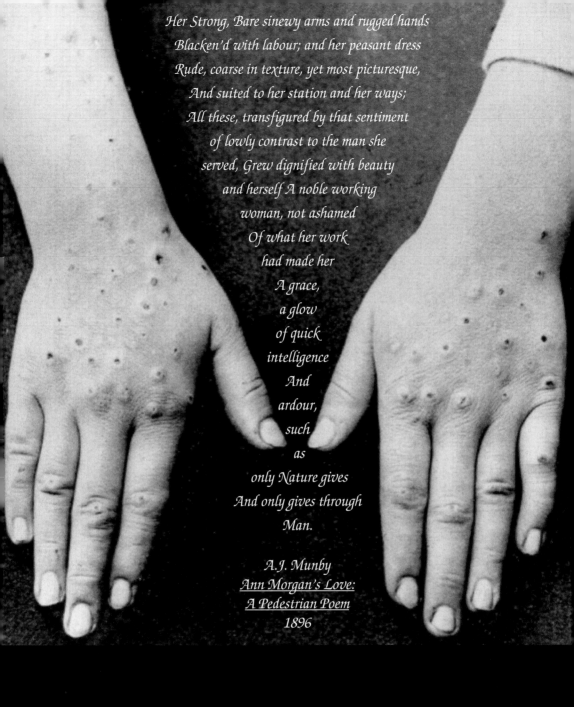

Her Strong, Bare sinewy arms and rugged hands
Blacken'd with labour; and her peasant dress
Rude, coarse in texture, yet most picturesque,
And suited to her station and her ways;
All these, transfigured by that sentiment
of lowly contrast to the man she
served, Grew dignified with beauty
and herself A noble working
woman, not ashamed
Of what her work
had made her
A grace,
a glow
of quick
intelligence
And
ardour,
such
as
only Nature gives
And only gives through
Man.

A.J. Munby
Ann Morgan's Love:
A Pedestrian Poem
1896

heard my mother scream at my father that he was driving her mad. I heard my mother scream at my sisters that we were all driving her mad. I overheard fragmented conversations between my mother and other women. I saw movies on television about women; women accused of inheriting their mother's madness. Were all women potentially mad? Would my mother, my sisters—would I myself end up behind the wall? I gradually realized, after many years of observing women enter and re-enter asylums, how fragile the line separating the sane from the insane; how telling the stains of insanity, visible upon the surfaces of women's bodies. For a women it seemed as though the inside-and-outside distinction was contingent. The weave of her dress, the perception of her desires and maternal inclinations determined when, how, and if she might be incarcerated.

...is not only found much larger than usual as a ... malformation, but ... requires the care of the surgeon from hypertroph... ...ral structure ...bid deposition into its tissue. Scarcely any organ is so lia... ...ment from ...ent excitation, and this in its turn prompts to a re... ...t. The ...mples on record are very numerous, and in some instances, it ... ...d of ...ormous size, in others more moderate, it has given rise to a doubt as ... the ...dividual. In the majority of these cases, however, it does not exceed ... in ...ength.

The primary symptoms, or those which arise from the mechanical disproportion of the ...rts, are trifling; in some cases, sexual intercourse has been impeded, and in most, from ...situation of the part and its great sensibility ... li... to irritation from motion, ...d the consequences of this susceptibility form ... far the most important feature of the ...case. The sexual desire naturally leads to its gratification, and this again aggra... ...complaint, and impels to further excess, until the pa...t at length ... nymphomania.

The hypertrophy may be congenital, or the result of inflamat... This part is als... found the seat of scirrhous depos...n, most fr... ... condition of the uterus, and ult...ely ru...ng ulcer... with lan...ng pain and foetid discharge, but givin... ...w or non of the sec...ry or nymphomaniacal symptoms.

Treatment. If the hypertroph... ...e slight and the symptoms not excessive ... ... sometimes be afforded by cooling or astringent lotions, or touch...g the ...art ... but if the enlargement be so considerable as to occasion physical inconvenience or excessive sexual indulgence, amputation will be necessary. Some blo... is usually lost, but cold or caustics wi... ... ...rhage. Astringent ...tons should be used for some time, and the patient kept in a state of absolute ... If, when the clitoris is enlarged from morbid de... ... is free of disease, we might, under favorable c...nce remove ... ...re are few cases which might be per... ...eeding, ...ease to be reproduced and extended. In ... ...great care ... taken to excise the whole of the disea...

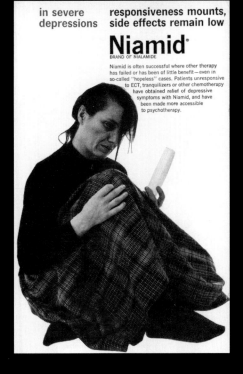

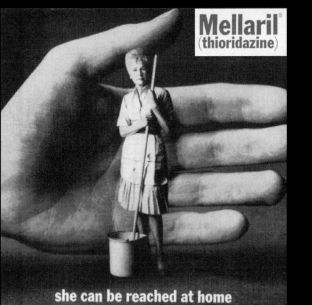

Many of the women in my family were diagnosed as mentally unstable. Aunt Dora committed suicide in 1978. She took an overdose of Mellaril. Her doctor had prescribed it for her "condition." Her husband was an alcoholic. He was often unemployed. He was seldom home. Aunt Rose was convinced she had throat cancer. Her husband always completed her sentences. She found it hard to swallow. He was a marriage-guidance counsellor in his spare time. He left her for a younger woman; one of his clients. Her doctor prescribed Niamid. He told her to take up knitting. Aunt Sadie disliked sexual relations with her husband. Her father had forced her to marry a man thirty years her senior. She was fifteen at the time. Her doctor prescribed Sinequan. He said it would help her to relax. Aunt Vera had insomnia. Her husband attended weekly business dinners Tuesday and Thursday nights. He didn't get home until the following evening. She discovered he had another "wife" in a neighboring town. He lived under a different name three days a week. Her doctor prescribed Placidyl. He said it would relieve her nervousness.

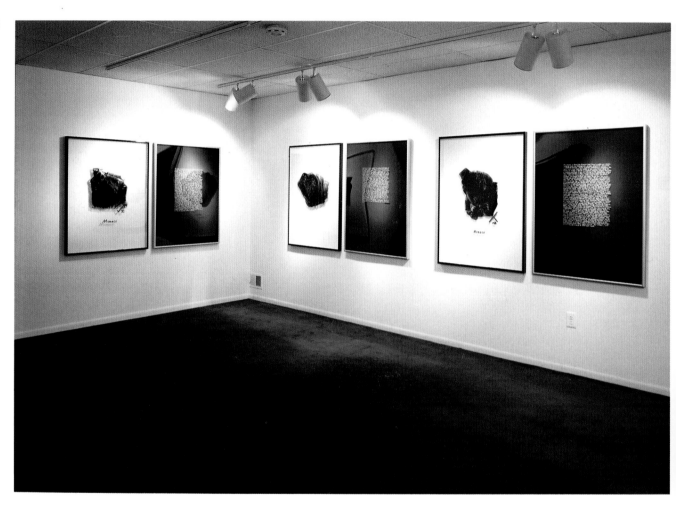

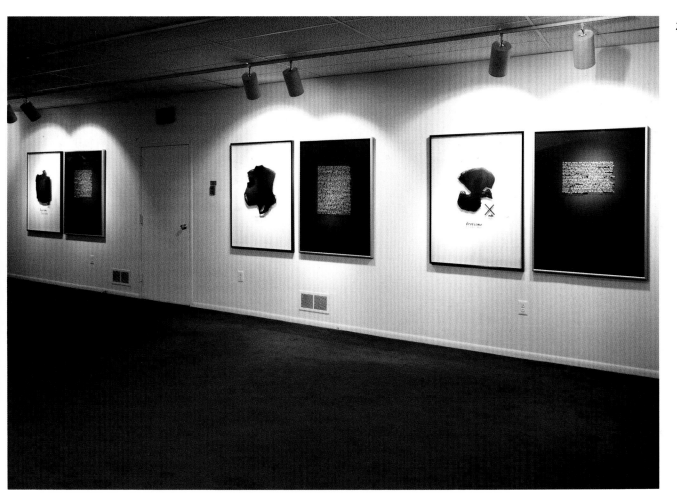

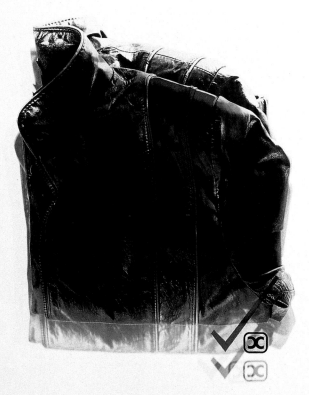

MENACÉ
MENACÉ

the room is crowded yet subdued, almost silent. No music, no dancing. Everyone is talking quietly in couples or small groups. Many are old friends, some I haven't seen for several years. They look different, not just greyer or fatter or more degenerate or less fashionable, just not the same. We are celebrating Lynn's fortieth birthday. "you look great," she says, kissing me on both cheeks, "haven't changed at all," then Anna mocks us but affectionately, "well preserved." She smiles. We laugh. I am content. Emboldened by the warmth, the comfort of their compliments, im-muddle, at least until Rod whispers, "How old are you anyway?" and I remember I am nearly forty-three. I hesitate and Sarah fills the gap with, "See, she can't even say it!" A possible re-prieve, Elizabeth comes over and asks me what I'm working on. I tell her its another long project and hope she won't pursue it. "On what," she insists. I fumble, knowing it will sound dreadful no matter how I say it. "Middle-age, well, that is, I suppose I mean women like us." "I dont feel middle-aged," she snaps, seems offended. I try to explain that its not so literal, more about the way we represent it to ourselves, almost before the fact. She says she has a phobia about it, trys to change the subject. Sarah interrupts to tell me the leather jacket is lovely but she distinctly remembers that I said I'd never wear one. I confess I finally gave in for professional reasons, that theres so much to think about now besides what to wear, that the older you are the harder it seems to be to get it right and that the uniform makes it a little easier. I look at Maya for confirmation but she disagrees, says theres a certain freedom attached to getting older, not caring so much, being able to get up in the morning and get dressed like a man, confidently, without wasting time primping. I notice she is dressed simply, hair hanging loosely on her shoulders, wearing very little make-up, nearly sixty and absolutely gorgeous. I say I'm not so sure most men are that secure but maybe her confidence comes from knowing she has always been a very attractive woman. She looks surprised. "No one is that confident," she protests, "I must admit I've never missed an opportunity to glance in a mirror as I passed it, or in a shop window, or any reflective surface for that matter, hoping to catch a glimpse of myself as others see me." Lynn is lighting the candles. "Watch me," she says, "I'm going to blow them out now." And she does, all forty, without a flicker.

296

[1] An obvious instance of representational politics, employed, for example, in the art and critical writing of Martha Rosler, Alan Sekula, and Sally Stein, is provided by the genre of so-called concerned documentary or photojournalism. In its most familiar manifestations, from the 1930s to the present, these practices represent those individuals or groups—the poor, the homeless, the famine victim, the ill, the deviant, the outcast, the primitive—who, not having themselves the means or even the motives for self-representation, are represented for the gaze of the relatively powerful. Irrespective of motive and ameliorative intention, the representational politics here are operative on two levels. On one level, insofar as such imagery can deal only with appearances, not with causes or determinations, structural or political explanation or analysis is precluded. Thus, what is in effect the result of a history, a politics, or a web of causality is congealed into an image, a spectacle, a decontextualized fragment that leaves unaddressed the question of structural redress rather than privatized response. At another level, the objectification and rendering into spectacle inseparable from conventional documentary modes operates to secure the otherness of the other while fostering an essentially voyeuristic relation to actuality on the part of the spectator. See Martha Rosler's now-classic "In, Around and Afterthoughts (On Documentary Photography)," in *Three Works* (Halifax: Press of the Nova Scotia College of Art and Design, 1981); Alan Sekula, "Dismantling Modernism: Reinventing Documentary," in *Photography Against the Grain*, ed. Alan Sekula (Halifax: Press of the Nova Scotia College of Art and Design, 1985); Sally Stein, "Making Connections with the Camera: Photography and Social Mobility in the Career of Jacob Riis," *Afterimage* 10, no. 10 (May 1981): 12–

In looking back at the art production of the past twelve years or so, it seems apparent that one of the characteristic features of the 1980s, namely, the emergence (and relatively prompt institutionalization) of practices concerned with the politics of representation, before the decade's end underwent a shift in emphasis to the politics of *self*-representation. In part, this would seem to be a consequence of production by and recognition of "minority," that is to say, nonwhite cultural producers for whom the enterprise of self-representation has a singular historical and political import. But a second factor has been the centrality of the problem of self-representation within feminist art and theory, understood, it should be said, precisely *as* a problem. For inasmuch as feminist aesthetics poses the question of how to represent the unrepresented (or unrepresentable), so too has the work of subaltern—in other words, subordinated—producers (artists of color, gay men and lesbians) hinged on the task of self-representation. But what is even meant by self-representation? And how do the politics of self-representation differ from the politics of representation *per se*?

The currency of the concept of a politics of self-representation is, of course, itself predicated on the antecedent politics of representation.[1] The politics of representation (which was elaborated in art criticism in the 1970s) presumes that relations of power are operative both in the act of representing and in the relations that govern the production and reception of cultural artifacts. A politics of representation, therefore, virtually by definition precludes any notion of autonomous, much less transcendent meanings in works of art and focuses attention instead on the generation of meanings as they operate to either affirm, contest, or subvert dominant ideological formations. At the same time, it questions "realist" modes of depiction and expression, assuming that reality is always and already ideologically marked and is thus in no simple way available to re-presentation.

Considered in relation to visual representation in general or to the specific project of self-representation, this explicitly political model of productive and viewing relations encompasses the two meanings of representation for which the German language helpfully provides two different words. Thus, in aesthetics and philosophy, where representation refers to the act of re-presenting a preexisting object, the verb is *darstellen*; the strictly political sense of representation—as in "taxation without representation is tyranny"—is *vertreten*, to speak for; it is this double sense that is invoked in the concept of representational politics. Both meanings of representation are germane to Foucault's injunction against "the indignity of speaking for others," signaling the ethical imperative that subaltern groups conscript the means for self-representation, rather than being the subject of others' representation. Thus, for artists of color, for gay and lesbian artists, and for (white) women artists, the possibilities (and difficulties) of self-representation can be said to represent the cultural analogue of struggles for political visibility and enfranchisement. Accordingly, the representational politics that govern the imagery of the subaltern subject—the woman, the black, the colonized, the deviant—engage both the field of vision and the field of power, which are understood to be mutually implicated. But while these terms of analysis provide conceptual models for understanding how relations of domination and subordination, mastery and appropriation, reification and objectification are operative in visual production, they do not in and of themselves provide guideposts—*modes d'emploi*—for cultural producers. For numerous nonwhite American artists in the present, as for women artists since the earliest emergence of the women's movement, the project of giving form to historically unrepresented subjectivities is, to a certain extent, shaped by formal, and indeed philosophical, choices. For some artists, the task is to appropriate realist forms in which to articulate the truth of the subject, a subject either historically demeaned (as in racial stereotypes), occulted, or "disappeared" altogether. Much feminist photographic production—and photography has historically functioned as the quintessential realist medium—is premised on the conviction that the camera can express authentic social and psychic truths, including the lived reality of female experience, merely by the act of imaging what has not been imaged, a truth guaranteed by the investment of its maker and the authority of her experience. For example, many lesbian photographers have photographed themselves, their lovers, and their communities motivated by the belief that photographic self-representations are not only empowering in and of themselves, but, even more important, further the process of political consolidation and mobilization.

For other artists, however, classic realist forms are themselves the problem, and in keeping with modern ideological critiques of realism (Roland Barthes is here an important figure, but the critique goes back to the 1920s),[2] the choice is for conceptual, occasionally self-consciously theoretical modes of production. Consider, for example, the difference between those photographs of Anne Noggle that unflinchingly document the physical inscription of aging on a woman's face and body (her own) and Mary Kelly's multimedia, multipart work *Interim*, which also takes as one of its concerns the experience of aging. Insofar as Noggle's photographs accept, and indeed have no quarrel with, the putative transparency of the photographic image—its ability to transcribe or document an external reality—their ideological "work," their transgressive intent, lies in their defiant exposure of what older women are conventionally expected to hide. For

14; and Abigail Solomon-Godeau, "Who Is Speaking Thus? Some Questions About Documentary Photography," in *Photography at the Dock: Essays on Photographic History, Institutions, and Practices* (Minneapolis: University of Minnesota Press, 1991). More recently, there have appeared a number of studies by African American scholars that examine the politics of representation in relation to race and racial politics. See Michele Wallace, *Invisibility Blues* (London: Verso, 1991), and bell hooks, *Black Looks: Race and Representation* (Boston: South End Press, 1992).

2 Barthes's dismantling of the pretensions of realist forms and styles to objectivity began as early as the 1950s with his essays "The Great Family of Man" and "Myth Today," both in *Mythologies*, trans. Annette Lavers (New York: Hill & Wang, 1957). See as well his other essays "The Rhetoric of the Image," in *Image, Music, Text*, trans. Stephen Heath (New York: Hill & Wang, 1977) and "The Reality Effect," in *The Rustle of Language*, trans. Richard Howard (Berkeley & Los Angeles: University of California Press, 1989).

3 Beginning with the groundbreaking anthology *Woman as Sex Object*, ed. Elizabeth Baker and Thomas Hess (New York: Newsday Books, 1973), the feminist bibliography concerned with sexual politics and representation has grown by quantum leaps. For a good introduction to these issues as they concern elite visual culture, see Linda Nochlin, *Women, Art and Power* (New York: Harper & Row, 1991); Rosemary Betterton, ed., *Looking On: Images of Femininity in the Visual Arts and Media* (London: Pandora Press, 1987); Roszika Parker and Griselda Pollock, eds., *Framing Feminism: Art and the Women's Movement 1970–1985* (London: Pandora Press, 1987); Norma Broude and Mary Garrard, eds., *Feminism and Art History: Questioning the Litany* (New York: Harper & Row, 1982); and Broude and Garrard, eds., *The Expanding Discourse: Feminism and Art History* (New York: HarperCollins, 1992).

4 The foundational essays here are by Laura Mulvey. See her "You don't know what's happening, do you Mr. Jones?" and "Visual Pleasure and Narrative Cinema," both in *Visual and Other Pleasures*, ed. Laura Mulvey (London: Macmillan, 1988).

5 The bibliography of feminist theory concerned with the construction of woman both as category and image (and within a range of media) is enormous. Among the earliest and most important works, however, are the following: Elizabeth Cowie, "Woman as Sign," in *The Woman in Question*, ed. Parveen Adams and Elizabeth Cowie (Cambridge: MIT Press, 1991); Griselda Pollock, "What's Wrong with 'Images of Women'?" in *Framing Feminism*, ed. Parker and Pollock; Griselda Pollock and Deborah Cherry, "Woman as Sign in Pre-Raphaelite Literature: The Representation of Elizabeth Siddal," in *Vision and Difference: Femininity, Feminism and the Histories of Art*, ed.

Kelly, who, with the exception of Jenny Holzer, is perhaps the premier iconoclast in feminist art, there is an a priori rejection of mimetic imagery, whether of the aging woman or, in the case of her earlier *Post-Partum Document*, the mother. In part, this rejection of mimetic representation follows from Kelly's understanding that both "aging" and "motherhood" should be approached not as visual facts or self-evident states to be truthfully rendered, but rather as the product of discursive constructions and social relations. In other words, far from being natural states of being, aging and motherhood are conceived as themselves a product of representational practices.

In this respect, the rejection of realist modes exemplified by Kelly has received further theoretical justification in the aggregate implications and conclusions of feminist theories of representation and feminist revisions within the discipline of art history. These have examined the mechanisms of power in visual culture with particular emphasis on the representation (and construction) of femininity in both elite and mass cultural forms.[3] Thus, feminist theorists, particularly those working in film, have variously demonstrated that the image of woman *qua* image is a function of masculine projections, fears, desires, and fantasies.[4] Consequently, the referent for the woman-as-representation can never be taken as that of real women in the real world, nor can the image be considered to manifest a more or less truthful correspondence to a preexisting category (real women). Rather, the image of woman is taken to be a semiotic object—a sign—whose meanings are generated within a larger semiotic system.[5] In thus shifting the terms from the truth or falsity of images of woman to the question of what Griselda Pollock termed woman-as-image, it becomes possible to analyze the mechanisms of fetishism, voyeurism, and objectification that form and inform the representation of woman. Relations of domination and subordination, of mastery, appropriation, and imaginary knowledge—the politics of representation par excellence—can thus be seen as independent of whether a given image is idealizing, eroticizing, or even demonizing.

By definition, an analysis of this nature precludes the (unproblematic) deployment of realist modes of expression, and it is in this regard that artists using film, video, and photography have obviously had the harder row to hoe. In this context, it is suggestive to observe the refusal of many African American artists such as Renee Green, Lorna Simpson, Adrian Piper, Pat Ward Williams, or Carrie Mae Weems to attempt "authentic," "realist," or ameliorative depictions of black subjects, to substitute "positive" for "negative" representations. Instead, their work may be said to be animated by a concern with the complex processes by which race and gender are variously constituted within representational systems.

Griselda Pollock (London: Routledge, 1988); and works by Laura Mulvey cited in note 4. A crucial essay for its argument about the sign status of woman (although not concerned with visual representation per se) is by Gayle Rubin, "The Traffic in Women: Notes on a 'Political Economy' of Sex," in *Towards an Anthropology of Women*, ed. Rayna R. Reitner (New York: Monthly Review Press, 1975).

6 To a certain extent, this is an analysis associated with French feminist theory. For a useful introduction see Elaine Marks and Isabelle de Courtivron, eds., *New French Feminisms: An Anthology* (New York: Schocken Books, 1981). See also Toril Moi, ed., *French Feminist Thought: A Reader* (London: Basil Blackwell, 1987) and Moi, *Sexual/Textual Politics: Feminist Literary Theory* (London and New York: Methuen, 1985).

7 The relations between specularity, fetishism, and the patriarchal construction of femininity are crucial issues in the work of Luce Irigaray and Sarah Kofman. See Irigaray, *Speculum of the Other Woman*, trans. Gillian C. Gill (Ithaca: Cornell University Press, 1985) and Irigaray, *The Sex Which Is Not One*, trans. Catherine Porter (Ithaca: Cornell University Press, 1985); Kofmann, *The Enigma of Woman: Woman in Freud's Writings*, trans. Catherine Porter (Ithaca: Cornell University Press, 1985).

8 My consistent use of quotation marks around the terms "realism" or "realist," and, in certain contexts, around the word "woman," indicates my own conviction that realism should not be automatically assumed to possess a privileged relation to the real. Similarly, I am in general agreement with feminist critiques of the use of the categorical term "woman" to encompass an imagined collectivity of undifferentiated female subjects. See, in this respect,

Crudely stated, the problem of self-representation posed by feminist art production from its first emergence in the early years of the women's liberation movement has been how to represent female subjectivity and experience when the artistic languages of form and expression are understood as themselves patriarchal constructions, inescapably marked by the symbolic order, which is itself inseparable from patriarchy.[6] In visual culture particularly, there has developed a substantial corpus of feminist theory that has suggested that the domain of the visual and its attendant psychic components (for example, fetishism, scopophilia, voyeurism) has been especially complicit in the processes by which women are constituted as bearers rather than makers of meaning.[7] The implications of such analyses are complex and wide-ranging for those feminists working in the mediums of photography and film, indexical and "realist" forms that by virtue of their illusory transparency have historically functioned to naturalize the ideologies of gender they are employed to convey.[8] Consequently, many feminist photographers have devised ways of working within these media that acknowledge their conventional instrumentalities even as these are variously subverted, destabilized, or politically "exposed." Examples of such practices in the past ten to fifteen years are legion—the work of Barbara Kruger or Cindy Sherman is perhaps the best known—but it is in the very nature of such (feminist) enterprises that they are compelled by the terms of their analyses to bracket altogether the issue of self-representation. In other words, to the extent that such mass media–based practices are concerned to reveal the constructedness of the category of "woman" and the ways in which this category is visually produced and articulated, any question of an authentic femininity outside of representation is necessarily deferred. This is in marked contrast to a parallel tributary in feminist art that has, on the contrary, concerned itself with the task of excavating and giving artistic form to the repressed or silenced truth of femininity, the truth of the body, what Clarice Lispector has described as the "unleashed tides of muteness." Often this is explicitly accompanied or implicitly underpinned by an appeal to the authority of experience, indeed to the bodying forth of that hitherto excluded or silenced experience. Such a tactic is perhaps most clearly and most influentially demonstrated in the use of the female body itself as both vessel and agent of meaning, as exemplified in women's performance art. Thus, when Carolee Schneeman, in a famous performance piece, drew a written scroll out of her body, literally out of her sex, or when Ana Mendieta physically enacted the incorporation of the female body to nature, the intention was to literalize and celebrate what was historically considered the grounds of its abjection, seeking to valorize what had been historically demeaned, inventing ways by which female subjectivity could be spoken.

The legacy of such approaches exists today in works such as Nancy Spero's or Kiki Smith's; a work such as Smith's *Tale*, whose title puns on woman's putative animality, features a sculpted female figure, which as it crawls secretes its own narrative from the hidden recesses of the body. Similarly, recent photographic work such as that by Judy Maber and Zoe Leonard, featuring genital imagery, or work by Jeanne Dunning, which evokes (using fruit and vegetables) bodily orifices and various organs, operates within a comparable context. On the level of form, too, this tendency within feminist art-making prompted the use of denigrated materials and processes, such as fabrics and quilting—as in the work of Faith Ringgold and Miriam Shapiro.

The desire to represent the truth of "woman" or female subjectivity has, however, proved vulnerable to critique on the grounds of essentialism, the bad object of much contemporary feminism.[9] For feminist projects that take as their theme the problematics of femininity, however construed, run not only the risk of universalizing (thereby paralleling the exclusionary and oppressive concept of the universal "man" as universal human being), they also circumvent the political and cultural fact of difference between women. Consequently, in defining feminist practice as predicated, to whatever degree, on the enterprise of "representing woman," her experience and her subjectivity, the question becomes how any one artist can speak *for* women, either in the sense of *darstellen* or in the sense of *vertreten*. Hence, the silencing and occlusion of women, *as* an abstraction and *as* a project of feminist art-making, does not in and of itself address the specific nature and modalities of the silencing and occlusion of women of color, of lesbians, of postcolonial subjects. Once one rejects the notion of woman—or women—as an undifferentiated category, the project of self-representation must be accordingly nuanced, specific, and local.

Whatever the difficulties it presents in other media, the project of self-representation encounters even greater difficulties within the inescapably specular constraints of photography. Nevertheless, an artistic commitment to this genre has been a recurring motif in the work of many women photographers; Ann Noggle, Bea Nettles, and the late Jo Spence, to take three very different artists, can all be said to operate in some relation to this project of self-representation. In the case of the first three examples, the practice of self-representation is ultimately predicated on the first person singular; the autobiographical I. It is the I who ages, the I who experiences the conflicts and joys of motherhood, the I who enacts the process of self-discovery and self-curing.[10] The specifically feminist component of such projects lies in the assumption that the experience of the singular, autobiographical I may be considered to have some kind of broader applica-

Denise Riley, *Am I That Name? Feminism and the Category of "Women" in History* (London: Macmillan, 1988) and Judith Butler, *Gender Trouble* (New York and London: Routledge, 1990).

9 An interesting discussion of the need to complicate the binary opposition essentialism/anti-essentialism may be found in Diana J. Fuss, *Essentially Speaking* (New York: Routledge, 1989).

10 See the following: Janice Zita Grover, *Silver Lining: Photographs by Anne Noggle* (Albuquerque, University of New Mexico Press, 1983), and *Anne Noggle*, exhibition catalogue (London: Photographers' Gallery, 1988); Bea Nettles, *Flamingo in the Dark* (Rochester: Inky Press Productions, 1979), and *Gifts: A Retrospective of Work by Bea Nettles 1969–1983*, exhibition catalogue (Bethlehem, Penn.: Payne Gallery of Moravian College, 1983); and Jo Spence, *Putting Myself in the Picture* (London: Camden Press, 1986).

bility. In this respect, such practices are the aesthetic descendants of the consciousness raising that was such a conspicuous feature of early seventies' feminism. Like consciousness raising too, such practices are equally predicated on the knowledge that the personal is political; that aging, maternity, and illness are themselves shaped by the subaltern status of women in patriarchal society. Generally speaking, we can consider this kind of production as an attempt to address the general (that is, a condition shared by women as a collectivity) through the representation of the particular (for example, the individual who incarnates, who emblematizes the condition). Nonetheless, photography—in its conventional usages—tends to resist emblematic or collective applications, in part because of its visual specificity, and it is undoubtedly for this reason that photomontage, didactic montage, phototext, and photo-installation work has been more frequently employed by artists concerned with political and social issues, feminist or otherwise.

But whatever the forms adopted by individual artists, what is at stake in the process of visual self-representation is, in the final instance, always political. The history of the artist's self-portrait (in easel painting) provides as good an example as any of the way particular genres can operate to convey particular ideological formations. In this respect, the fact that the artist's self-portrait was for all intents and purposes invented in the Renaissance is itself significant. For even as it attests to the new status of the artist, rising from the relative anonymity of artisan to the relatively exalted status of humanist—even, at the apex represented by a figure such as Michelangelo, to *Übermensch*—the figure of the artist stands for that individual and sovereign (male) subject who will henceforth serve as a privileged signifier of the primacy of "man" in the culture at large. And while there are as many different forms of artists' self-portrait as there are individual artists, schools, and styles, and while the artist's self-portrait has different ideological significance at different moments, it is nonetheless possible to argue that the cumulative effect of this pictorial tradition has operated to secure and reaffirm a mutually reinforcing set of propositions. For example, whether the artist presents himself as gentleman/humanist, messiah or martyr, worker or outcast, what remains consistent is the self-evident co-identity of masculinity with cultural creation, a model, moreover, that posits the individual, rather than collective nature of such creation. This is, of course, a crucial element in the ideology of mainstream art history; to the degree that cultural creation is understood as individually rather than collectively produced, the individual artist's personality is the very emblem of bourgeois individualism.[11] This explains why the designation "artist" is an unmarked term; it would be absurd—because usually redundant—to qualify the genre

[11] For a good corrective to the bourgeois mythology of cultural production, see Janet Wolff, *The Social Production of Art* (New York: New York University Press, 1984). See also Griselda Pollock, "Artists, Mythologies, and Media: Genius, Madness and Art History," *Screen* 21, no. 3 (1980): 57–66.

with the adjectives "white, male." This is especially clear when we consider the obviously far more limited realm of the women artists' self-portraiture. Whatever the visual or social terms in which the woman artist represents herself, it is the gender of the artist that predominates for the spectator, just as it did for the woman artist's own contemporaries.

But the ideological "work" of the artist's self-portrait goes beyond reaffirming the equivalence of masculinity with cultural creation. For the artist—in keeping with contemporary theorizations, let us call him the author—stands as the linchpin for a complex set of beliefs about the function of the work of art. These include, but are by no means limited to, the notion of art as, in T. S. Eliot's influential formulation, an unbroken series of monuments passed down through time in the institutional form of the canon. Furthermore, the canon itself can be thought of as a "single-sex" model of cultural production. But the endlessly engrossing visage of the artist/author has another, albeit fantasmatic function. I refer here to the mystical belief in psychological access, a one-to-one relation, as between persons, that the artist's self-portrait is believed to offer. This perception of a psychic transparency between representation and spectator plays its own, by no means negligible role, fostering a relation in which the viewer thinks to read or discover or excavate a personal, individuated, and unified identity through the agency of representation. In one sense, then, the artist's portrait is a surrogate, not merely in the obvious fact of its positive presence in the artist/author's actual absence, but as a mirror of the (male) viewer's own presence and subjectivity, an alter ego of sorts. In modern myths of the artist—that is to say, from the nineteenth century on—those elements that constitute *Homo ludens*—free play, creative expression, as well as sexual license and practical irresponsibility—are located in the figure of the artist, just as they are foreclosed to the bourgeois male citizen. Finally, and equally important, the integrity and authority of the author, confirmed in his portrait, secures the value—in all senses of the term—of the oeuvre. This is in fact the strongest correspondence to the Foucaultian model of authorship whereby the image of the artist is perceived to be the self-present, intentional, and originating locus of meaning. In the light of such massive ideological labor, it is hardly surprising that the genre has been strikingly durable. Its consistent appeal and unbroken currency—think of Robert Mapplethorpe's self-portraits—testifies to its continued ideological utility.

Needless to say , for women artists the enterprise of self-representation has been a much more complicated affair, and it is in fact through the problems encountered in women's attempts at self-representation that certain of the terms and difficulties of self-representation for all subaltern groups can be concretely grasped. For women, themselves a subaltern group within patriarchy, notions of authenticity, autonomy—indeed, the honorific of authorship itself—are obviously not analogous, much less comparable to, those of men. More pointedly, to the extent that much feminist work has focused on the task of inventing formal and expressive languages in which to signify *difference*, the project of self-representation, with its political as well as aesthetic implications, goes well beyond the substitution of one content for another. Much of my own work as a feminist scholar has focused on women's attempts at self-representation in the medium of photography, a medium whose putative transparency can be understood paradoxically to expose the dense accretion of already circulating meanings that always and already underpin the representation of femininity.[12] Insofar as feminism understands visual culture to collectively produce concepts of the feminine, of "woman," artists and theorists have had to address the terms and possibilities of a counterdiscursive practice; that is, forms of art-making that either avoid, contest, subvert, or transform the existing terms by which femininity is produced in representational systems.

One possible strategy, associated largely with British art of the 1970s and 1980s, was a form of feminist iconoclasm such as that associated with the work of Mary Kelly. Far more prevalent, in literary as well as visual culture, was the attempt, from the early 1970s on, to forge or invent new languages to express the repressed truth of femininity.[13]

But the strategy that has come to exemplify the marriage, so to speak, of critical postmodernism and feminism is most clearly represented in the work of such artists as Sarah Charlesworth, Cindy Sherman, and, perhaps most famously, Barbara Kruger. These artists have tended to put to one side the issue of an authentic self-representation in order to expose the signifying codes by which the feminine is discursively produced and the psychic and cultural codes of investiture by which woman-as-sign is mobilized. In this respect, Cindy Sherman's work can be viewed as a kind of exemplar of this type of feminist postmodernism, insofar as her lexicon of images of femininity, despite her ubiquitous presence, can in no sense be said to be "authored" by an individual sensibility (or psychology) but only by the culture at large. Obviously too, the illusory presence and authority of the titular author is consistently undercut by the conspicuous absence of a "self," an absence particularly appropriate insofar as femininity is programmatically presented in her work as a parade of personae, masks, and masquerades. Such work conforms readily to the terms of critical postmodernism; it brackets if not jettisons issues of lived subjectivity; it takes its cue from mass cultural forms; it traffics in quotation, citation, and pastiche; it presumes no truth of the subject, no author/father as locus of meaning.

But like Nancy Miller's important critique of the death-of-the-author

12 Abigail Solomon-Godeau, "The Legs of the Countess," *October* 39 (Winter 1986), and Solomon-Godeau, "Just Like a Woman" and "Sexual Difference: Both Sides of the Camera," in *Photography at the Dock: Essays in Photographic History, Institutions and Practices* (Minneapolis: University of Minnesota Press, 1991).

13 One important and influential example of the attempt to write "otherly ," to invent a distinctively feminine language (and myth), is represented by Monique Wittig. See Wittig, *The Lesbian Body*, trans. Peter Owen (New York: Avon Books, 1977), and Wittig, *Les Guérillères*, trans. David Le Vay (New York: Avon Books, 1976). See as well the discussions of *écriture féminine* in Moi, *French Feminist Thought*.

position, we may ask whether this paradigm holds good as either a descriptive or prescriptive model for the practices of subaltern groups across the board. For as Miller argued in 1984, "The removal of the Author has not so much made room for a revision of the concept of authorship as it has, through a variety of rhetorical moves, repressed and inhibited discussion of any . . . identity in favor of the (new) monolith of anonymous textuality or, in Foucault's phrase 'transcendental anonymity.' "[14] But more even more forcefully, she pointed out that "[t]he postmodernist decision that the Author is Dead and the subject along with him does not . . . necessarily hold for women, and prematurely forecloses the question of agency for them. Because women have not had the same historical relation of identity to origin, institution, production that men have had, they have not, I think, (collectively) felt burdened by *too much* Self, Ego, Cogito, etc. Because the female subject has juridically been excluded from the polis, hence, decentered, 'disoriginated,' deinstitutionalized, etc., her relation to integrity and textuality, desire and authority, displays structurally important differences from that universal position."[15] And in an analogous questioning of the dispatchal of the author, Andreas Huyssen commented: "Isn't the 'death of the subject/author' position tied by mere reversal to the very ideology that invariably glorifies the artist as genius, whether for marketing purposes or out of conviction or habit? . . . Doesn't poststructuralism, where it simply denies the subject altogether, jettison the chance of challenging the ideology of the subject (as male, white and middle-class) by developing authoritative and different notions of subjectivity?"[16]

It is in fact precisely the question of the existence of "alternative and different notions of subjectivity" that suggests new paradigms of and for self-representation. In this respect, it is one of the conspicuous and recurring features of what I will awkwardly and provisionally call subaltern postmodernism that it deploys a form of self-representation that exceeds the personal, can even be considered *impersonal.* And while much work by African American women artists specifically invokes the autobiographical, it lodges and locates the personal within a larger (and longer) history. A continuing series of works by Howardina Pindell, for example, has the overall title *Autobiography*; one of the works from the series, entitled *Water/Ancestors/Middle Passage/Family Ghosts*, features a blank white silhouette of a slave ship, the deathlike emblem of the historical past, which is itself contained within the conceptual frame of autobiography, signaling the refashioning of the notion of individual subjectivity to encompass the historical determinations that cumulatively shaped it. Many of Faith Ringgold's narrative quilts counterpoint the private memories of community or milieu with individual perception and experience. These modes of self-

[14] Nancy Miller, "Changing the Subject: Authorship, Writing and the Reader," in *Subject to Change*, ed. Nancy Miller (New York: Columbia University Press, 1988), 000–000.
[15] Miller, "Changing the Subject," 106.
[16] Andreas Huyssen, "Mapping the Postmodern," in *After the Great Divide: Modernism, Mass Culture, Postmodernism* (Bloomington and Indianapolis: Indiana University Press, 1986), cited in Miller, "Changing the Subject," 106.

representation, identifiable with what Cornel West has called "the new cultural politics of difference," can be thought of as collective and explicitly political forms of self-representation, offering, unlike the classic self-portrait, not so much the revelation of a singular self, but the retrieval and revelation of the historical and social forces that forged that self. Thus, even when the work makes reference to the specifically autobiographical, this aspect of the work is integrated into larger frames that are entirely historical, and thus, social and collective. It is therefore precisely this assimilation and refiguration of the personal into the social and the historical, and the individual into the collective that I want to propose as an important paradigm for representing women, both in the sense of women who represent (that is, women artists) and for their feminist project (that is, the embodiment, the giving form to women's experience and subjectivity).

By way of a more detailed consideration of the kind of practice I am outlining here, I want to discuss two recent works, both from 1989, by Renee Green and Lorna Simpson that go farther than the other works thus far cited in dissolving the personal into the social, but that nonetheless may be considered to engage with the issue of self-representation. What is at stake in both works is the ways in which the historical past remains a shaping force in the historical present. Put somewhat differently, both works can be said to frame black women's subjectivity in the present through reference to its prior determinations and circumstances, producing a hybrid form of self-representation.

I begin with Renee Green's installation work entitled *Sa Main Charmante* (Her Charming Hand). Its components consist of a wooden box, rubber-stamped texts on wooden slats, two images attached to masonite board, a viewer fitted with a lens mounted on a wooden base, a klieg light, and a small, empty frame above the slats. This is a work "about," among other things, the public spectacle that was the woman Saarjie or Saat-Jee or Sarah Bartmann, a Khoi woman from the Cape of Africa known to posterity as the Hottentot Venus.[17] Born in 1790, the daughter of a drover killed by Bushmen, Baartman was brought by Dutch farmers to the Cape, where she became the servant of one Peter Cezar, who brought her to England in 1810 to serve as a profit-making exhibit—upon arrival in England she was immediately put on public display in Piccadilly. After a long tour in England she was taken to Paris, where an animal trainer exhibited her for fifteen months. For the price of admission Europeans came to gape, fascinated especially by her steatopygia—the large, protruding, oblong buttocks, a physiological characteristic of Khoi women. Although exhibited clothed, she posed in the nude for scientific paintings in the *jardin de roi*. She died in Paris in 1815 of a respiratory inflammation. What Baartman thought, or felt,

[17] The information given here as been derived from the following sources: Stephen J. Gould, "The Hottentot Venus," *Natural History* 91 (1982): 20–27, and Sander Gilman, "The Hottentot and the Prostitute: Towards an Iconography of Female Sexuality," in *Difference and Pathology: Stereotypes of Sexuality, Race, and Madness* (Ithaca: Cornell University Press, 1985), 000–000.

306 Renee Green
Sa Main Charmante, 1989
mixed media installation.

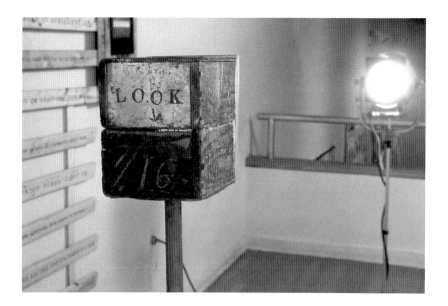

or indeed ever said about her life, including her years as a living specimen, is unrecorded and uncommemorated. Because she had become a subject of intense curiosity for the scientific community, an autopsy was performed in 1816 by Henri de Blainville, and a year later a more famous dissection was performed by the great anatomist Georges Cuvier. While Cuvier, like most of his scientific contemporaries, believed Baartman to represent a kind of monstrous missing link between human and ape, he admitted that her upper body "had grace" and wrote of her *main charmante*—hence, the title of Green's work. Of central concern for these dissections was not only the characteristic steatopygia—was it fat, muscle or even a distinctive bone?— but, as well, the appearance of her genitalia, which during her life Baartman refused to display, and which after her death and Cuvier's dissection remain preserved in the collection of the Musee de l'Homme. The "scientific" importance of Baartman's genitals for Cuvier and other contemporaries lay in Cuvier's description of the "development of the labia minoria or nymphae which is so general a characteristic of the Hottentot and Bushman race" and were "sufficiently well marked to distinguish these parts at once from any of the ordinary varieties of the human species."[18] As Sander Gilman has analyzed this fixation on Baartman's buttocks and genitalia—the so-called Hottentot apron—what was at stake was the support of the poly-genetic theory of racial origins that professed to prove that black Africans had had a wholly different genetic origin from Caucasians. The fixation on

[18] Gilman, "Hottentot and Prostitutes," 183.

the secondary sex characteristics of African women was, moreover, connected both to the pathologization of female sexuality across the board, and, with respect to black women, the function of the genitalia as a metonym for the black female throughout the nineteenth century.

Inscribed in this cruel and sordid historical anecdote of Sarah Baartman as Green has given it artistic form are three overarching themes: the silence of the subject, her status as spectacle, as an object of representation, and the reduction of a black woman to an icon of bestial sexuality. In Green's installation we are provided with the apparatus of the spectacle but denied its content. Instead, we are provided with a replica of the small platform where Baartman might be imagined to stand, marked with footprints—an indexical sign of presence; an empty frame, signaling again the absence of the subject. The slats are inscribed with alternating texts—the scientific, empirical commentary from the dissection of her genitals by Cuvier, and a straightforward account of the circumstances of her life, like the one I just provided. The formal organization of *Sa Main Charmante* obviously restages the structures of voyeurism and display that were the terms of Baartman's original exhibition. The viewer is further enjoined to peer through the peephole viewer, marked with the exhortation "look," but is then assaulted by the beam of light from the kleig, becoming herself the object of illumination. The texts, a melange of scientific observation and contemporary commentary, are not only inscriptions on the absent or the imaged body, but the matrix in which that historical body was made to signify its blackness, its sexuality, its fantasized bestiality. Intended, as Green has described it, to compel the spectator to "read between the lines," *Sa Main Charmante* is for all its historical specificity not really limited to the critical representation of Sarah Baartman. In fact, there were a number of generic Hottentot Venuses in the early nineteenth century, including, in 1829, a nude Hottentot Venus as the prime attraction at a ball given by the Duchesse de Berry. It would seem as though Green was fully aware of the way in which Sarah Baartman may be thought of as a metonym for black women in the white imaginary, and *Sa Main Charmante* suggests that this metonym is still in play.

The second work—Lorna Simpson's—is entitled *Three Seated Figures.* It consists of three color Polaroids with five plastic text panels. Unlike the nominally specific female subject of *Sa Main Charmante,* Simpson's faceless black woman is, as in all Simpson's work, to be understood as a generic rather than individuated subject. The simple white shift worn so frequently by Simpson's models functions to reduce temporal specificity; it is an article of clothing that could as well be worn in the nineteenth as in the twentieth century, although the use of white clothing on a black model also thema-

308 **Lorna Simpson**
Three Seated Figures, 1989
three color Polaroids with five plastic
plaques, 30″ × 97″.

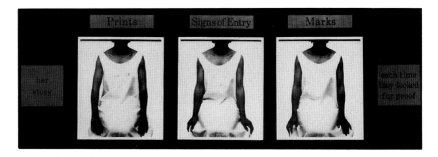

tizes whiteness and blackness. And, as photographers know, in photography you can either expose for the whites or for the blacks, but not for both. In this particular work, the texts guide but in no way rigidly fix a certain reading: "prints," "signs of entry," and "marks" signify evidence of criminal trespass, violation, "signs of entry" evoking both trespass and rape. Where trespass, however, denotes property, and "marks" the damaged body, the generic historical African American women is the fulcrum of both; chattel slave in the former, raped woman in the latter. "Signs of entry," evoking both, is thus appropriately the middle term. "Her story" flanking the three nearly identical Polaroids (only the hand changes position) is, of course, not forthcoming, neither spoken nor imaged; it is the viewer's share to imagine or project it. But the closing panel—conventionally we read from left to right—"each time they looked for proof" suggests nothing so much as a repetition without closure—each time. And who are "they"—and what is the proof they look for? Is it the proof of the violation that is "her" story? A proof that, neither spoken nor imaged, they never find? Is the looking for proof a looking at the body, the investment being in the looking rather than in the elusive proof? And confronted with this gnomic triptych that gives us a "her" and a "they," in what relation to both are we to locate ourselves?

There are obviously any number of ways in which *Sa Main Charmante* and *Three Seated Figures* may be discussed in relation to one another. There is, most obviously, a shared artistic exploration of black women as lost subjects of history and the myriad violences that constituted their histories. There is in both works also a shared concern with the intersections of sexuality, specularity, and representation in which imagery of black women has played a particular role. There is as well a shared concern with languages of science and evidence, surveillance and power that may be justly described as Foucaultian. Nevertheless, they seem equally illustrative of an expanded notion of self-representation that has fully integrated the politics of representation on the level of form as well as content. Insofar as both works comprehend in advance the pitfalls of specularity and spectacle, they construct their works in ways that make these mechanisms visible and thus available to critique and analysis. Significantly too, both artists are deeply concerned with the historic construction of black women's subjectivity, but in ways that can be said to be antipsychological, indeed, anti-individualistic. This approach to self-representation is applicable as well to artists such as Carrie Mae Weems, who even when she appears in the photographs is no more literally herself than is Cindy Sherman in *her* photographs. Rather, the artist uses herself to stand for a collectivity that is not the universal (black) woman, but the historical African American one.

That such practices emerge from the space of subaltern cultural production, a space only recently accorded recognition, is itself significant. In this respect, it conforms in suggestive ways to what Gilles Deleuze and Felix Guattari described as a "minor literature." Using Franz Kafka as their example ("minor" is, within the terms of their argument, by no means a deprecatory characterization), they argue that the cultural production of outsiders—ethnic, religious, racial minorities—who function within the dominant culture, and must perforce use its languages, produce work that is, virtually by definition, political and collective: "The second characteristic of minor literatures is that everything in them is political . . . its cramped space forces each individual intrigue to connect immediately to politics. . . . The third characteristic of minor literature is that in it everything takes on a collective value. . . . But above all else, because collective or national consciousness is often inactive in external life and always in the process of 'breakdown,' literature finds itself positively charged with the role and function of collective, and even revolutionary, enunciation."[19]

It is in this regard that I want to suggest that artists such as Greene, Simpson, and Weems express an identifiable tendency in contemporary art; not, as some have suggested as producers of an identifiable form of "black art," but rather as a quintessentially postmodern and feminist reworking of self-representation. Thus, Green's and Simpson's works that explore the histories of Sarah Baartman or, in a related work by Green, the representation of the African American entertainer Josephine Baker, as well as unnamed and unremembered black women, remind us that the regimes of spectacle and objectification that entrapped these women are no less active in contemporary life.

In hazarding the notion that work such as this may be critically framed, so to speak, as a category of self-representation, I am conscious of the risk of implying a separate-but-equal designation between those artists (white) who may be expected to deal with the cultural politics that postmodernism has designated as the task of critical practice and those other artists (people of color, gay people) who are expected to deal with race, ethnicity, sexu-

[19] Gilles Deleuze and Felix Guattari, "What Is a Minor Literature?" in *Out There: Marginalization and Contemporary Cultures*, ed. Russell Ferguson, Martha Gever, Trinh T. Minh Ha, and Cornel West (New York and Cambridge: The New Museum of Contemporary Art and MIT Press, 1990), 60–61.

ality, and so forth. This is not my meaning or intention, especially since in keeping with the arguments of such scholars as Hazel Carby, bell hooks, Michele Wallace, and Cornel West I believe that "whiteness" is our own unmarked term, the invisible but authoritative ground from which the multicultural is discursively distinguished, just as art—as in H. W. Janson's *The History of Art*—is the foundational entity from which non-Western art is adjectivally distinguished, just as the word artist is unmarked so as to exclude women producers. Nonetheless, it seems to me that one can, justifiably, identify an impulse—widely manifest in the art production of subaltern producers—toward a recuperation, a redemption, even, of the notion of self-representation that makes it something altogether different from the dominant modes of self-representation that have traditionally figured so prominently in art history.

If indeed the project of representing women remains an important project for feminism, it must be with the awareness that the women who represent, and the subject of their representations, must navigate on the one hand the legacy of bourgeois individualism that exalts the individual producer, and on the other, the risk of a totalizing or universalizing assumption that the category "woman" is equivalent to the plurality and difference that constitute the category "women." And where it is a question of the representation of women of color or lesbians, groups who by definition give the lie to all universalisms, the nature of self-representation itself is given new meanings. It is therefore precisely in the emergence of these new modes of self-representation, and indeed in the heightened visibility of new subjects of self-representation, that we glimpse the utopian possibility of a world of equally empowered, heterogeneous, and different subjectivities.

Laura Aguilar

from *Latina Lesbians*
black-and-white phototexts, 1987–90
Reference in Catherine Lord *Reframings* essay

S. A. Bachman

from *It's All There in Black and White*
"Patrilocality"
"Come and get it"
"Finding an Outlet"
color phototexts, 1988–92

Are you telling yourself a little white lie?
silkscreen on nylon, public art banner created at the Fabric Workshop, Philadelphia, 1988

Nancy Barton

from *Live and Let Die*
mixed media installation, 1992

Deborah Bright

The Management of Desire
black-and-white montage, 1993
Reference in Lucy R. Lippard *Reframings* essay

Kaucyila Brooke

from *Making the Most of Your Backyard: The Story Behind an Ideal Beauty*
black-and-white phototext, 1990

Linda Brooks

from *between the birthdays*
black-and-white phototext, 1981–ongoing

Martha Casanave

Untitled Pinhole Photographs
black-and-white pinhole photographs, 1988–92

Dorit Cypis

from *X-Rayed (Altered)*
installation view, Intermedia Arts, Minneapolis, April 1989
installation view, San Francisco Museum of Modern Art, March 1991
installation view, San Francisco Museum of Modern Art, March 1991
installation view, Intermedia Arts, Minneapolis, April 1989
mixed media installation, 1989–91
Reference in Moira Roth *Reframings* essay

Ann Fessler

Ancient History/Recent History
black-and-white phototext, 1993

Nan Goldin

from *The Ballad of Sexual Dependency*
"Mark and Mark, Boston 1978"
"Philippe M. and Rise on their wedding day, New York City 1978"
"Greer and Robert on the bed, New York City 1982"
"Philippe H. and Suzanne kissing at Euthanasia, New York City 1981"
"Joey and Andres in bed, Berlin 1992"
"The Hug, New York City 1980"
Cibachrome color photographs, ongoing since 1978
Reference in Catherine Lord *Reframings* essay

Sarah Hart

from *Valley Girls: The Construction of Feminine Identity in Consumer Culture*
color photographs, 1991

Connie Hatch

from *The DeSublimation of Romance*
black-and-white photographs, 1975–ongoing

Susan Jahoda

from *Theatres of Madness*
black-and-white phototext, 1989–ongoing

Tamarra Kaida

from *Tremors from the Faultline*
black-and-white photographs and text, 1989

Leigh Kane

from *A Legacy of Restraint*
black-and-white photomontage, 1993

Mary Kelly

from *Corpus*
screenprint and Plexiglas on acrylic; laminated photopositive, acrylic, and screenprint on Plexiglas, 1985

Barbara Kruger

Recent Public Works
Public Art Fund, New York City, bus shelter, 1991
Campaign for Legal Abortion and Women's Reproductive Rights, New York City, poster, 1990
Public Art Fund, New York City, billboard, 1989
London, billboard, 1986
Against the AntiGay Referendum, Portland, Oregon, bus placard, 1992
New York City, poster campaign, 1991
Campaign Against Domestic Violence, San Francisco, billboard, 1992
Reference in Moira Roth *Reframings* essay
Reference in Abigail Solomon-Godeau *Reframings* essay

Adrian Piper

from *Decide Who You Are*
"Decide Who You Are #21: Phantom Limbs"
Courtesy of John Weber Gallery, New York
"Decide Who You Are #6: You'r History"
photomontage: pencil drawing, photographs, graph paper and text, 1992
Courtesy of Brody's Gallery, Washington D.C.
Reference in Valerie Soe *Reframings* essay
Reference in Abigail Solomon-Godeau *Reframings* essay

Gail S. Rebhan

from *The Family Tapes*
color photographs, 1989

Carol Simon Rosenblatt

Is This How I Look?
color photomontage, 1989–93

Martha Rosler

from *Bringing the War Home: House Beautiful*
color montage, 1967–72
The portfolio of images from *Bringing the War Home: House Beautiful* is published by Simon Watson, New York.
Reference in Moira Roth *Reframings* essay

Hinda Schuman

from *Dear Shirley*
black-and-white photomontage, 1985

Cindy Sherman

Untitled
color photographs, 1992
Courtesy of Metro Pictures, New York
Reference in Moira Roth *Reframings* essay
Reference in Abigail Solomon-Godeau *Reframings* essay

Coreen Simpson

from *Aboutface*
black-and-white constructed images, 1991

Lorna Simpson

Three Works
"Same"
color polaroids and plastic plaques, 1991
Collection of the J.B. Speed Art Museum, Louisville, Kentucky
"Figure"
black-and-white and plastic plaques, 1991
"Guarded Conditions"
color polaroids and plastic plaques, 1989
Collection of the Museum of Contemporary Art, San Diego
Courtesy of Josh Baer Gallery, New York
Reference in Moira Roth *Reframings* essay
Reference in Abigail Solomon-Godeau *Reframings* essay

Clarissa Sligh

from *Reframing the Past*
"She Sucked Her Thumb"
cyanotype collage, 1989
"Kill or Be Killed"
cyanotype with pastel, 1991
"Slept With Her Brother"
Vandyke brown print, 1984
"Waiting for Daddy"
Vandyke brown print, 1987
non-silver photographic processes, 1983–ongoing
Reference in Valerie Soe *Reframings* essay
Reference in Deborah Willis *Reframings* essay

Margaret Stratton

Justice on TV, from *A Guide to the Wasteland*
black-and-white interactive installation, 1991–93
Reference in Deborah Willis *Reframings* essay

Diane Tani

Hard Glance: Asian American Image and Identity
color photomontage, 1989–ongoing
Reference in Valerie Soe *Reframings* essay

Hulleah Tsinhnahjinnie

from *Native Programming*
black-and-white photocollage, 1990
Reference in Theresa Harlan *Reframings* essay
Reference in Lucy R. Lippard *Reframings* essay
Reference in Moira Roth *Reframings* essay

314 **Linn Underhill**
from *Claiming the Gaze*
black-and-white photographs, 1992–ongoing

Carrie Mae Weems
from *Untitled* (*Kitchen Table Series*)
black-and-white photographs and text, 1990
Courtesy of P.P.O.W., Inc., New York
Reference in Theresa Harlan *Reframings* essay
Reference in Lucy R. Lippard *Reframings* essay
Reference in Abigail Solomon-Godeau *Reframings* essay

Carla Williams
from *How to Read Character*
gilt-framed black-and-white photographs paired with photocopy transfers, 1991
Reference in Deborah Willis *Reframings* essay

Pat Ward Williams
Two Installations
  I Remember It Well, Smith College Museum of Art, Northhampton, Massachusetts
  WHAT YOU LOOKN AT, Whitney Museum of American Art 1993 Biennial Exhibition, New York
dot screen mural print with paint, attached color snapshots, texts, 1993
Reference in Theresa Harlan *Reframings* essay
Reference in Moira Roth *Reframings* essay
Reference in Abigail Solomon-Godeau *Reframings* essay

Laura Aguilar is a photographer who lives in Rosemead, California.

S. A. Bachman is an artist who works with photographs and text. She lives in Boston, where she is on the faculty of the School of the Museum of Fine Arts.

Nancy Barton is an installation artist who lives in Los Angeles, where she is the Chair of the Photography Program at Otis School of Art and Design. She is represented in Los Angeles by Christopher Grimes Gallery and in New York by American Fine Arts Co., Colin Deland Fine Art.

Deborah Bright is a photographer and writer who lives in Somerville, Massachusetts, and is on the faculty of Rhode Island School of Design.

Kaucyila Brooke is a phototext and video artist who lives in Los Angeles and is on the faculty of the California Institute of the Arts.

Linda Brooks is a photographer who lives in St. Paul, Minnesota, and is on the faculty of St. Paul Academy and Summit School.

Martha Casanave is a photographer who lives in Monterey, California. She is a commercial photographer and photography instructor.

Dorit Cypis is an installation and performance artist who lives in Minneapolis, Minnesota.

Ann Fessler is an installation and book artist who lives in Providence, Rhode Island. She is Head of the Graduate and Undergraduate Photography Program at Rhode Island School of Design.

Nan Goldin is a photographer who lives in New York. She is represented by Matthew Marks Gallery, New York.

Sarah Hart is a photographer who lives in New York City and Friday Harbor, Washington, and teaches at the Rhode Island School of Design.

Connie Hatch is an artist photographer who is on the faculty of California Institute of the Arts.

Susan Jahoda is an artist who works with photographs. She lives in Amherst, Massachusetts, and is on the faculty of the University of Massachusetts.

Tamarra Kaida is a photographer who works with text. She lives in Mesa, Arizona, and is on the faculty of Arizona State University.

Leigh Kane is an artist photographer who lives in Northfield, Minnesota, and is on the faculty of Carleton College.

Mary Kelly is a mixed media artist who uses photography. She lives in New York City, teaches in the Whitney Museum Independent Study Program, and is represented by Postmasters Gallery.

Barbara Kruger is an artist who works with pictures and text. She lives in New York City and Los Angeles and is represented by Mary Boone Gallery.

Betty Lee is a photographer who lives in Los Angeles and teaches at the University of California, Irvine.

Jin Lee is a photographer who lives in Chicago and teaches at the School of the Art Institute of Chicago and at Columbia College.

Carm Little Turtle is a photographer who lives in Prescott, Arizona, and is an operating room nurse.

Susan Meiselas is a photographer who lives in New York City and is a member of Magnum Photos.

Ann Meredith is a photographer who lives in New York City.

Sherry Millner is a video-maker and collage artist. She lives in New York City and is on the video faculty of Hampshire College.

Yong Soon Min is a mixed media artist who lives in Brooklyn, New York.

Marilyn Nance is a photographer who lives in Brooklyn, New York, and teaches at the International Center of Photography.

Anne Noggle is a photographer who lives in Albuquerque, New Mexico.

Catherine Opie is a photographer who lives in Los Angeles and is on the staff of the University of California, Irvine.

Esther Parada is a photocollage artist who usually works with a computer. She lives in Chicago and is on the faculty of the University of Illinois at Chicago.

Adrian Piper is a conceptual artist who uses a variety of media including photography, text, and drawing. She is on the philosophy faculty of Wellesley College and is represented by John Weber Gallery.

Gail S. Rebhan is a photographer and video-maker. She lives in Washington, D.C., and is on the faculty of Mount Vernon College.

Carol Simon Rosenblatt is a painter and photocollage artist who lives in Providence, Rhode Island.

Martha Rosler is a video artist, writer, and photographer. She lives in Brooklyn, New York, is on the faculty of Rutgers University, and is represented by Jay Gorney Modern Art.

Hinda Schuman is a photographer who lives in Philadelphia and is on contract with *The Philadelphia Inquirer.*

Cindy Sherman is a photographer who lives in New York City and is represented by Metro Pictures.

Coreen Simpson is an artist who works with photography and design. She lives in New York City, where she operates her own commercial studio.

Lorna Simpson is a phototext artist who lives in Brooklyn, New York, and is represented by Josh Baer Gallery.

Clarissa Sligh is an artist who uses words, photography, and drawing in her installations, books, and prints. She lives in New York City.

Margaret Stratton is an installation photographer who lives in Iowa City and is on the faculty of the University of Iowa.

Diane Tani is a photographer who lives in San Francisco.

Hulleah Tsinhnahjinnie is a photographer who lives in Vallejo, California.

Linn Underhill is a photographer who lives in Lisle, New York, and is on the visiting faculty of Colgate University.

Carrie Mae Weems is an artist who lives in Oakland and New York City and is represented by P.P.O.W.

Carla Williams is a photographer who lives in New York City. She is Curator of Photography and Prints at the Schomburg Center for Research in Black Culture.

Pat Ward Williams is an installation artist who uses photography. She lives in Los Angeles, is on the faculty of the University of California, Irvine, and is represented by P.P.O.W., Inc.

Julia Ballerini is a writer and historian who lives in New York City.

Theresa Harlan is curator at the CN Gorman Museum, Native American Studies Department at the University of California at Davis. She lives in Vallejo, California, and is also a freelance curator and writer.

Lucy R. Lippard is an independent writer and cultural organizer who lives in New York City and Boulder, Colorado.

Catherine Lord is a writer who lives in Los Angeles and is on the faculty of the Studio Art Department of the University of California, Irvine.

Moira Roth is an art historian and critic who lives in Berkeley, California, and is the Trefethen Professor of Art History at Mills College, Oakland.

Valerie Soe is a writer and experimental video-maker who lives in San Francisco and teaches at the University of California, Santa Barbara.

Abigail Solomon-Godeau is a historian, curator, and critic who lives in Santa Barbara, California, and is on the art history faculty of the University of California, Santa Barbara.

Deborah Willis is a photographer, curator, and historian who lives in Washington, D.C., and is the Collection Coordinator of the National African American Museum Project, Smithsonian Institution.

Diane Tani
Duel,   1989
color photograph, 20″ × 16″.

Yong Soon Min
from *Defining Moments* #4: *Kwang Ju
Massacre*,   1992
black-and-white photograph,
20″ × 16″.

Abigail Solomon-Godeau
*"Representing Women: The Politics of
Self-Representation"*

Renee Green
Sa Main Charmante,   1989
mixed media installation.

Lorna Simpson
Three Seated Figures,   1989
three color Polaroids with five plastic
plaques, 30″ × 97″.

Deborah Willis
*"Women's Stories/Women's Photo-
biographies"*

Carla Williams
installation view
How to Read Character,   1990–91
gilt frames, black-and-white photographs, photocopy transfer, pushpins.

Margaret Stratton
*Item #2, Item #127, Item #17, Item
#211, Inventory of My Mother's House*,
1992
from an installation of 190 black-and-
white photographs.

Clarissa Sligh
two views, *What's Happening with
Momma?*,   1988
mixed media with Vandyke brown,
11″ × 36″.

Fay Fairbrother
detail from *The Quilt Shroud Stories*,
1991–92
cotton and photolinen, 60″ × 70″
overall.